POSTCARD HISTORY SERIES

Lakeland

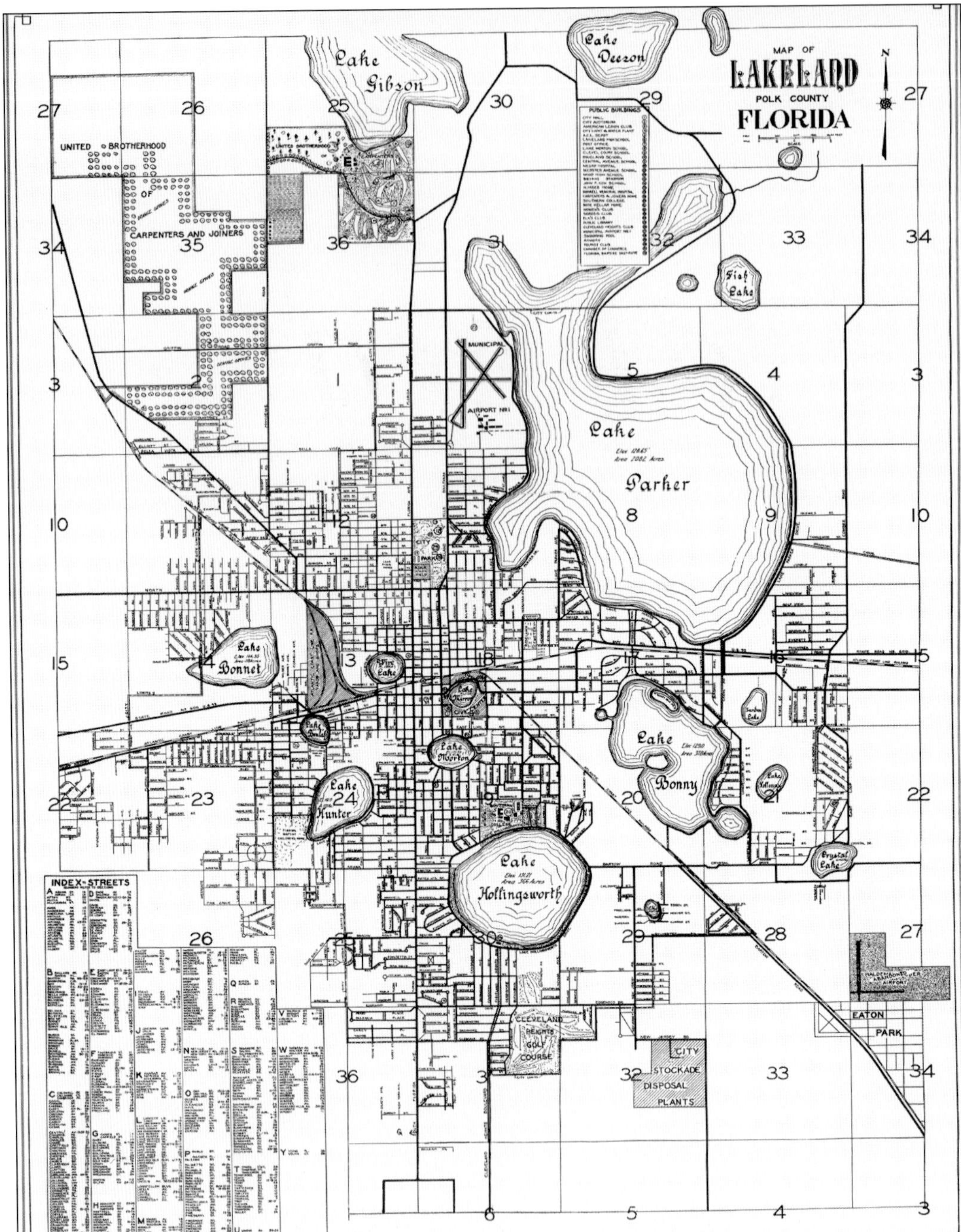

Map of Lakeland, Polk County, Florida. This undated map from the late 1940s illustrates the layout of Lakeland. Prominent are the many lakes from which the city takes its name. Other features are the municipal airport, lands owned by the United Brotherhood of Carpenters and Joiners, Atlantic Coast Line Railroad yard and shops, the Florida Baptist Children's Home, local parks, Florida Southern College, the Cleveland Heights Golf Course, and the city stockade disposal plants. Modern Lakeland encompasses dozens of named lakes. (Courtesy Florida Southern College Library.)

POSTCARD HISTORY SERIES

Lakeland

Mary M. Flekke and Randall M. MacDonald

ARCADIA PUBLISHING

ISBN 978-0-7385-4183-9

Published by Arcadia Publishing
Charleston, South Carolina

Printed in the United States of America

Library of Congress Catalog Card Number: 2005930925

For all general information contact Arcadia Publishing at:
Telephone 843-853-2070
Fax 843-853-0044
E-mail sales@arcadiapublishing.com
For customer service and orders:
Toll-Free 1-888-313-2665

Visit us on the Internet at www.arcadiapublishing.com

MMF: To my mother, Muriel, and other loved ones who support me in all my endeavors.

RMM: With love to Lakeland natives Susan Priest MacDonald and Sarah Elizabeth MacDonald.

Contents

ACKNOWLEDGMENTS

Inspiration for this volume came from the many fine local history titles produced by Arcadia Publishing. Many thanks to Barbie Langston Halaby and Kathryn Korfonta of Arcadia, both of whom offered us reassuring encouragement and advice.

This work could not have been attempted without the generous assistance of Kevin Logan and Carol Juchau of the Lakeland Public Library Special Collections Department. Many of these postcards are from the library's collections, and we appreciate greatly the opportunity to share them with a wide audience.

Florida Southern College alumna Brittany Melson connected us with Larry Gray, who generously agreed to allow inclusion of some of his wonderful postcards. It was a profound pleasure to meet such an avid and knowledgeable local historian. We thank you.

To our colleagues at the Florida Southern College Library, we appreciate your affable spirit and professionalism. Andrew Pearson, Nora Gabraith, Eridan J. McConnell, Anne Rogers, and Sally Gullage: our thanks to you all.

LAKELAND

(By R. A. Ward, Lakeland, Fla.)

I'm glad I live in Lakeland,
That highly-favored land,
Where Nature strews her blessings
With such a generous hand.
With her lakes of crystal beauty,
Few others can compare,
Her gently rolling uplands,
The ocean breezes share.

Deep wells with sparkling water,
Abundant full and pure,
Secure us health and comfort,
And joys that will endure.
Let others climb the mountains,
And canyons deep explore,
But give us a home in Lakeland,
And we will ask no more.

I love to live in Lakeland,
Where tourists find a home,
Where the invalid and aged,
Will always gladly come.
Her ripe and luscious berries,
And melons rich and rare,
Furnish a dish fit for a king,
Which all who come may share.

I'm glad I live in Lakeland,
And all its blessings share,
Its oranges and grapefruit,
Are far beyond compare.
And then our glorious climate,
Of which we proudly boast.
Has not a peer in all the realm,
Reaching from coast to coast.

LAKELAND. This whimsical poem by Lakeland resident R. A. Ward extolls the virtues of his beautiful community. (Courtesy Larry Gray.)

INTRODUCTION

Much of Florida remained a rural frontier in the first years following the Civil War, though in the midst of west central Florida, a small community was taking hold at the intersection of two rail lines. Settled by the 1870s, Lakeland was perfectly named in 1883 by her citizens; the small town was surrounded by and now encompasses dozens of lakes. Lakeland was incorporated in 1885, and it eventually developed into the agricultural and commercial center of Imperial Polk County.

The community grew from the town square around Munn Park to an eclectic mix of downtown buildings, the grand Polk Theatre, elegant hotels, roadways, handsome parks, and picturesque neighborhoods. By mid-century, Lakeland had grown to support small industry, churches, many schools, an airport, and two small colleges, one of which features the largest single-site collection of Frank Lloyd Wright architecture. The temperate climate and proximity to larger cities drew retirees and winter residents, while business interests and academia brought a substantial contingent of permanent residents. The Cleveland Indians held baseball spring training here in the 1920s, indirectly leading to construction of the prestigious Cleveland Heights development, and the Detroit Tigers have called Lakeland their spring training home since 1934.

Lakeland is the historic hub of Florida's citrus industry, and the city adopted the moniker "World's Citrus Center." The Marsh seedless grapefruit originated in the Lakeland area in the 1860s and by the 1890s was in extended commercial production. By the end of the 19th century, local strawberry farms were benefiting immensely from Lakeland's busy rail service. Polk County is centered in Florida phosphate mining and processing territory, and the Florida phosphate boom of the late 1800s affected Lakeland's fortunes in dramatic fashion, driving up land prices and reshaping the landscape through the 1900s. Phosphate companies existed in and around the city, and extensive portions of modern Lakeland were mined.

Picture postcards enjoyed increasing popularity during Lakeland's first years. Advances in photography, which occurred during the Civil War, coupled with sophisticated German lithography to bring postcards to life in the 1890s. Not only did postcards help document the growth of the community, but they have an intrinsic beauty that belies their historic importance. Hundreds of Lakeland-area postcards were published, advertising the young city's charm and offering a glimpse into what Lakeland and Lakelanders were like. Unique personalized messages added a touch of familiarity to a vista that was but a distant memory of a place once visited or never seen.

These postcard images evoke a time long past, when horse and buggy traversed dirt paths around lakes teeming with wildlife, when high school cadets marched on the outskirts of a bustling downtown, and when Munn Park was a favorite gathering place. Bountiful fishing, posh golf and country clubs, active rail and air service, and changes in architecture, transportation, and fashion were all captured on film and shared on postcards. Cultural, industrial, and technological progresses have transformed the small, neighborly community into a thriving modern city, which today continues to retain its small town atmosphere.

Regrettably postcards do not tell the entire story of Lakeland. The personal homes featured on old published postcards were not typical of all homes but were owned by affluent businessmen. Only the largest churches published postcards, and the lives of African American residents were better documented in regular photographs. Were there postcards of the Washington Park High School or other important landmarks? None are known to exist. As far as can be determined, no published postcards of the Moorhead community west of downtown—site of the Lakeland Center—were produced.

Drawn from local library collections and personal collections, the postcards in this volume were generally published before 1950. Bold text is from the postcard title or reverse caption. Excerpts from messages are reproduced in quotation marks. We hope you enjoy this postcard glimpse of Lakeland's history.

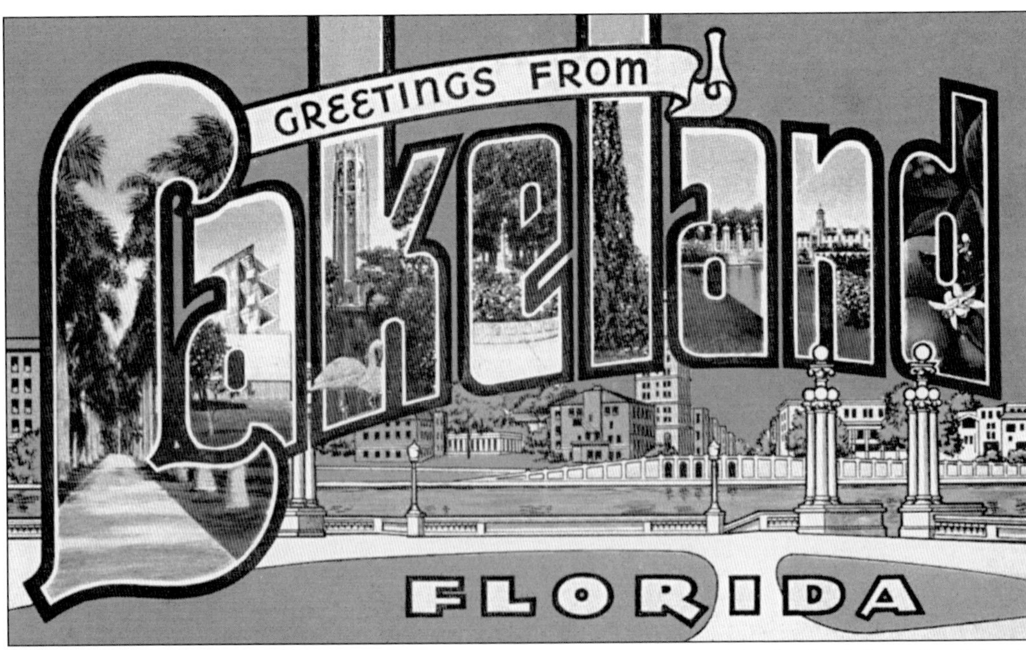

GREETINGS FROM LAKELAND FLORIDA. Local area images provide the backdrop for this big letter postcard. As noted on the reverse, these pictures make up the city's name: "L: An Avenue of Royal Palms. A: Annie Pfeiffer Chapel. K: Flamingos at the Singing Tower. E: Munn Park. L: Flame Vine (Pyrostegia Venusta). A: Mirror Lake and Bandstand. N: National Home of Carpenters & Joiners. D: Oranges and Orange Blossoms." (Courtesy Lakeland Public Library.)

One

Downtown Lakeland

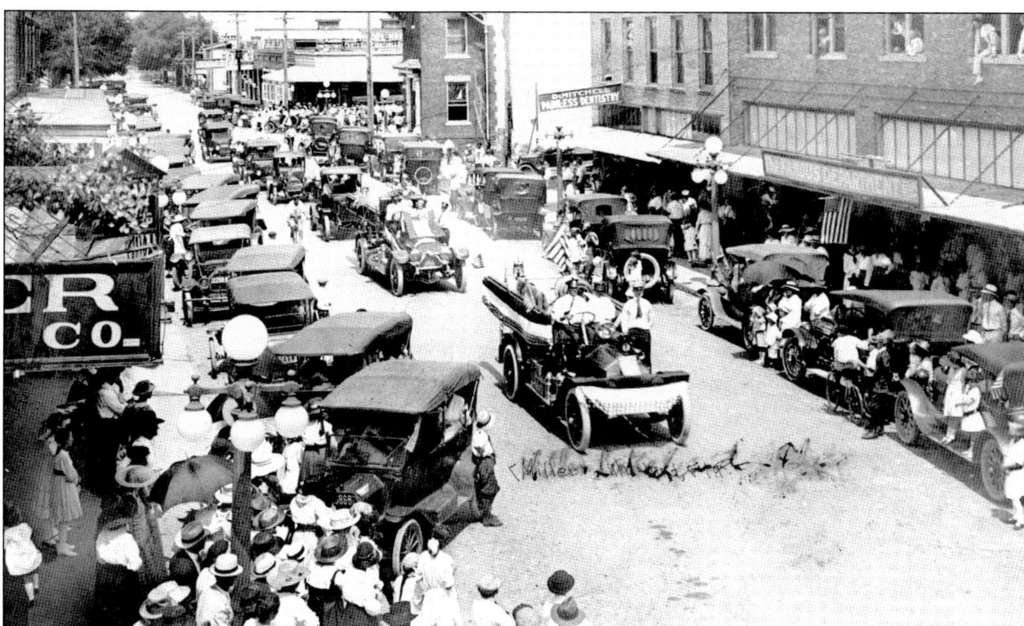

Miller, Lakeland, Fla. This view looks west on Main Street past Florida Avenue. Portions of this undated real-photo postcard are identical to a photograph depicting a September 16, 1917, parade through the heart of Lakeland. City Hall is visible in the center past two fire trucks. Famous Department Store and Doctor Mitchell's Painless Dentistry are on the right. (Courtesy Lakeland Public Library.)

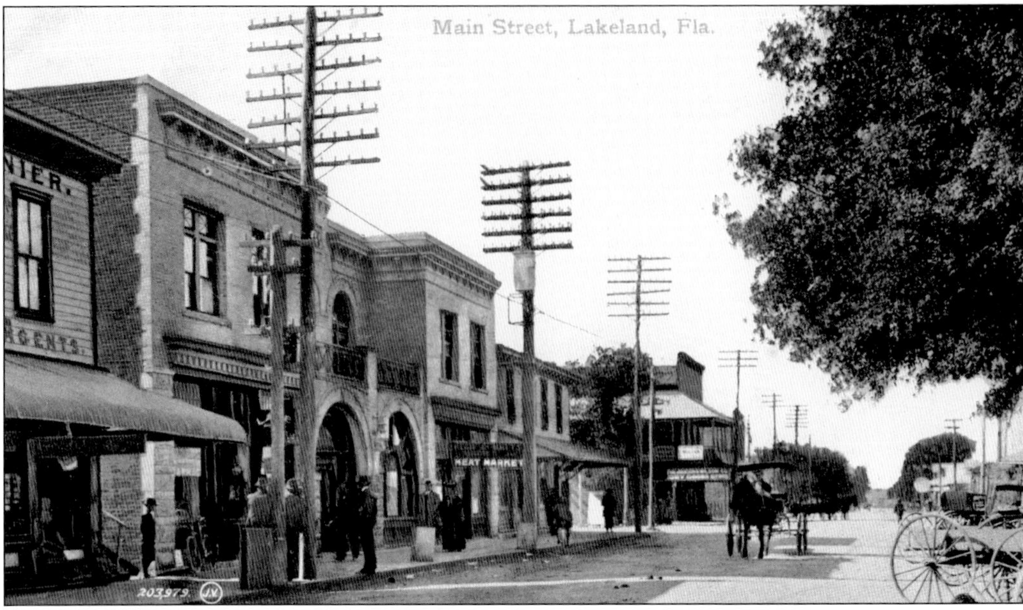

Main Street, Lakeland, Fla. Munn Park is to the right in this westward view from Kentucky Avenue. The landmark 1903 Kentucky Building, designed by architect W. B. Talley, is visible behind the nearest electric pole. Following the arrival of railroads linking Lakeland with other locales in Florida, the town grew as businesses sprung up around Munn Park. (Courtesy Lakeland Public Library.)

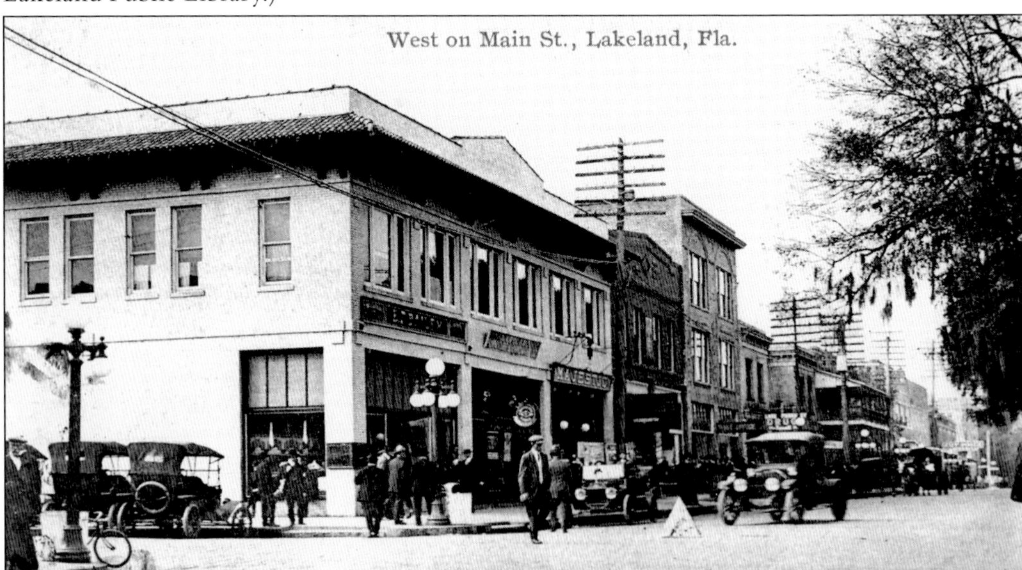

West on Main St., Lakeland, Fla. Earlier wood-frame structures had been replaced by durable brick buildings by the time this postcard was mailed in January 1917. The post office was located in the three-storey building in the center of the block. The prominent corner building is the Deen-Bryant Building, constructed around 1912. Sam wrote to South Akron, Ohio: "Dear Lottie! Here is a card from Lakeland, Florida. We drove over yesterday in Mr. King's Ford. Had a nice ride but it jarred up my rheumatism some. It is a nice place but not as much fruit there as around Winter Haven. . . . Sam." (Courtesy Lakeland Public Library.)

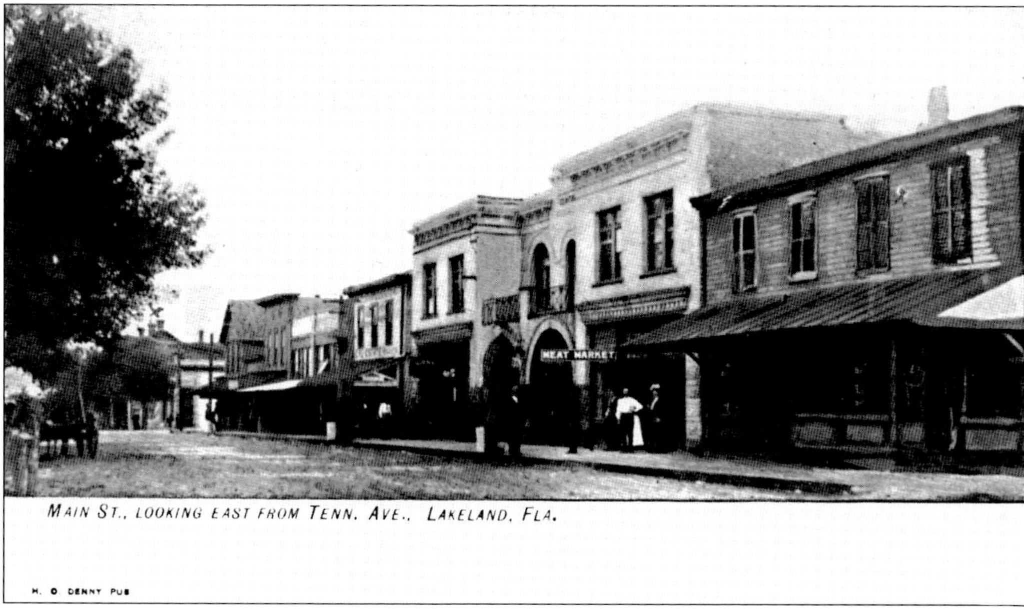

MAIN ST., LOOKING EAST FROM TENN. AVE., LAKELAND, FLA. The southern edge of Munn Park is visible on the left in one of the earliest postcard views of this block. Wood-frame structures flank the Kentucky Building, which was home to an early meat market. Although most of these structures were replaced, downtown pedestrians still get a wonderful look at buildings that figured in the city's fortunes. (Courtesy Larry Gray.)

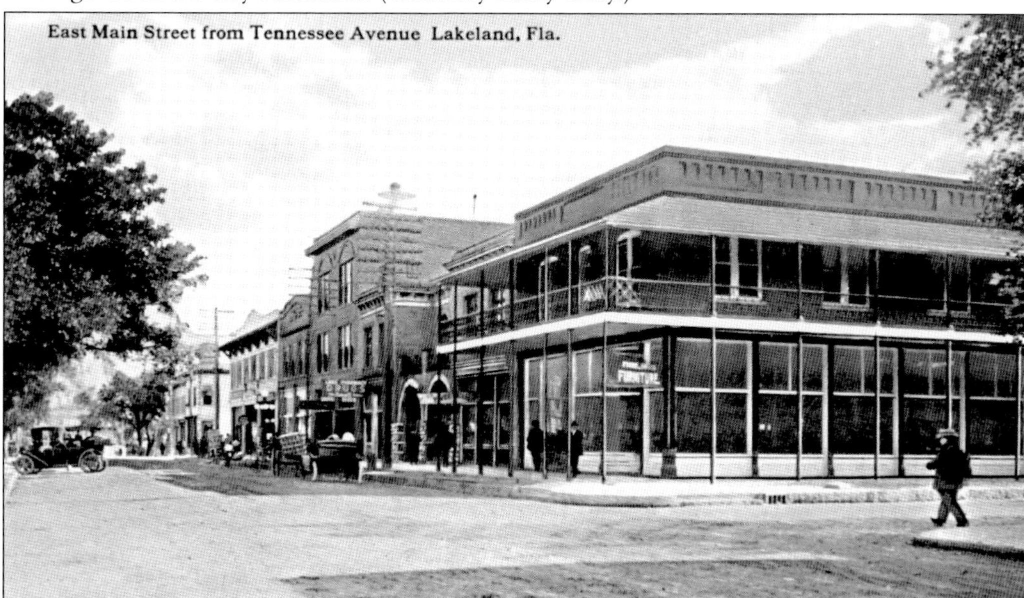

EAST MAIN STREET FROM TENNESSEE AVENUE, LAKELAND, FLA. This undated pre-1916 postcard shows continued development of Main Street with brick buildings replacing wood-frame structures. The Munn Building is visible in the distance at the southeast corner of Kentucky Avenue and Main Street. Lake Pharmacy Drugs was in the center of the block, and a furniture store was on the southeast corner of Tennessee Avenue and Main Street. (Courtesy Lakeland Public Library.)

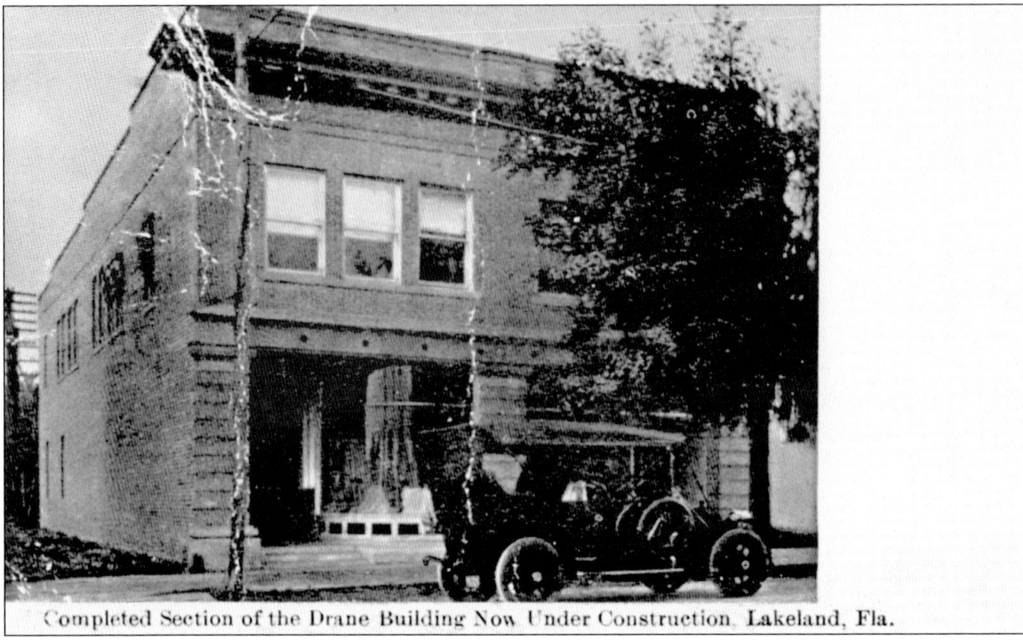

COMPLETED SECTION OF THE DRANE BUILDING NOW UNDER CONSTRUCTION, LAKELAND, FLA. The Drane Building was located on the south side of Main Street between Kentucky and Massachusetts Avenues—adjacent to the Munn Building—and was constructed by Herbert Jackson Drane (1863–1947). Postmarked in Lakeland on September 29, 1909, the postcard advertised a "Millinery Opening—October 1st, 2nd, 4th, and 5th, 1909. Mrs. J. M. Bass, Lakeland, Florida." (Courtesy Lakeland Public Library.)

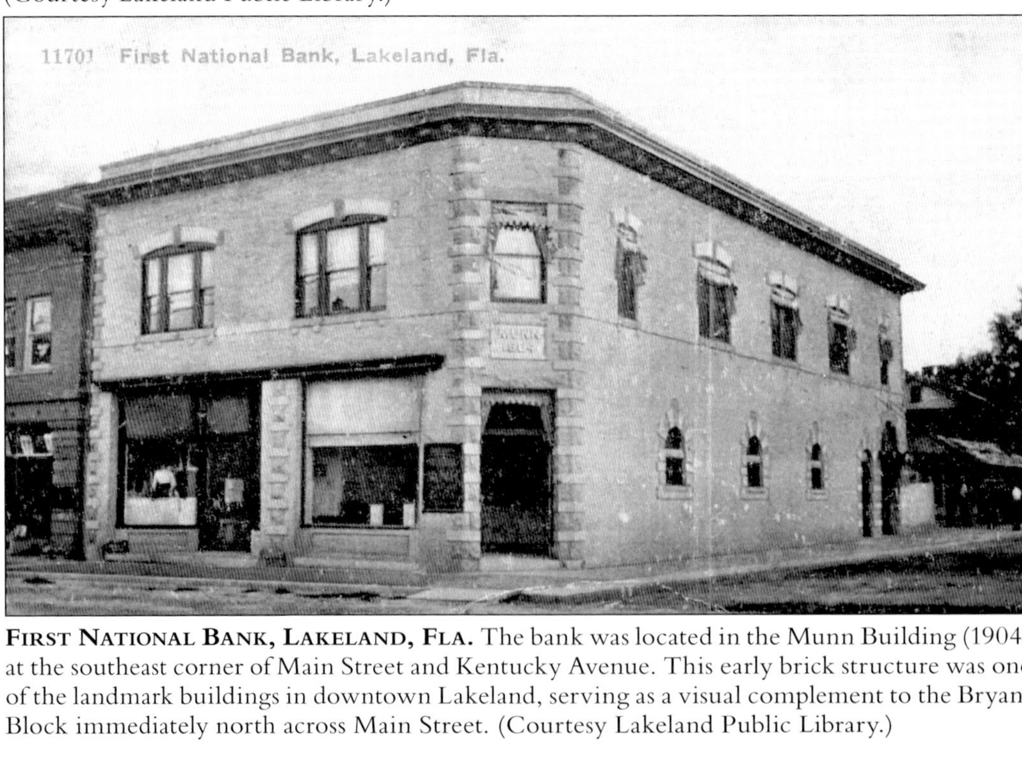

FIRST NATIONAL BANK, LAKELAND, FLA. The bank was located in the Munn Building (1904) at the southeast corner of Main Street and Kentucky Avenue. This early brick structure was one of the landmark buildings in downtown Lakeland, serving as a visual complement to the Bryant Block immediately north across Main Street. (Courtesy Lakeland Public Library.)

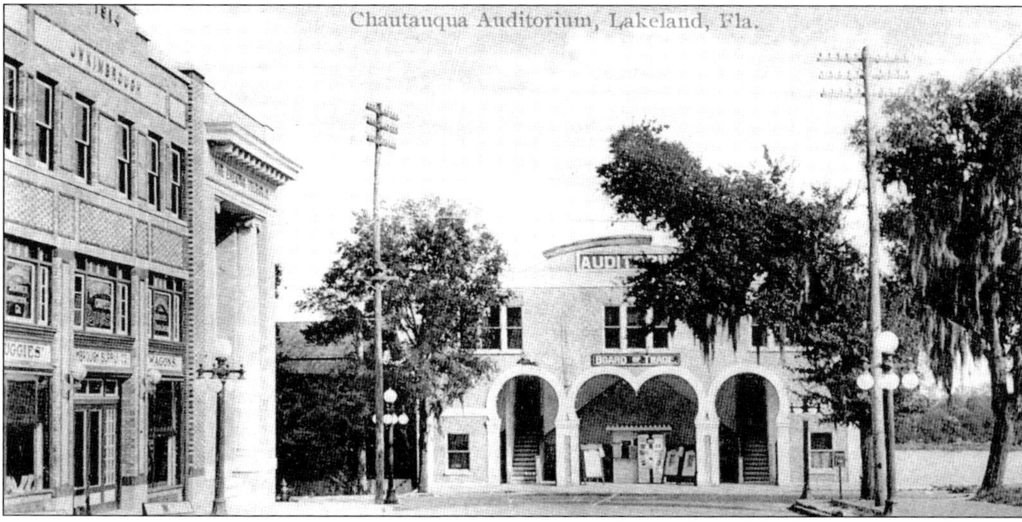

CHAUTAUQUA AUDITORIUM, LAKELAND, FLA. The 1,700-seat auditorium (1912–1928) stood on the east side of Massachusetts Avenue at the base of Main Street and was constructed at a cost of $30,000. The buildings on the left of the card include the J. W. Kimbrough Building and the Evening Telegraph Building. The message recounts daily life in the young town: "Mar 6, 1915. Dear Samuel—This has been a beautiful day, five children and a Mrs. Strasnider and I walked out to Lake Parker, the children gathered violets, cowslips, and other wild flowers, & I gathered some specimens to press. I attended Episcopal Lenten service with Miss Barclay last night. Met Senator Drane's wife she is the organist down there. The folks are still enjoying this Florida climate." (Courtesy Lakeland Public Library.)

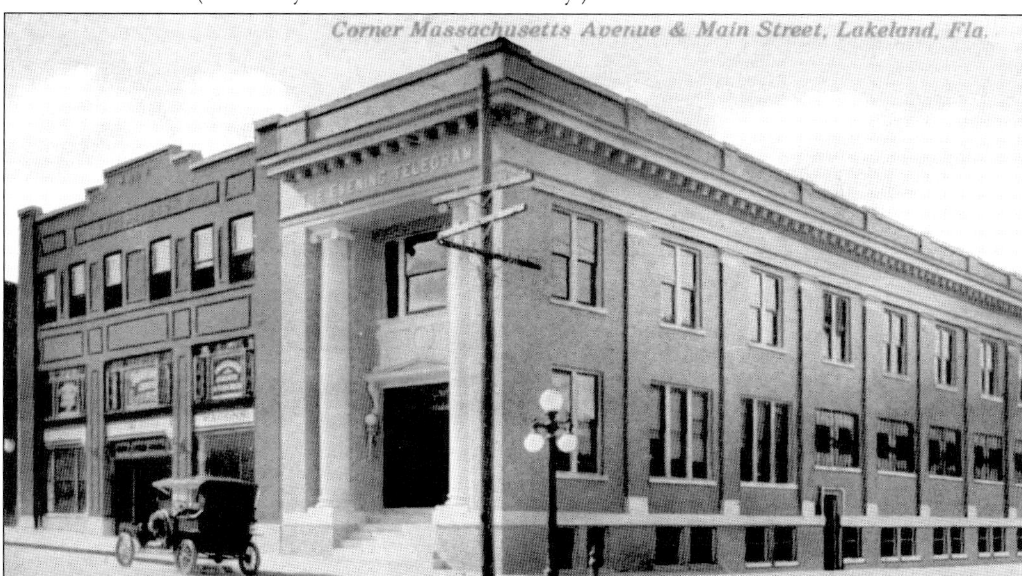

CORNER MASSACHUSETTS AVENUE & MAIN STREET, LAKELAND, FLA. The J. W. Kimbrough Building (1914) and the Evening Telegram Building (1913) were situated on the northwest corner of Main Street and Massachusetts Avenue. The Kimbrough Supply Company sold everything from wagons and buggies to rugs and furniture. Both buildings were demolished by the late 1970s to make way for a parking garage constructed in 1985–1986. (Courtesy Lakeland Public Library.)

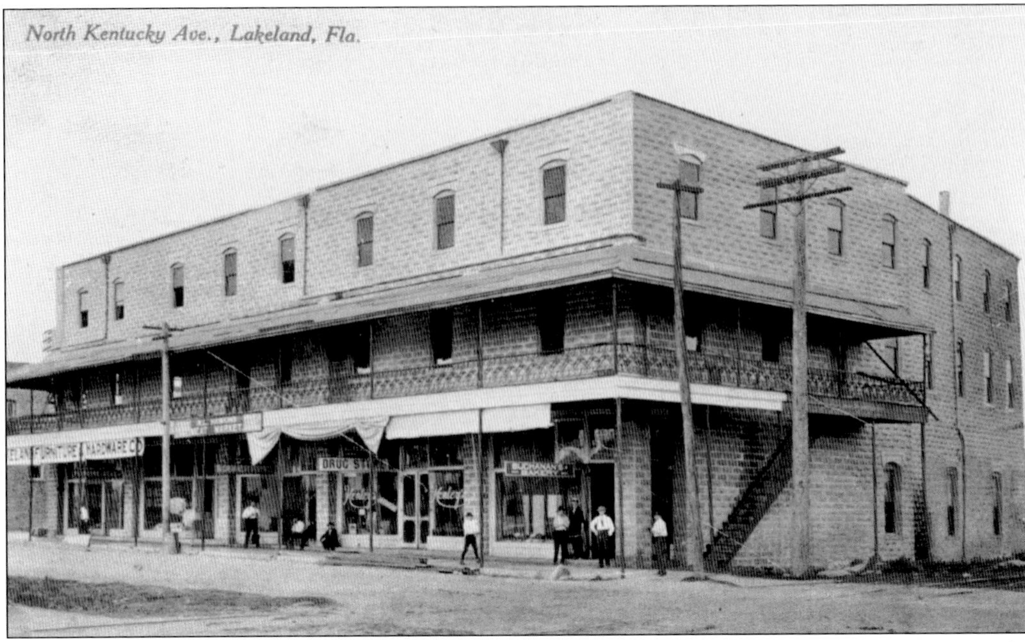

NORTH KENTUCKY AVE., LAKELAND, FLA. On the east side of North Kentucky Avenue, the building housed the Lakeland Furniture and Hardware Company, a meat market, drug store, and Buchanan's Bakery. This card was mailed from Lakeland on September 23, 1911, describing travels around the South. (Courtesy Lakeland Public Library.)

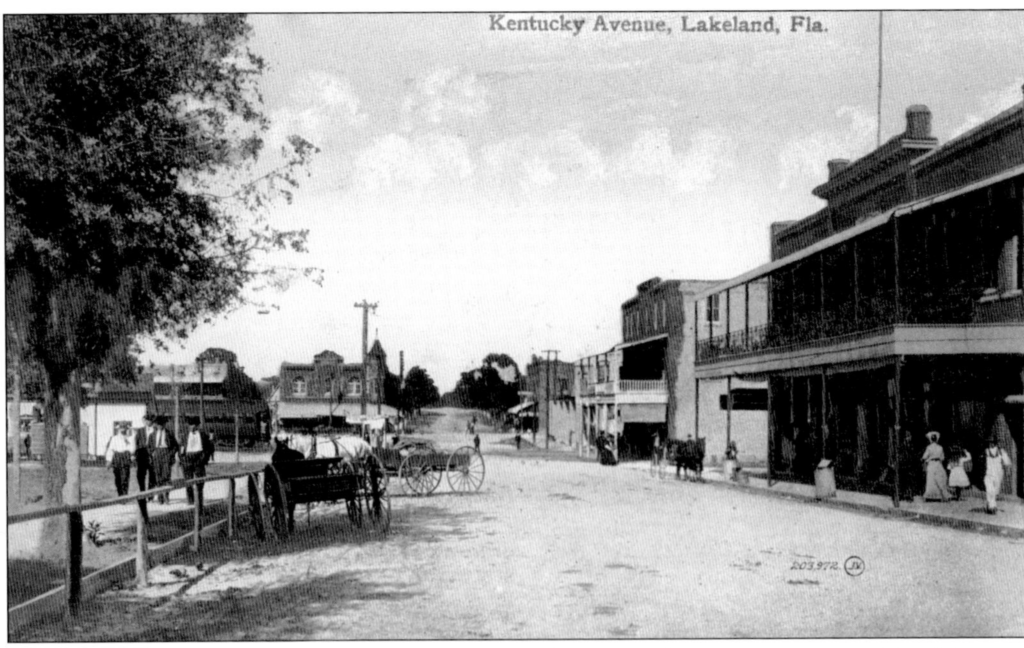

KENTUCKY AVENUE, LAKELAND, FLA. North Kentucky Avenue was unpaved in this view, showing Munn Park and the Atlantic Coast Line Railroad station to the left. The distinctive Clonts Building (224–228 East Pine Street) is visible past the railroad station. (Courtesy Lakeland Public Library.)

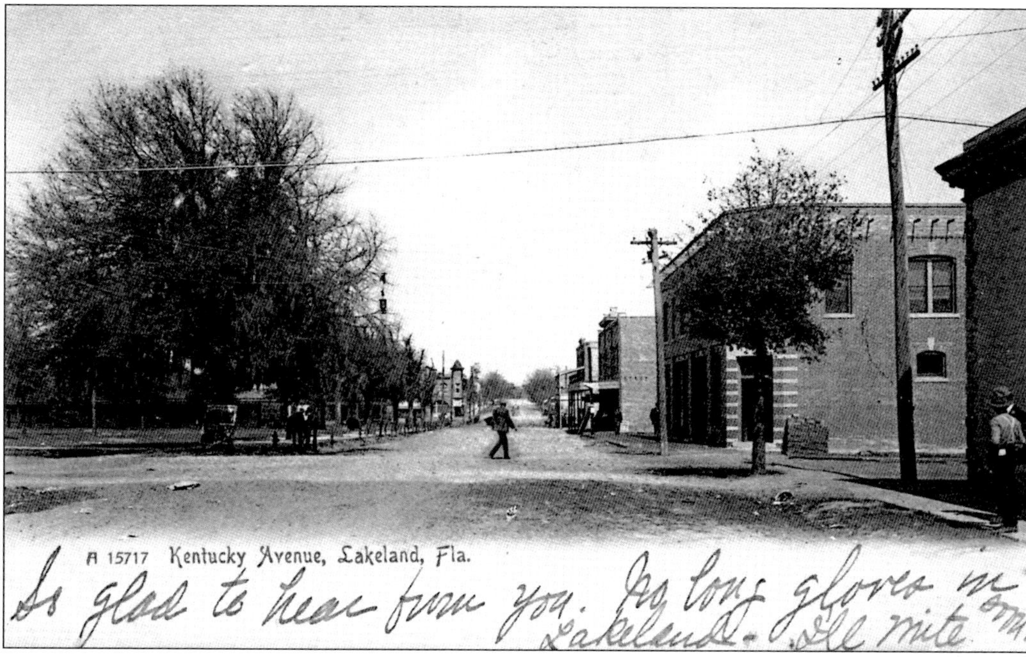

KENTUCKY AVENUE, LAKELAND, FLA. This view north along North Kentucky Avenue shows with the Bryant Block on the right and the Munn Building at near right. Main Street crosses through the foreground. The postcard was mailed in Lakeland, January 12, 1906, to Washington, D.C.: "So glad to hear from you. No long gloves in Lakeland. I'll write soon." (Courtesy Larry Gray.)

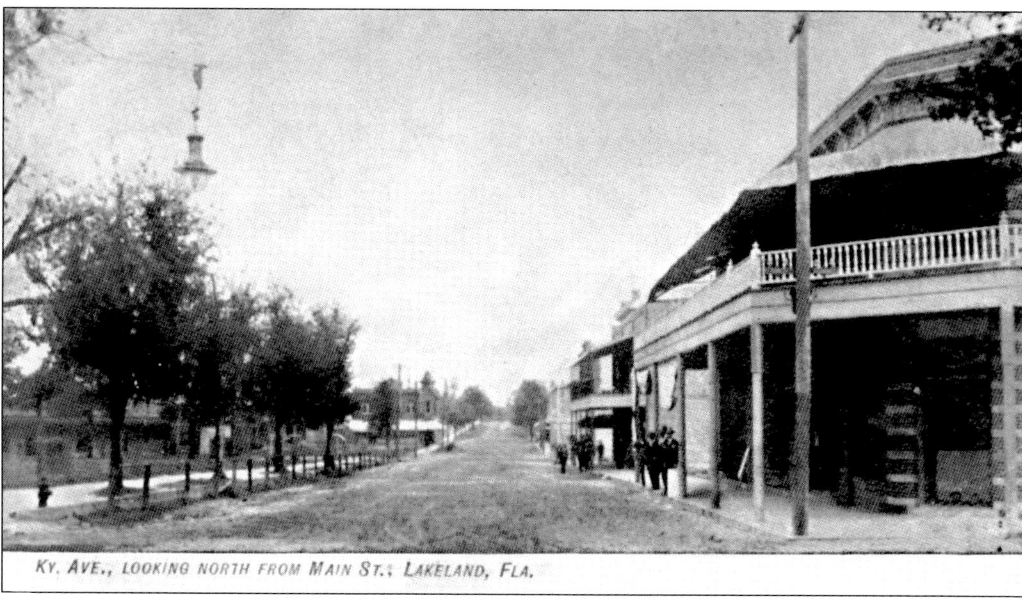

KY. AVE., LOOKING NORTH FROM MAIN ST., LAKELAND, FLA. Munn Park is on the left, and the streets are still unpaved, but the Bryant Block now has a porch and balcony. Lakeland began paving the business district with bricks in 1913. An electric light is visible over the intersection. The postcard shows Lakelanders assembled in front of the businesses for the photograph. (Courtesy Larry Gray.)

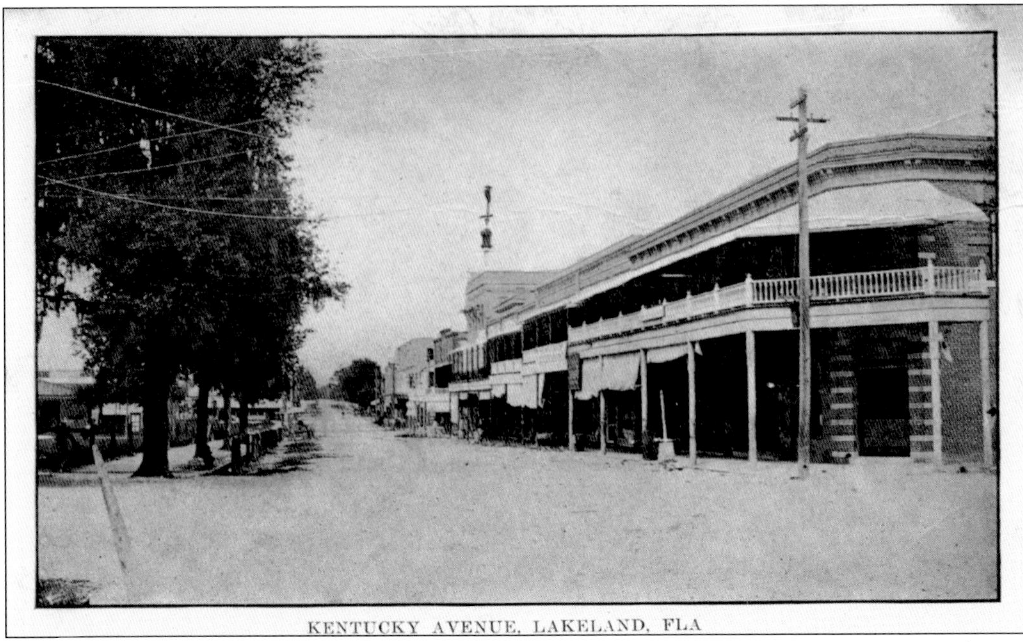

KENTUCKY AVENUE, LAKELAND, FLA. The city continued to grow, and the business district along the east side of Kentucky Avenue continued to flourish. Hitching posts are visible along the edge of Munn Park bordering the street. Horse-drawn buggies were seen in town as late as the 1940s. (Courtesy Lakeland Public Library.)

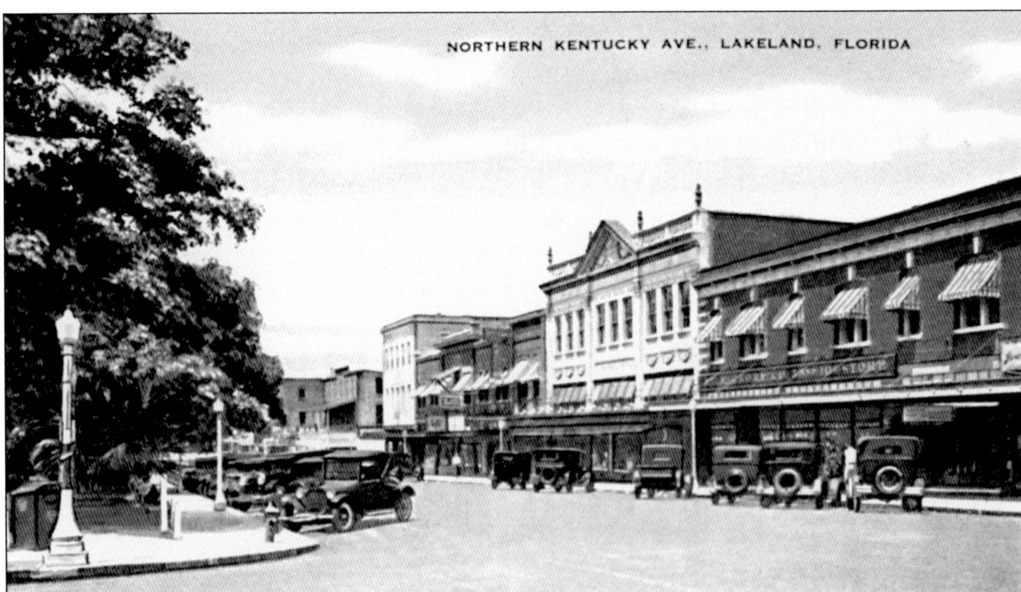

NORTHERN KENTUCKY AVE., LAKELAND, FLORIDA. North Kentucky Avenue bordering the east side of Munn Park was part of the central business district and remains a recognizable sight to Lakeland residents. The Kress Building, constructed in 1929 on what was known as the "Raymondo Block," adjoined the J. G. McCrory 5 and 10 Cent Store. Jewett Drug Store occupied the southern end of the block for over 50 years. (Courtesy Lakeland Public Library.)

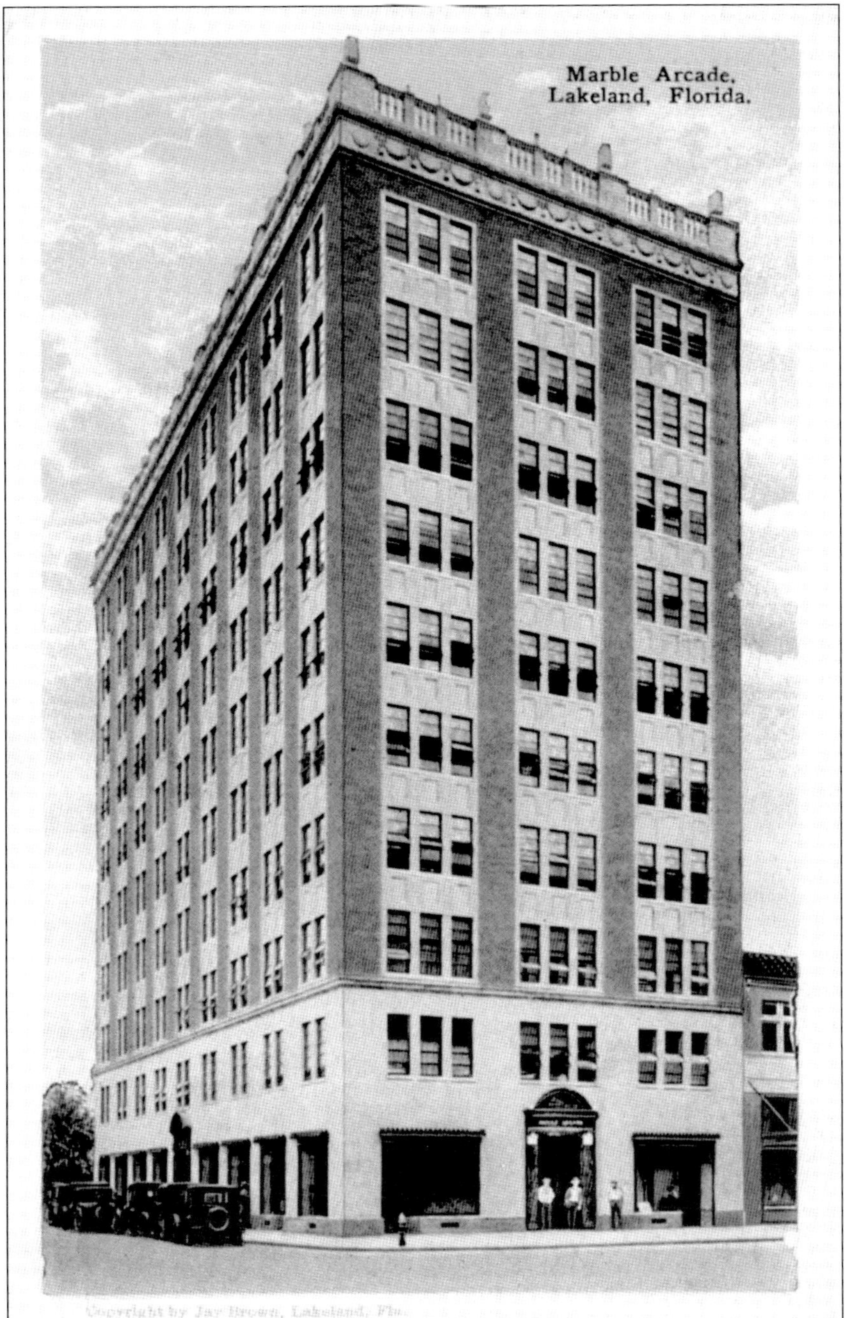

Marble Arcade, Lakeland, Florida. Completed in 1928, this 10-storey building remains one of the tallest in the city. Today it houses the MidFlorida Federal Credit Union, Mitchell's Coffee House, and other businesses. The postcard advertised the new building: "The Marble Arcade, Lakeland's new 10-story office and store building constructed last year at a cost of more than $800,000, is one of the finest office buildings in the state. It faces Kentucky Avenue and the Hotel Thelma and is but one block removed from the main business street." (Courtesy Lakeland Public Library.)

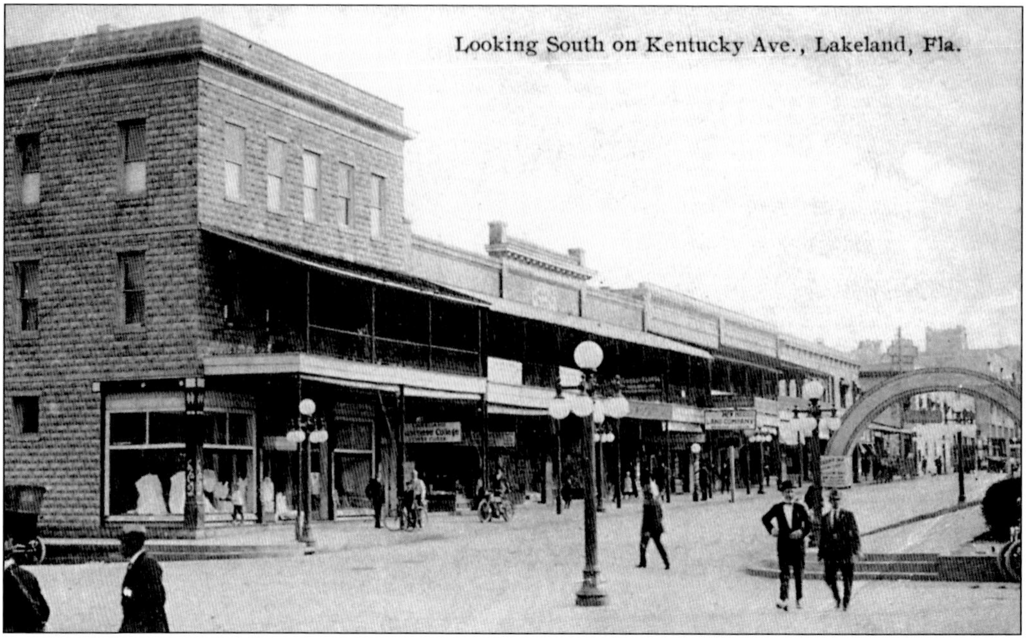

Looking South on Kentucky Ave., Lakeland, Fla. The arch visible on the right side of this undated postcard was constructed for the United Confederate Veterans Reunion in late 1914. Local establishments include the Lakeland Business College, the Kansas-Florida Highlands Company, and the New Mexico Land Company. (Courtesy Lakeland Public Library.)

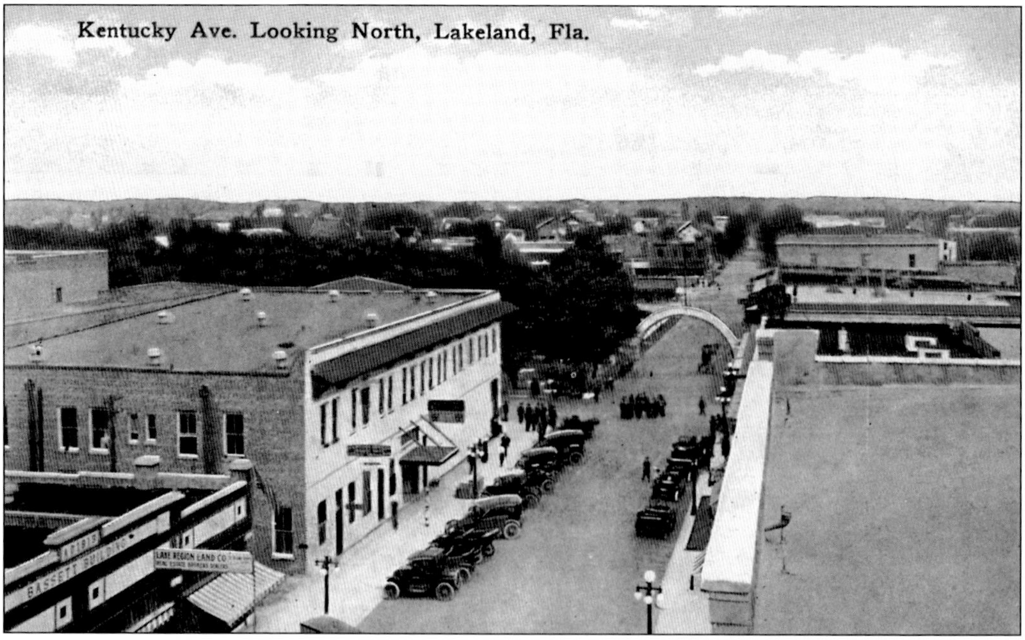

Kentucky Ave. Looking North, Lakeland, Fla. This photograph was likely taken from atop the Hotel Kibler looking toward the welcome arch. From left to right are the Bassett Building (1913), home of the Lake Region Land Company (real estate brokers and dealers), and the Deen-Bryant Building, current home of Nathan's Men's Store. The roof of the Munn Building is prominent in the right foreground. (Authors's Collection.)

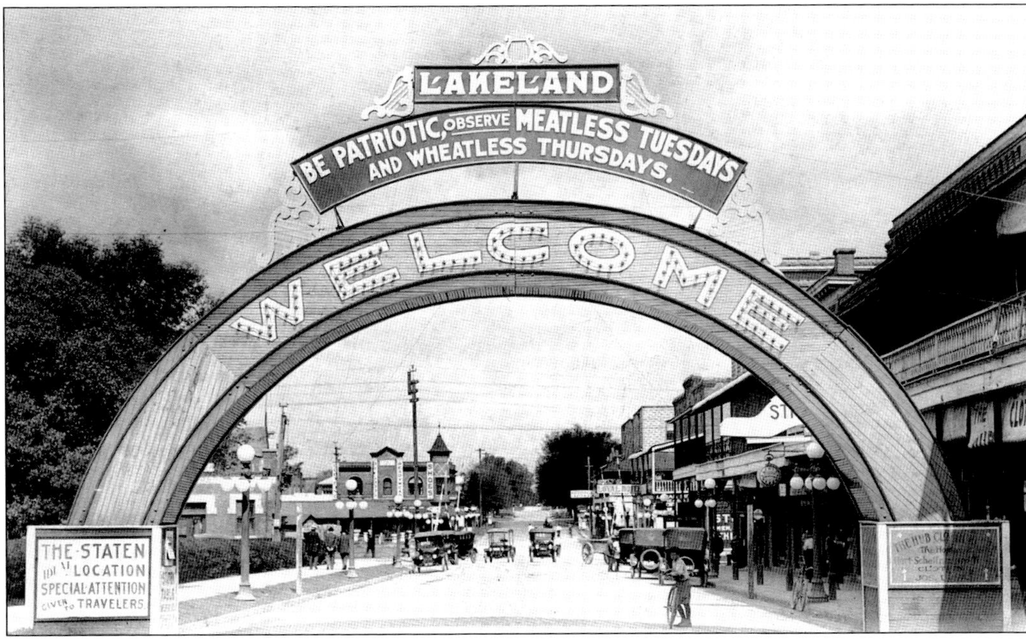

Welcome Arch. This rare World War I-era real-photo postcard features Lakeland's welcome arch. The arch stood some 100 feet north of Main Street and was illuminated with electric lights at night. Advertisements for local businesses were displayed at the base of the arch. At the far left are the railway station and the Clonts Building (1903). Signs for the Loyal Hotel, the Hub Clothing Company, and a photography studio are visible. (Authors's Collection.)

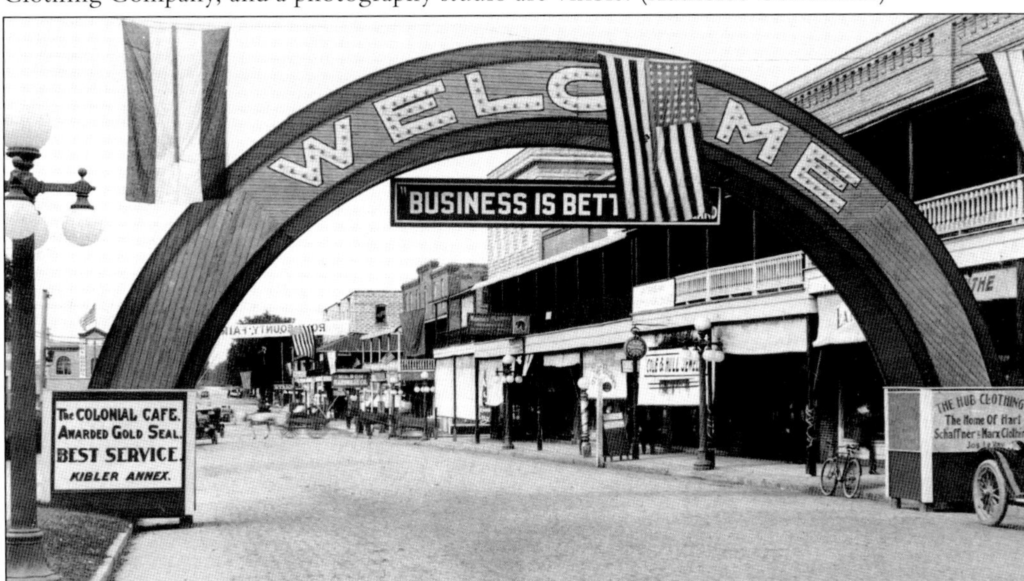

Welcome Arch. The appearance of the arch evolved over the years. Here it displayed the slogan "Business is Better in Lakeland." Flags and a banner advertising the Polk County Fair hung across the street. Wilson Hardware Company, Cole and Hull Jewelry, a bookstore, picture framing services, and barbershop could be found along this busy avenue. (Courtesy Lakeland Public Library.)

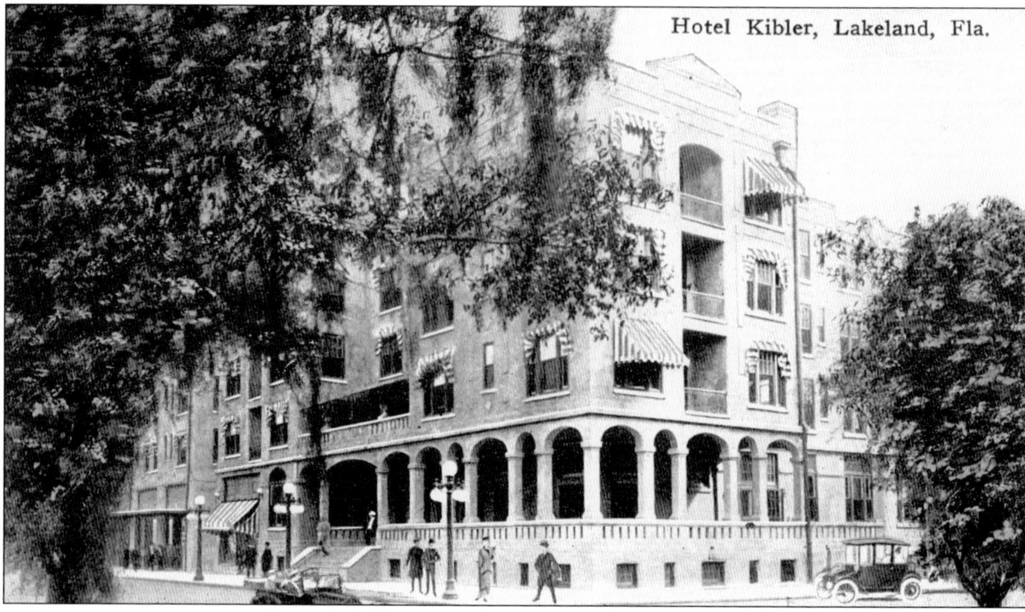

HOTEL KIBLER, LAKELAND, FLA. The magnificent Hotel Kibler, located at the northeast corner of Kentucky Avenue and Lemon Street, catered to Florida's growing tourist trade. The hotel was built by A. B. and D. B. Kibler at a cost of $125,000 and opened November 10, 1913. (Courtesy Lakeland Public Library.)

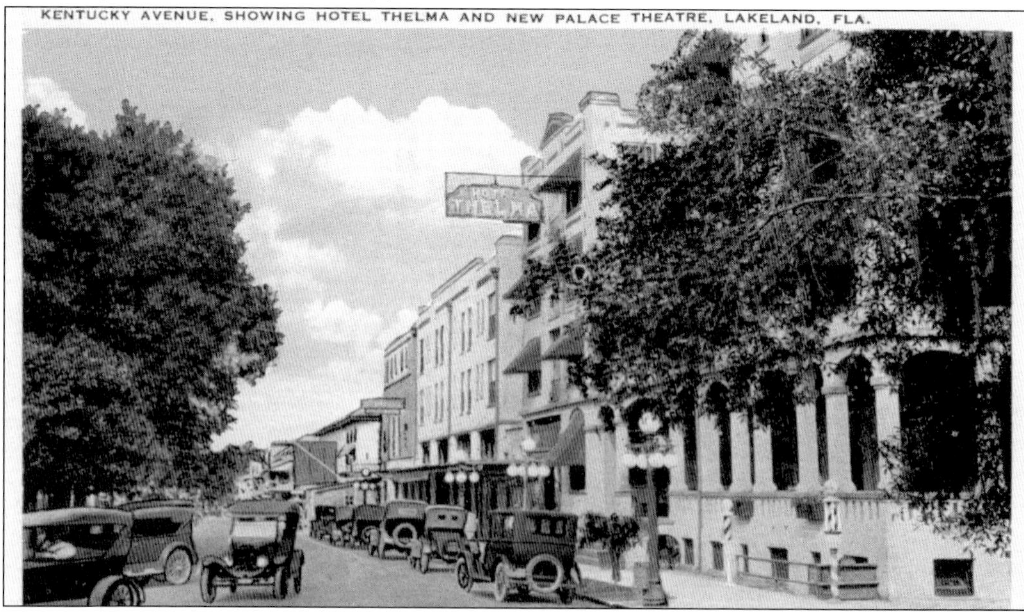

KENTUCKY AVENUE, SHOWING HOTEL THELMA AND NEW PALACE THEATRE, LAKELAND, FLA. The Hotel Kibler was purchased by Henry B. Carter in 1919, and he renamed it the Hotel Thelma in honor of his daughter. The hotel was a Lakeland landmark until it closed and was razed in 1962. The undated message evokes a time long past: "Dear Mr. Hacket, please be sure that the ice house is filled just as full as possible and covered with plenty of sawdust. Maurice Chase will fill it as usual. Have them get more sawdust if necessary. Today is just like an August day in NH. Best regards to all. CAB." (Courtesy Lakeland Public Library.)

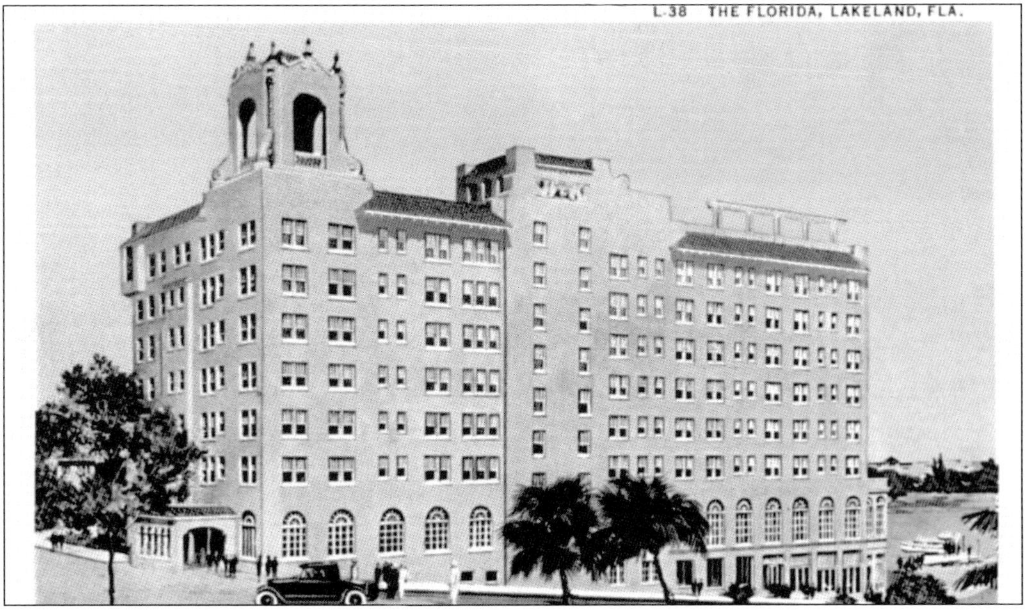

THE FLORIDA, LAKELAND, FLA. Ground was broken for the New Florida Hotel at 128 South Massachusetts Avenue in 1926 during the height of Florida's land boom. Construction was not completed until 1935, a result of the land bust and the Depression. The hotel served for a time as a retirement center before extensive renovation and reopening in 2005 as luxurious living spaces. This peculiar postcard may have been produced as a pre-construction promotional postcard; the hotel is missing the top floor. (Courtesy Lakeland Public Library.)

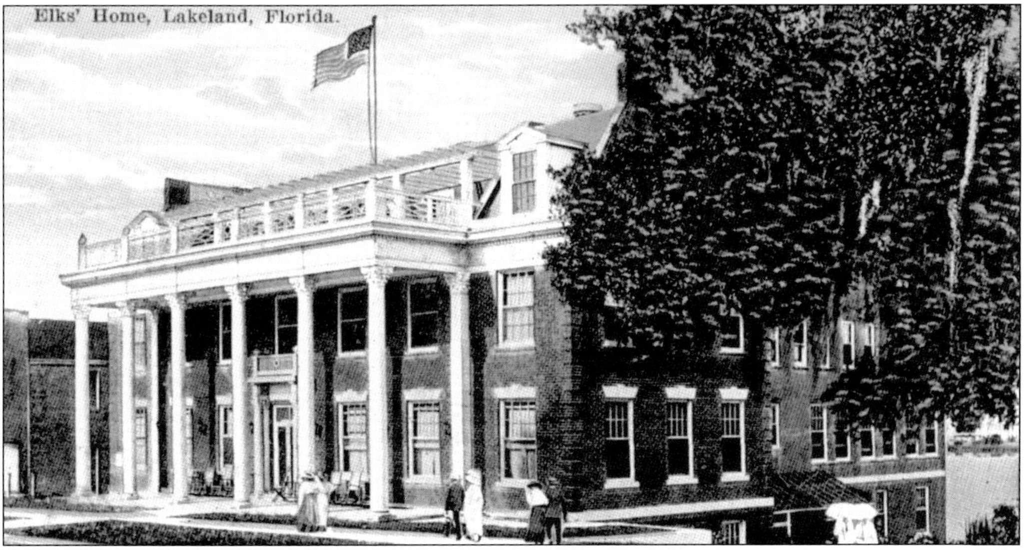

ELKS' HOME, LAKELAND, FLORIDA. The Elks' Home was on the east side of Massachusetts Avenue north of First Presbyterian Church and the New Florida Hotel. The Elks' Home cornerstone was laid March 29, 1917, and the grand opening was the following year. The cost of the facility including furnishings was nearly $75,000. According to a 1922 *Lakeland Morning Star* advertisement, the Elks Grill was "Positively the Best Place to Eat in Lakeland. . . . Our regular noonday full meal is a winner. You can't beat it—50¢. The Elks Grill is Open to All, A. A. Rahner, Prop." (Courtesy Lakeland Public Library.)

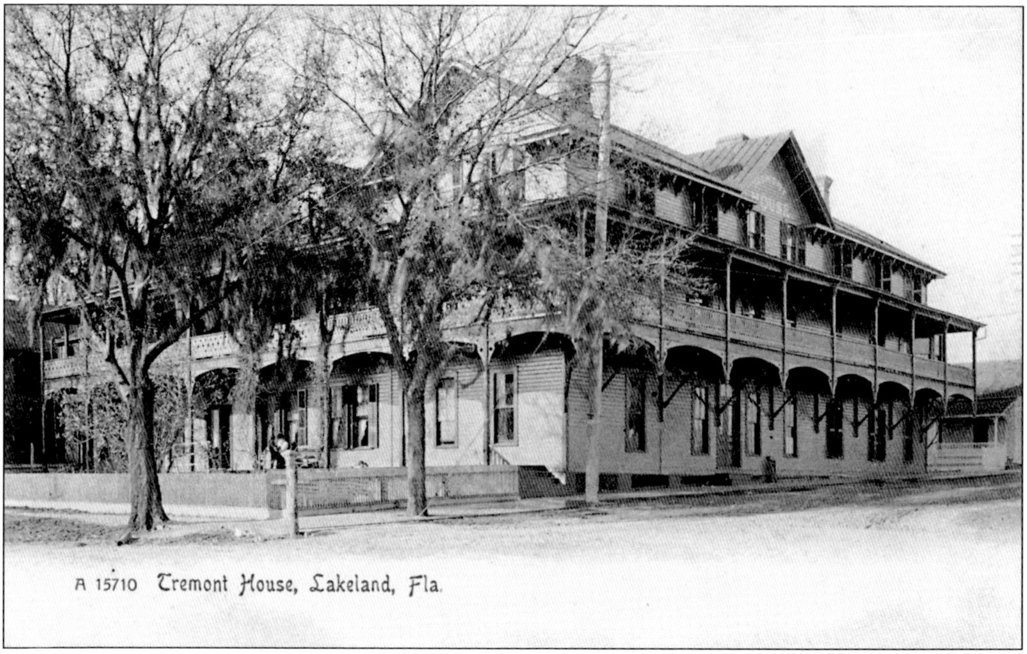

TREMONT HOUSE, LAKELAND, FLA. Tremont House was constructed in 1885 by Abraham G. Munn on the southwest corner of Main Street and Massachusetts Avenue, and it was widely regarded as the city's finest hotel by the time this postcard was mailed in July 1906. Known later as the Tremont Hotel, the building was enlarged before being moved to make way for the Hotel Lakeland Terrace. (Courtesy Lakeland Public Library.)

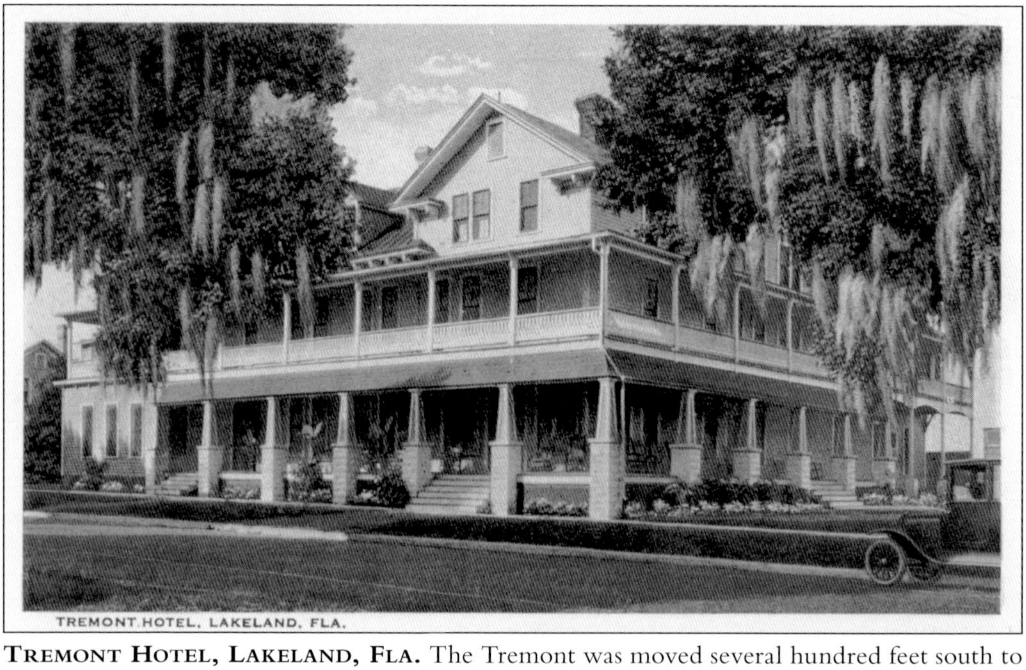

TREMONT HOTEL, LAKELAND, FLA. The Tremont was moved several hundred feet south to 113 South Massachusetts Avenue by 1924. Renovations were made to the façade of the hotel before it was demolished in 1936. (Courtesy Lakeland Public Library.)

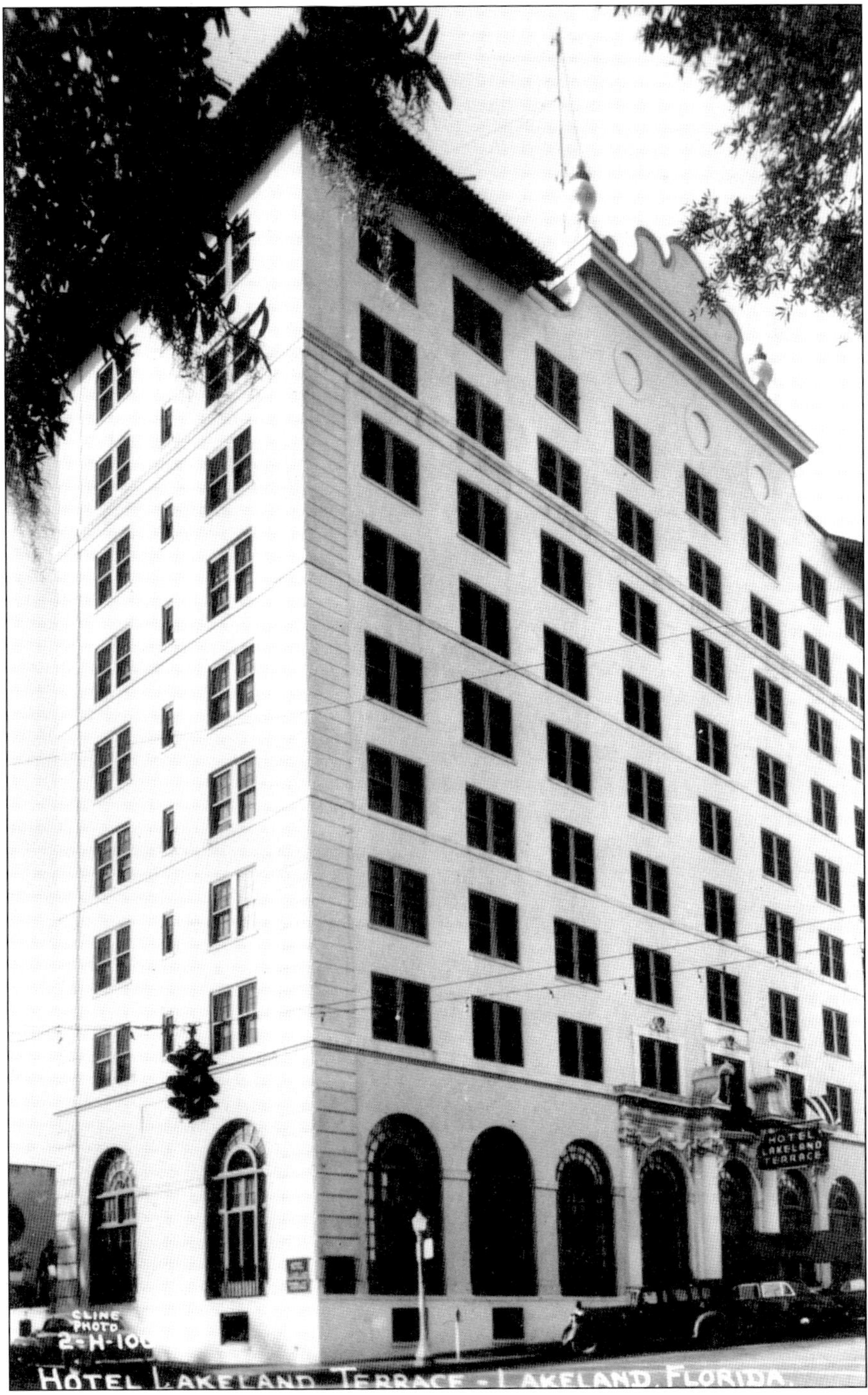

HOTEL LAKELAND TERRACE—LAKELAND, FLORIDA. This distinctive Lakeland landmark was constructed on the southwest corner of Massachusetts Avenue and Main Street, on the site previously occupied by the Tremont Hotel. The hotel opened in October 1924. Following a period of neglect, the hotel was renovated and reopened in 1998 as Lakeland's most elegant hostelry. (Courtesy Lakeland Public Library.)

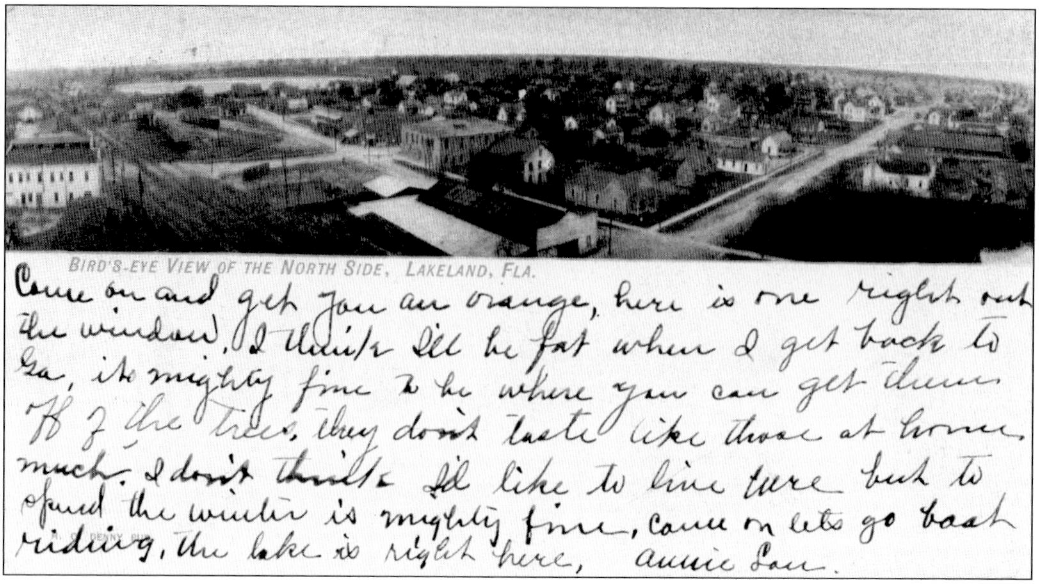

Bird's Eye View of the North Side, Lakeland, Fla. Early aerial views of Lakeland were taken from the municipal water tower at the southeast corner of Massachusetts Avenue and Cedar Street. Mailed in December 1906, this postcard shows the railroad lines on the left, and the Bowyer Building (1902)—current home of Brooke Pottery—is visible in the center. Lake Wire and numerous residences are visible in the distance. The delightful message reads: "Come on and get you an orange, here is one right out the window. I think I'll be fat when I get back to Ga., it's mighty fine to be where you can get them off of the trees, they don't taste like those at home much. I don't think I'd like to live here but to spend the winter is mighty fine. Come on let's go boat riding, the lake is right here. Annie Lou." (Courtesy Lakeland Public Library.)

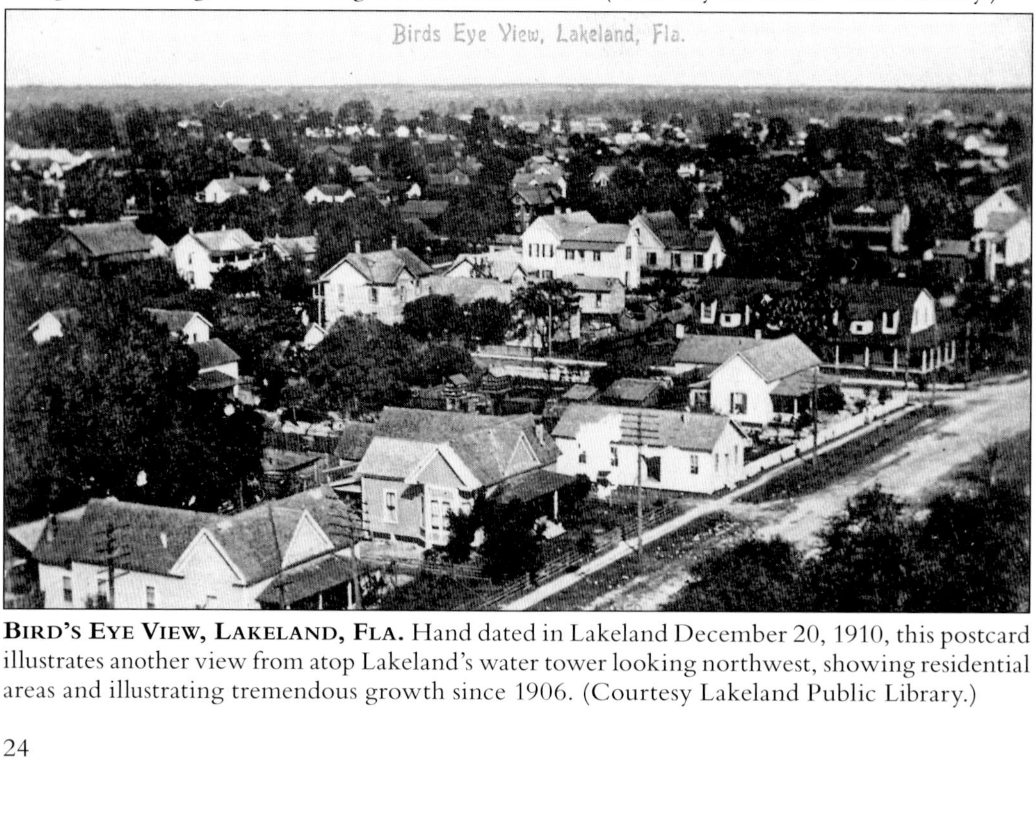

Bird's Eye View, Lakeland, Fla. Hand dated in Lakeland December 20, 1910, this postcard illustrates another view from atop Lakeland's water tower looking northwest, showing residential areas and illustrating tremendous growth since 1906. (Courtesy Lakeland Public Library.)

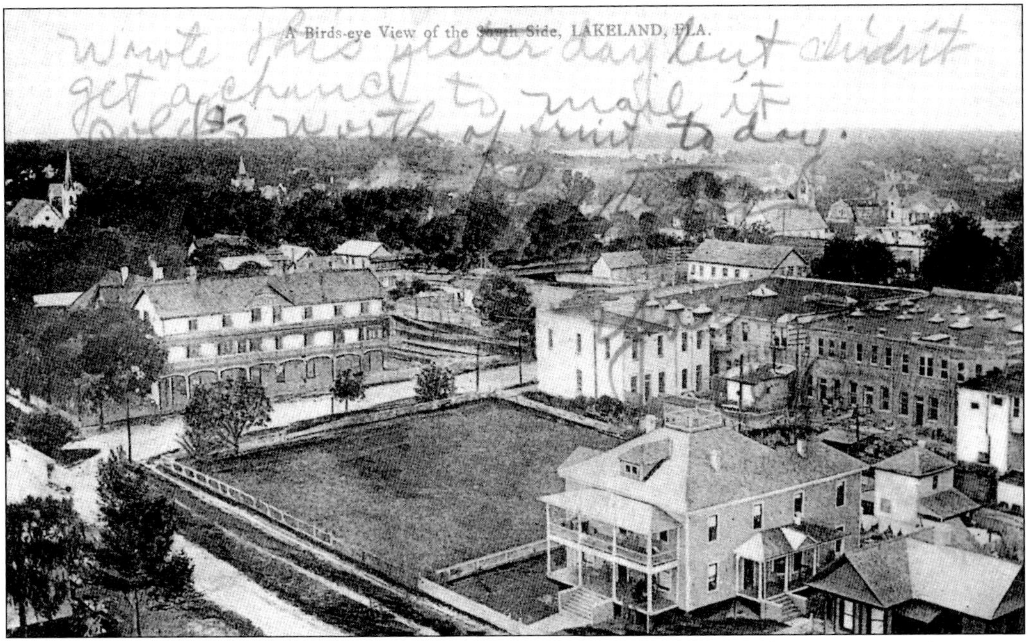

BIRD'S EYE VIEW OF THE SOUTH SIDE, LAKELAND, FLA. Postmarked in November 1911, this view from atop the downtown water tower looks toward the southwest. Massachusetts Avenue runs from left to right in the foreground, and Main Street borders the Tremont House. The wood-frame building in the right foreground was the Florida Hotel, predating the New Florida Hotel. (Courtesy Lakeland Public Library.)

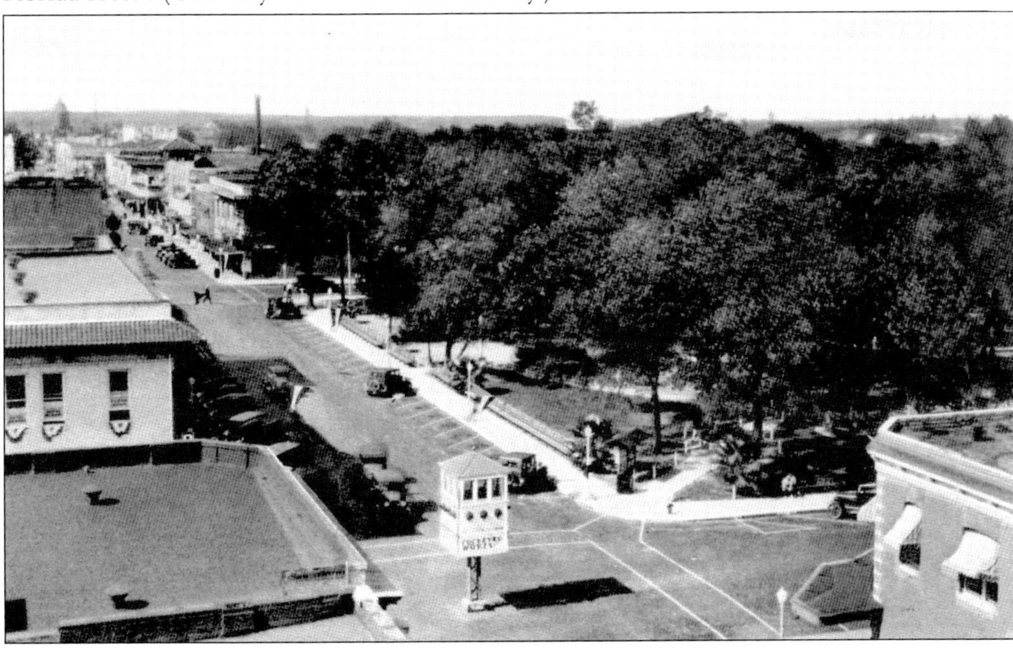

MAIN STREET FROM THE LAKELAND TERRACE HOTEL, LAKELAND, FLORIDA. This is an unusual view looking westward on Main Street. The traffic-control tower in the center of Kentucky Avenue and Main Street was a familiar sight to Lakelanders in the late 1920s and 1930s. (Courtesy Larry Gray.)

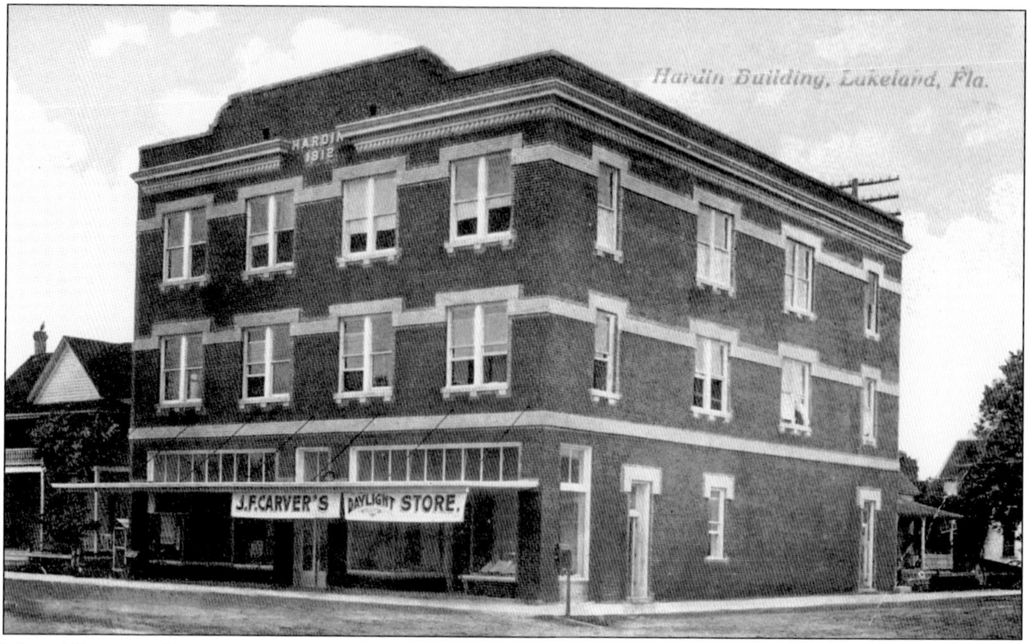

THE HARDIN BUILDING, LAKELAND, FLA. The Hardin Building (1912) stood at the corner of Florida Avenue and Main Street and housed J. F. Carver's Daylight Store. (Courtesy Lakeland Public Library.)

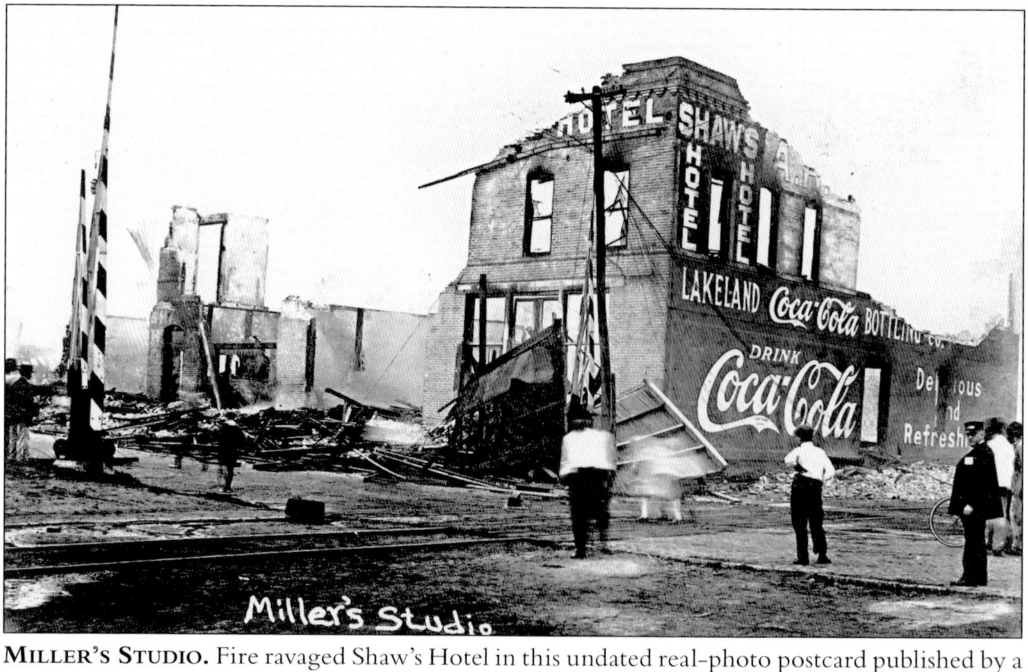

MILLER'S STUDIO. Fire ravaged Shaw's Hotel in this undated real-photo postcard published by a Lakeland photographic studio. The hotel was also known as the New Southern Hotel, with L. C. Shaw as proprietor, and was located at 301 North Kentucky Avenue. (Authors's Collection.)

Two

Munn Park and Train Depot

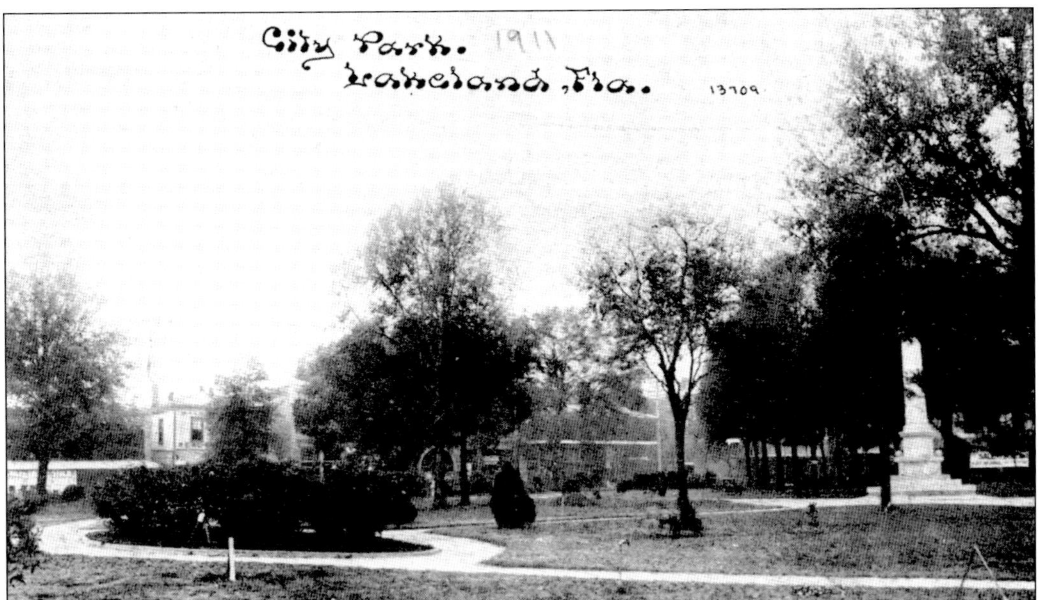

City Park, Lakeland, Fla. Kentuckian Abraham Godwin Munn is regarded as the "Father of Lakeland," although he never lived here permanently. His Lakeland Improvement Company was an influential real estate and development concern, and in 1898 he donated land to the new town for the public park, which, since 1908, bears his name. This postcard was postmarked August 1911 and reads: "Was pleased and a little surprised to receive your card. I thought you had forgotten your Lakeland acquaintances by now. I don't see how things could be much duller there than here, however when school begins one has no time to be dull—Every day is a full one. The next L-social meets at my house. Sorry you can't be here. B. H." (Courtesy Lakeland Public Library.)

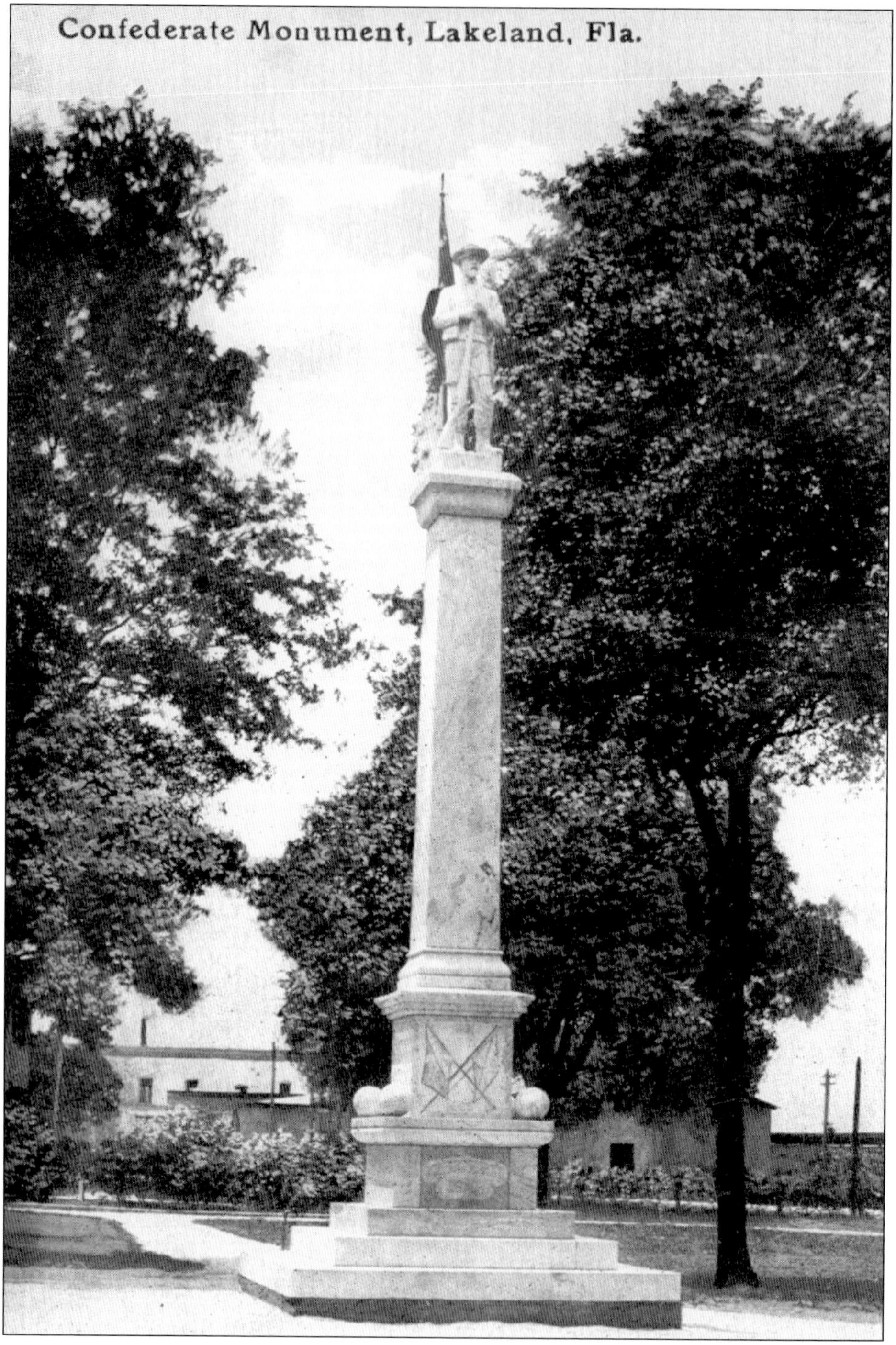

CONFEDERATE MONUMENT, LAKELAND, FLA. The Confederate monument is located in Munn Park. The monument, featuring a Confederate soldier atop an ornate marble column, was dedicated in Munn Park on June 3, 1910, by the Lakeland chapter of the United Daughters of the Confederacy. This postcard shows a Confederate flag flying atop the monument. (Courtesy Lakeland Public Library.)

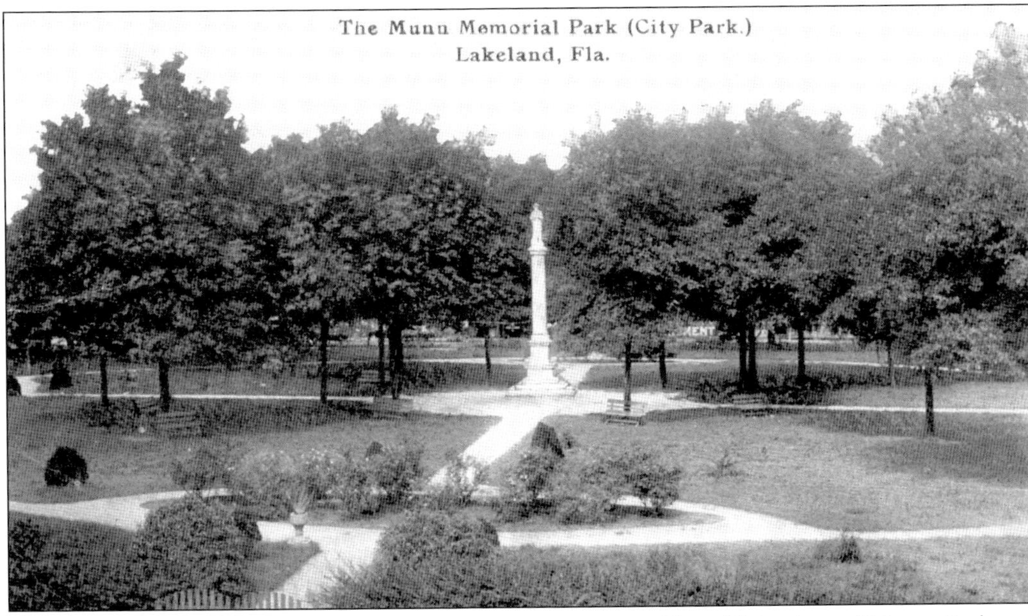

THE MUNN MEMORIAL PARK (CITY PARK) LAKELAND, FLA. This view of Munn Park was from the east (North Kentucky Avenue) side of the park. This postcard was mailed in October 1912 and reads: "Your card, with the lovely sentiment, has been received. Many thanks for the same. We have been having beautiful weather for the past week. Mr. H. has been busy making garden & setting out strawberry plants; ought to be eating ripe berries by Jan. or Feb. We are counting on seeing our dear ones this winter. Hope nothing will prevent them coming. Lovingly, Mrs. C. M. Keene." (Courtesy Lakeland Public Library.)

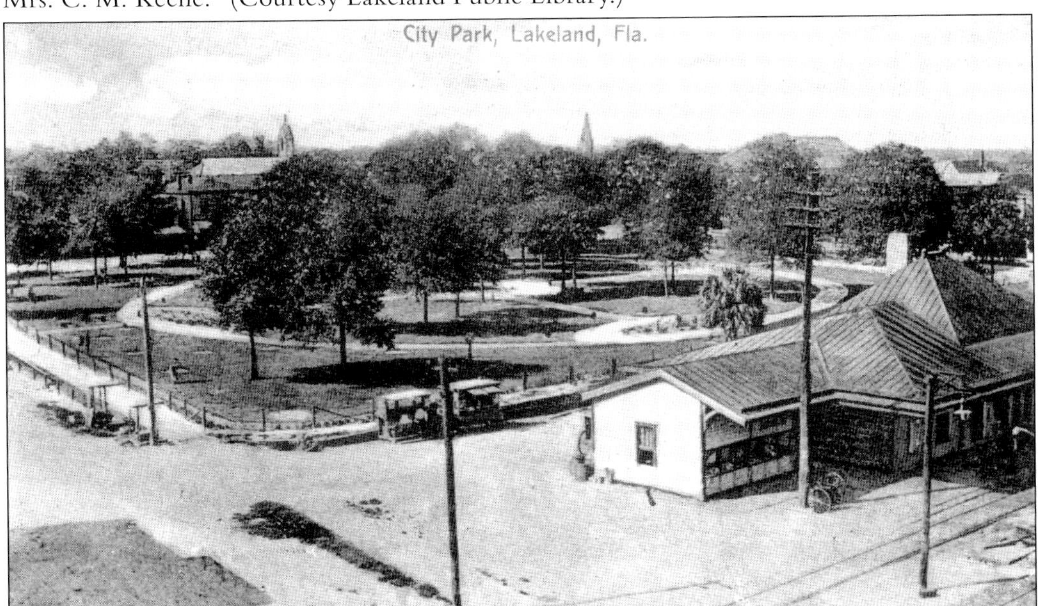

CITY PARK, LAKELAND, FLA. This unusual view toward the southwest shows the fenced park and an early series of walking paths, with the Atlantic Coast Line Railroad station at the right. Pres. Theodore Roosevelt addressed a large crowd of citizens in Munn Park in 1917 regarding the world war. (Courtesy Larry Gray.)

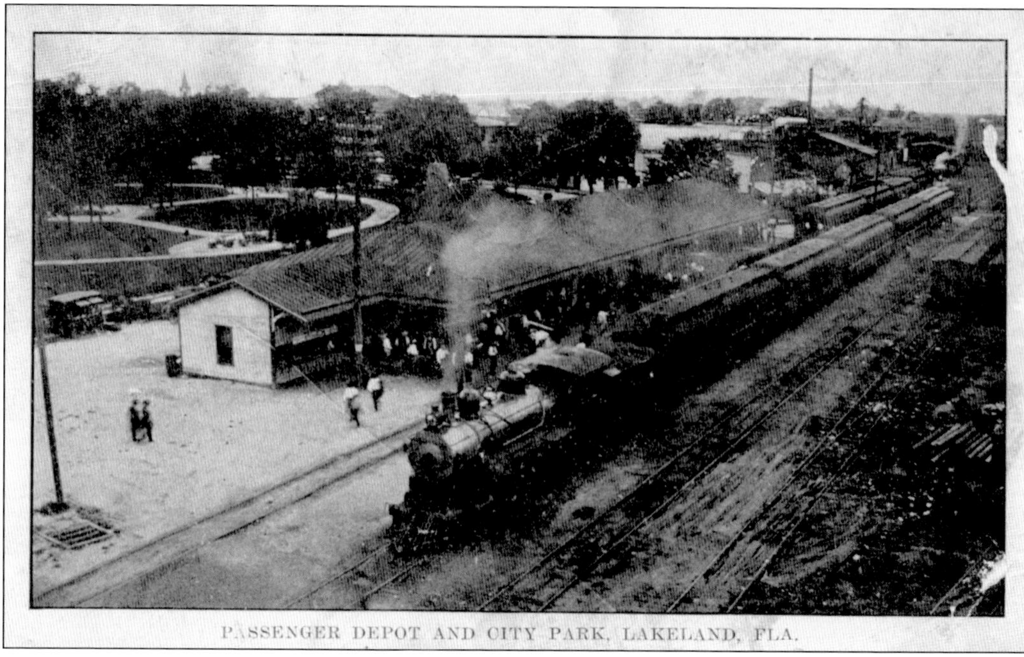

PASSENGER DEPOT AND CITY PARK, LAKELAND, FLA. All aboard! A train leaves Lakeland for points east on one of the oldest postcards showing Lakeland's train station. (Courtesy Lakeland Public Library.)

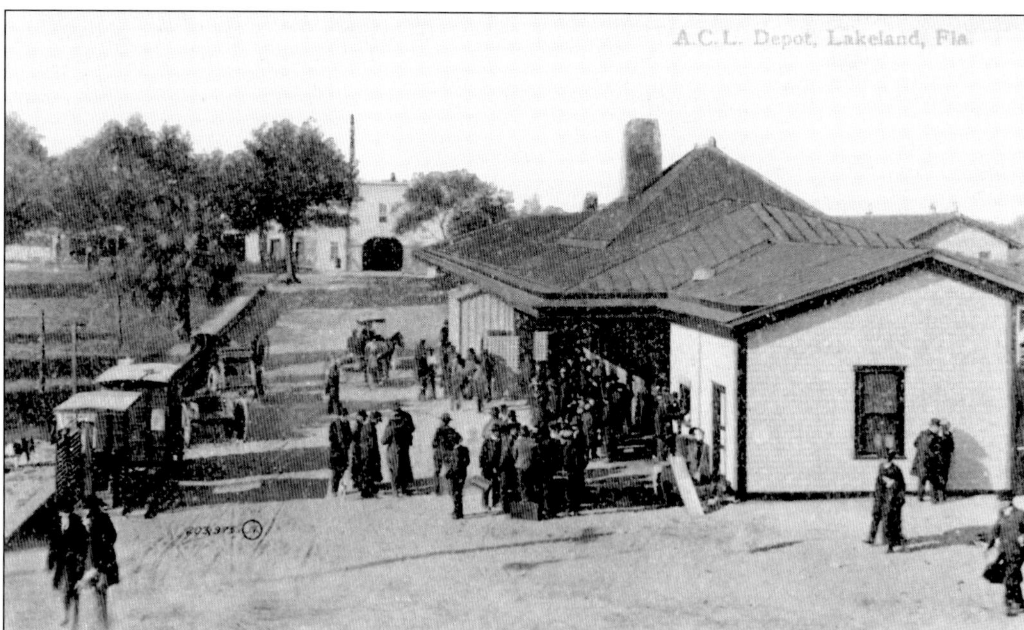

A. C. L. DEPOT, LAKELAND, FLA. Lakeland experienced a gradual transformation from a remote settlement to a bustling city that is centered around a dynamic downtown. The importance of the railroad was paramount, as rail traffic brought goods and visitors directly to the town's center and provided a reliable shipping point for local agricultural products. This is a view from across North Kentucky Avenue looking west. (Courtesy Lakeland Public Library.)

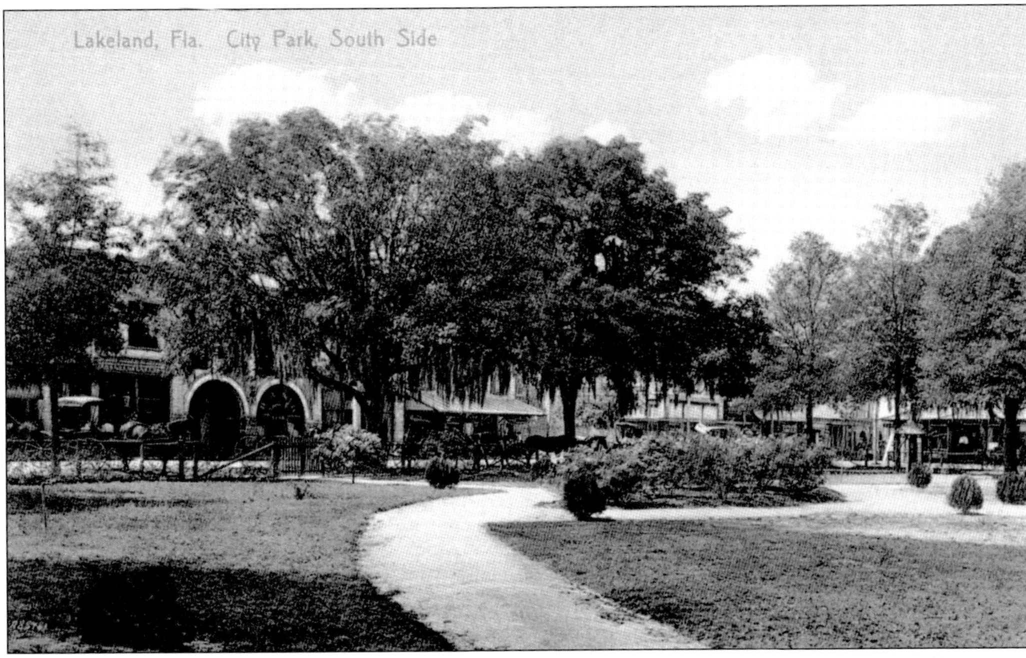

LAKELAND, FLA. CITY PARK, SOUTH SIDE. The Kentucky Building on the south edge of Main Street is visible in this early view of Munn Park. A number of horse-drawn buggies line the park's edge. (Courtesy Lakeland Public Library.)

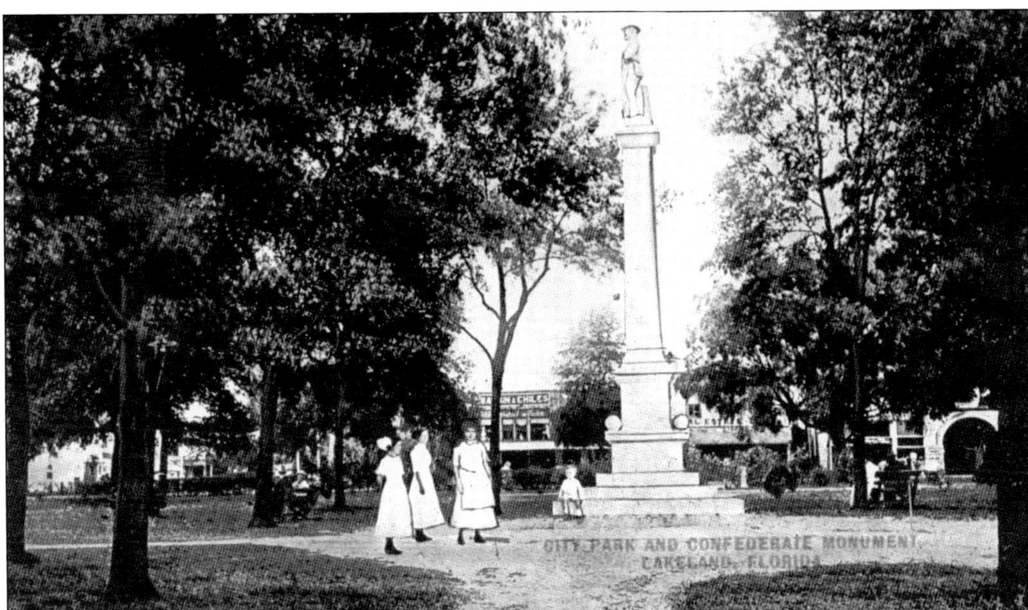

CITY PARK AND CONFEDERATE MONUMENT, LAKELAND, FLORIDA. Businesses along Main Street are visible at the south edge of Munn Park. This postcard was mailed from Lakeland December 23, 1911: "Dear Friend I thought I write you a line we are all well hope this finds you the same. This is a scene at the depot it is nice & warm here I wish you a Merry Xmas & Happy New Year Clifford & I will write soon. Georgia Taft." (Courtesy Lakeland Public Library.)

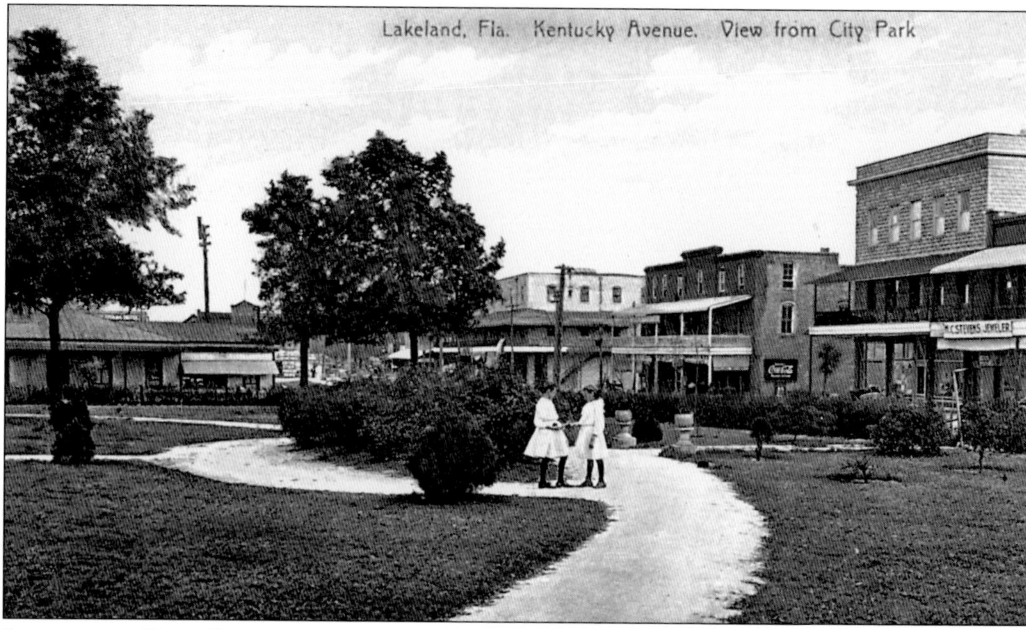

LAKELAND, FLA. KENTUCKY AVENUE. VIEW FROM CITY PARK. This rich view from within Munn Park looks northeast toward the train station and North Kentucky Avenue. Some of the earliest brick buildings surrounding the park are extant: the Bowyer Building (1902), Kentucky Building (1903), Clonts Building (1903), Bryant Block (1904), part of the Raymondo Building (*c.* 1904), and the Deen-Bryant Building (*c.* 1912). (Courtesy Lakeland Public Library.)

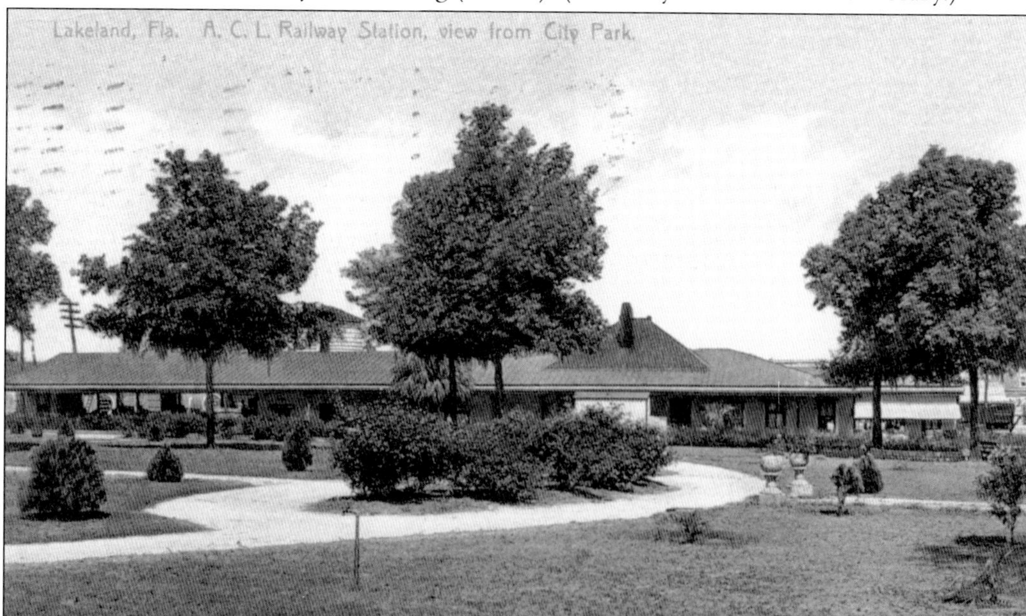

LAKELAND, FLA. A. C. L. RAILWAY STATION, VIEW FROM CITY PARK. The train station's water tower is visible over the rooftop. This card was mailed to Chicago-area LaGrange, Illinois: "Jan. 27, 1910. Home next week Monday we think—it has been a great trip. Have seen lots of Florida but it has been a great deal of riding on some poor track. Can hardly believe there is no snow at home. Wish you had been with us, Lida." (Courtesy Lakeland Public Library.)

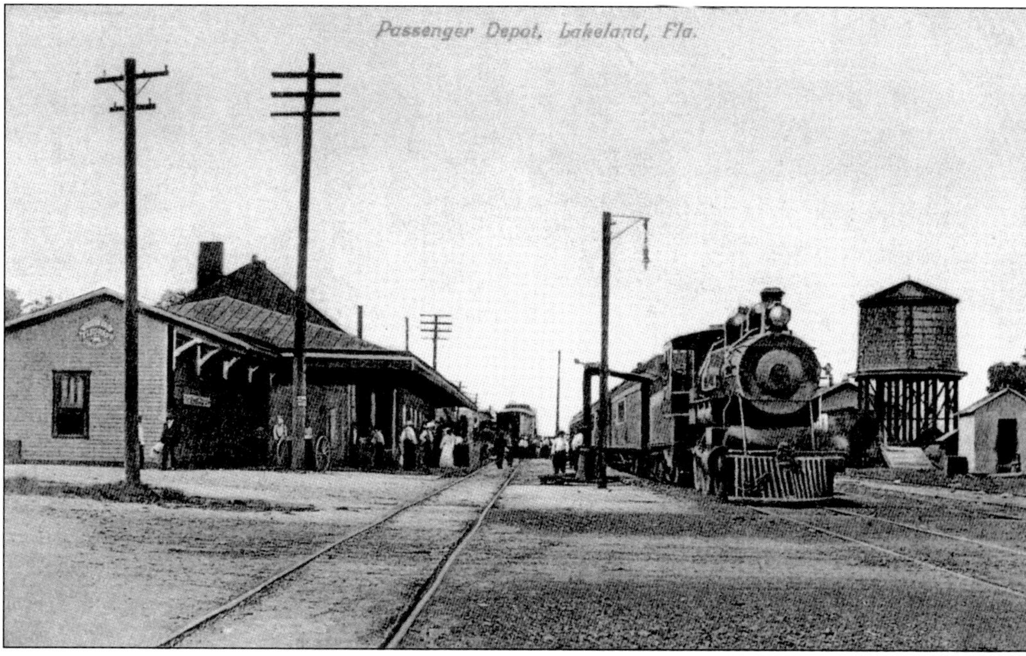

PASSENGER DEPOT, LAKELAND, FLA. Lakeland was situated on the main rail line between Tampa and Jacksonville and was the highest point between those cities. (Courtesy Larry Gray.)

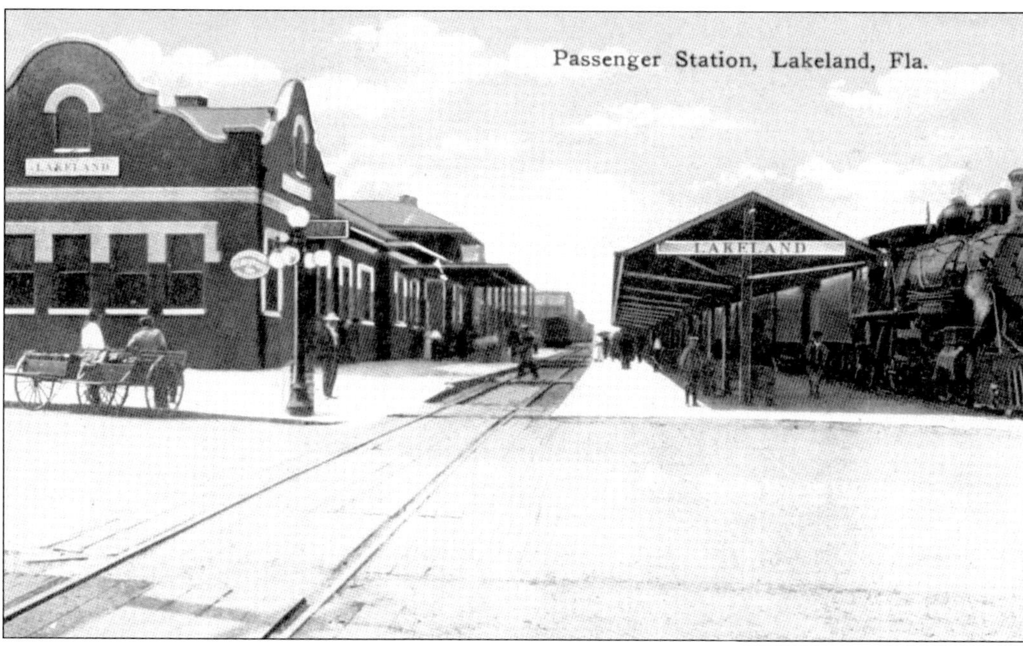

PASSENGER STATION, LAKELAND, FLA. This station was completed in 1912 at a cost of $35,000. By this time, 30 passenger trains passed through Lakeland daily. (Courtesy Lakeland Public Library.)

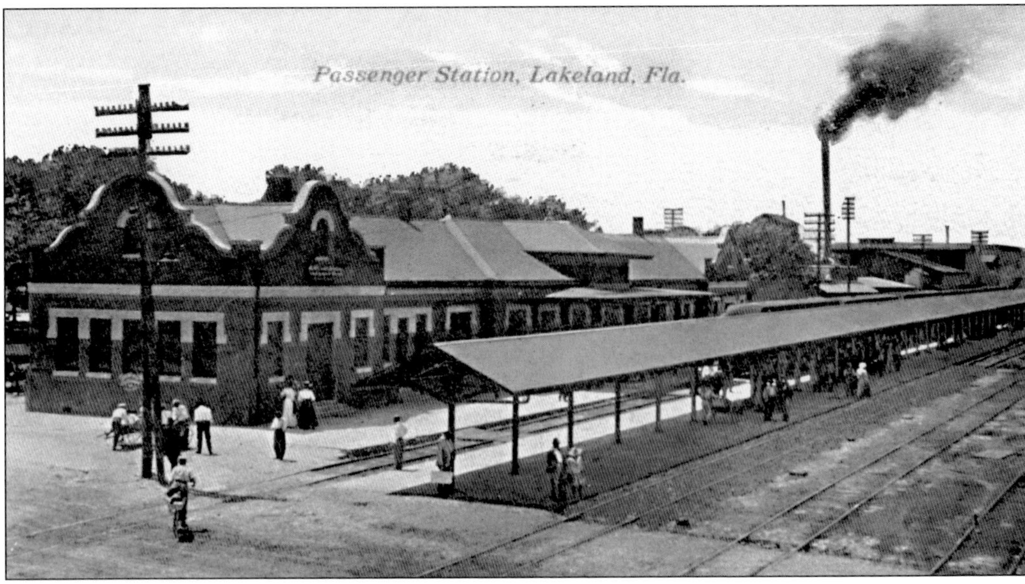

PASSENGER STATION, LAKELAND, FLA. The smoke stack visible on the horizon was part of Norman Riggins' sawmill. Mailed from Lakeland in early 1915, the postcard carried news of everyday life: "Friend Ed, I am camped here for a day or two. Called at the old barbershop saw your friend Weaver—he sent his regards to you. . . . They have improved this town quite a little with new Depot new hotels paved streets. I saw Ed Spencer he is looking good it is cold here and the weather has been bad. All winter I am wearing my heavy overcoat." (Courtesy Lakeland Public Library.)

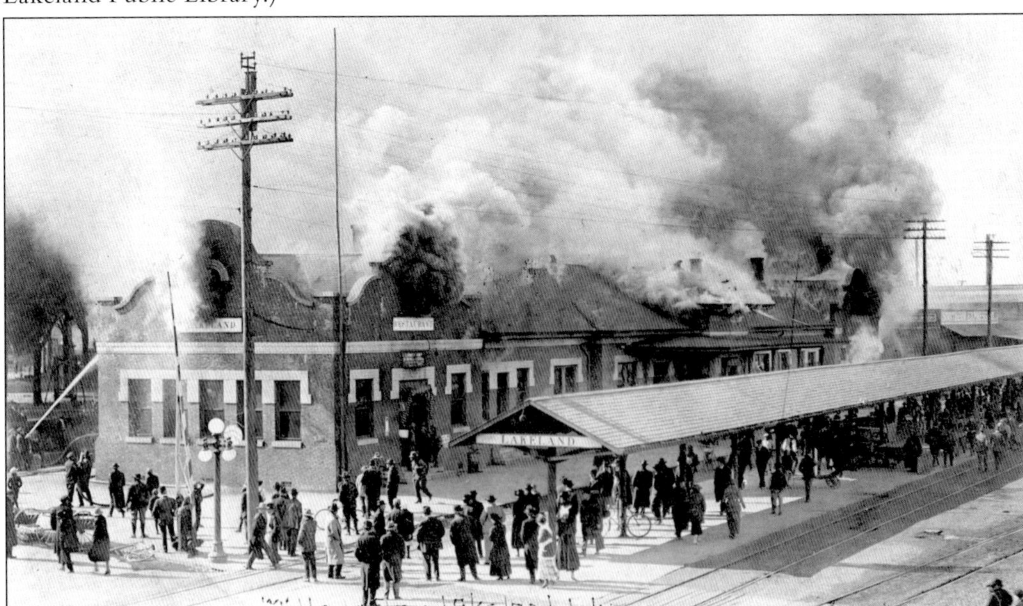

MILLER AND BAY, LAKELAND, FLA. In February 1918, fire destroyed much of the Atlantic Coast Line Railroad station, which is seen in this dramatic real-photo postcard. Luckily the shell of the building was largely salvaged, and the station reopened in January 1919 having been rebuilt to incorporate the walls of the damaged structure and with a new second story. (Courtesy Lakeland Public Library.)

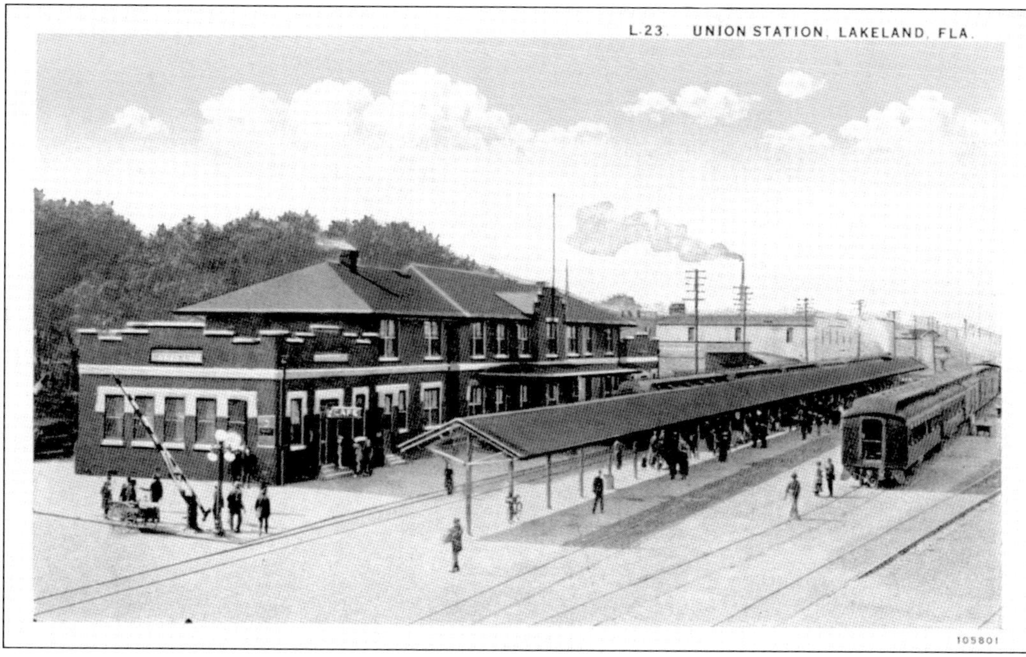

UNION STATION, LAKELAND, FLA. After reopening in 1919, the station served until it was razed in 1961 and replaced by a new terminal on the New Tampa Highway. Trains still rumble past Munn Park, but without the terminal, the park doubtless lost some of the flavor early citizens were accustomed to. (Courtesy Lakeland Public Library.)

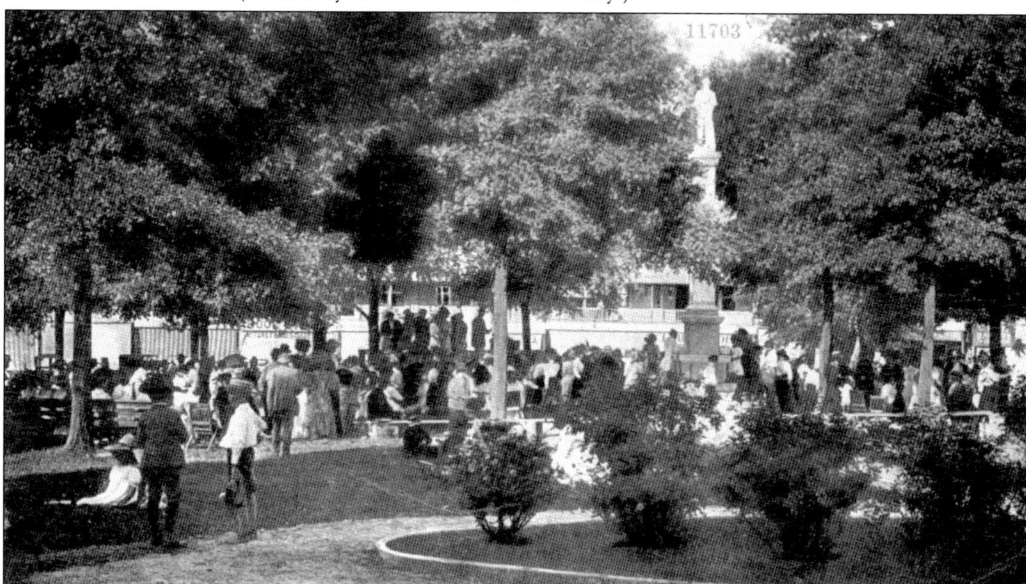

CITY PARK, LAKELAND, FLA. This undated postcard shows a large gathering in Lakeland's oldest park. Cultural and civic activities have long attracted local residents to the city's center. Concrete walks were installed in Munn Park in 1921. The evolution of the park grounds has continued, as today's wide brick walkways wind through a mature, lightly wooded area. Many other parks exist within the city today, but none approach the historical importance of this large block. (Courtesy Lakeland Public Library.)

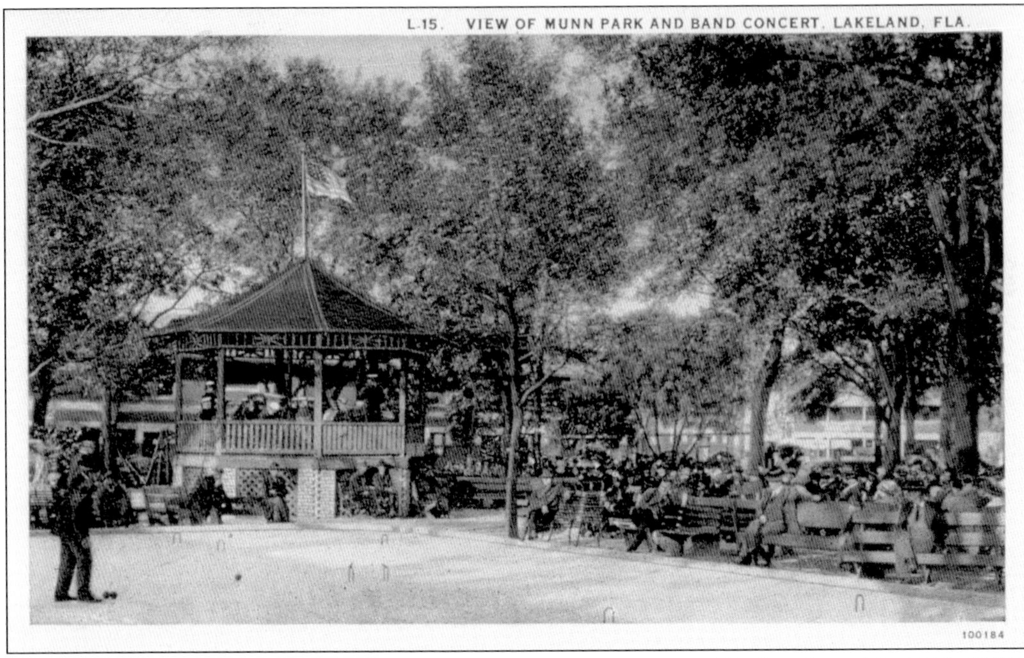

VIEW OF MUNN PARK AND BAND CONCERT, LAKELAND, FLA. The bandstand (*c.* 1915–1950s) is long gone, but Munn Park remains a traditional community gathering spot, hosting concerts, politicians, and other public events. (Courtesy Lakeland Public Library.)

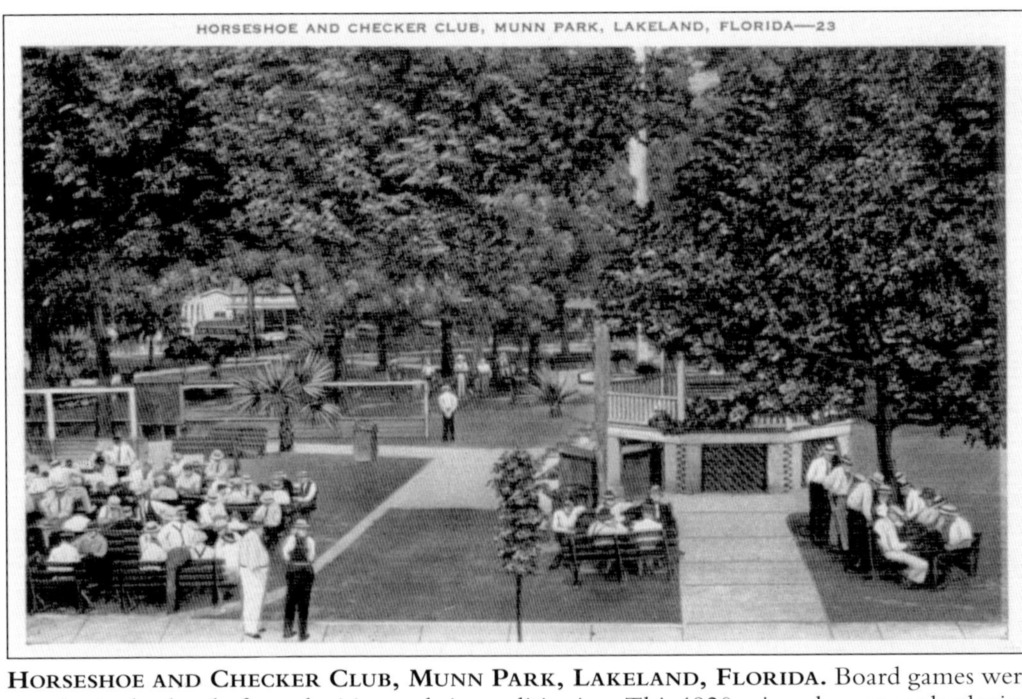

HORSESHOE AND CHECKER CLUB, MUNN PARK, LAKELAND, FLORIDA. Board games were popular in the days before television and air conditioning. This 1920s view shows people playing checkers when tournaments were popular year-round. (Courtesy Lakeland Public Library.)

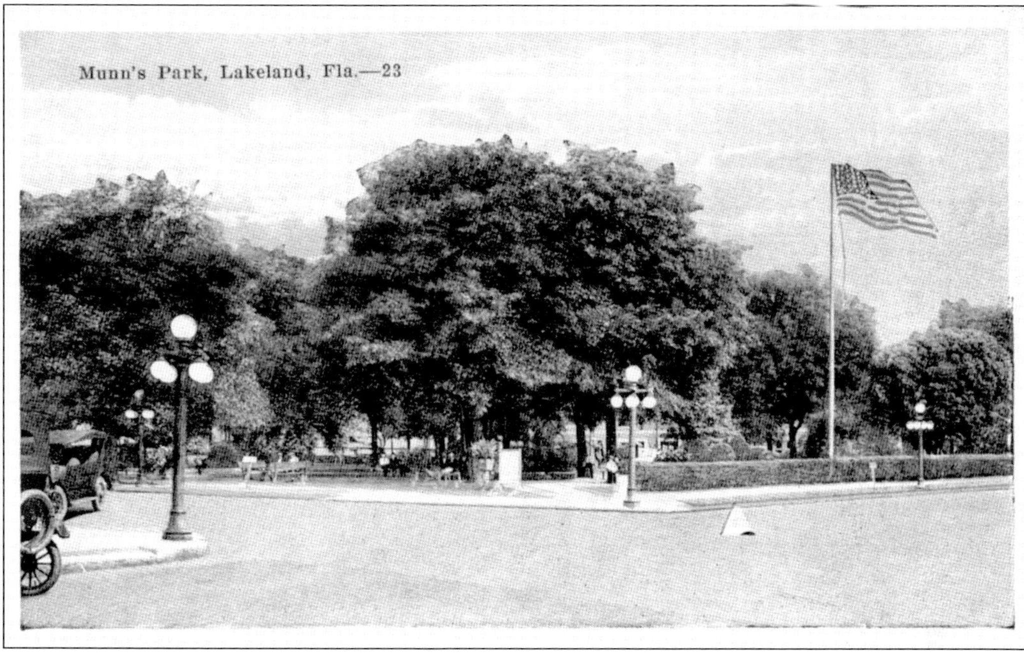

MUNN'S PARK, LAKELAND, FLA. The southeast corner of the park is shown in one of many existing postcards published by the Lakeland Bookstore in the early 1920s. (Courtesy Lakeland Public Library.)

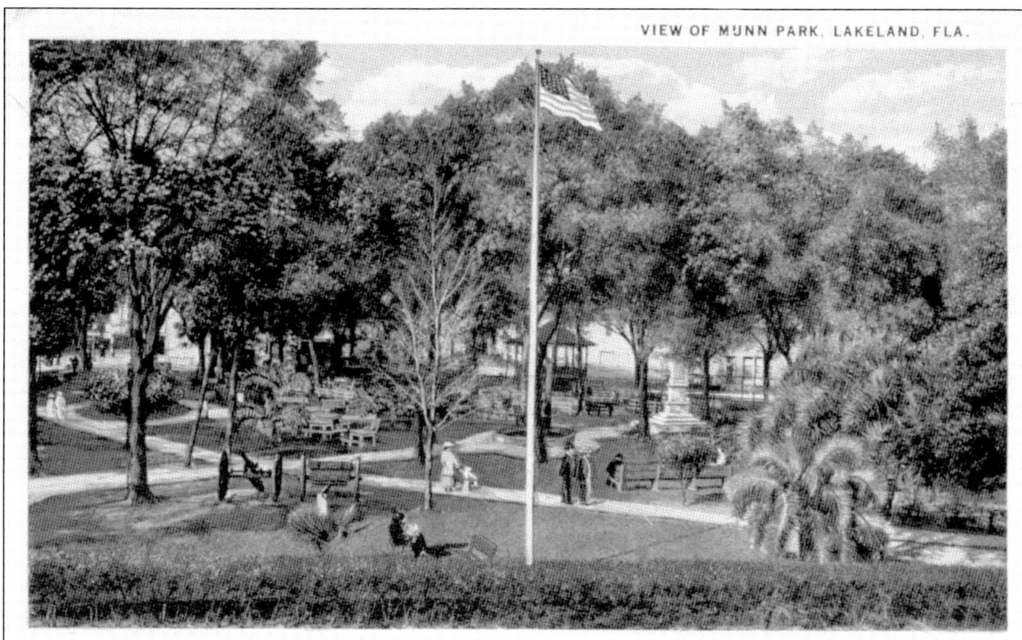

VIEW OF MUNN PARK, LAKELAND, FLA. Lakeland was living up to its reputed average of mid-70s temperatures if one would sit comfortably in the park in January 1926. Leila A. Kelsey wrote: "315 W. Magnolia St. Lakeland, Florida Jan. 18, 1926. This is where we went and sat without wraps this afternoon. The flowers are much nicer than they look here. Leila A. Kelsey." (Courtesy Lakeland Public Library.)

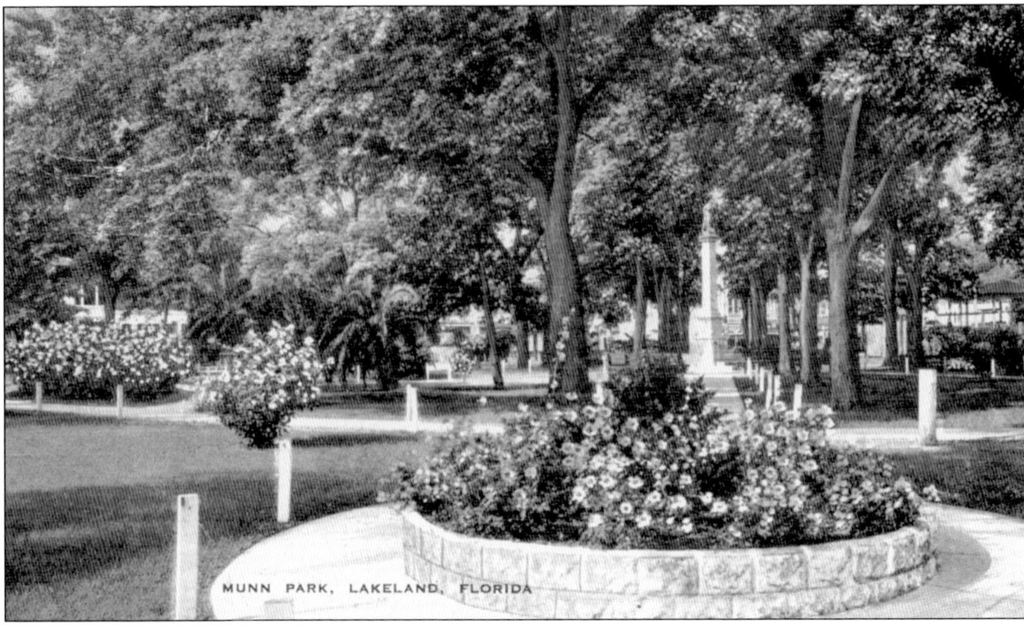

MUNN PARK, LAKELAND, FLORIDA. Central-Florida visitors mailed this postcard in December 1947 telling of their journey: "Hi Folks, On the go each day Saw Orlando, Tampa. Yesterday we went to St. Pete. Lovely flowers and palms so beautiful. Real warm here. See you soon. Lou & Bill." (Courtesy Lakeland Public Library.)

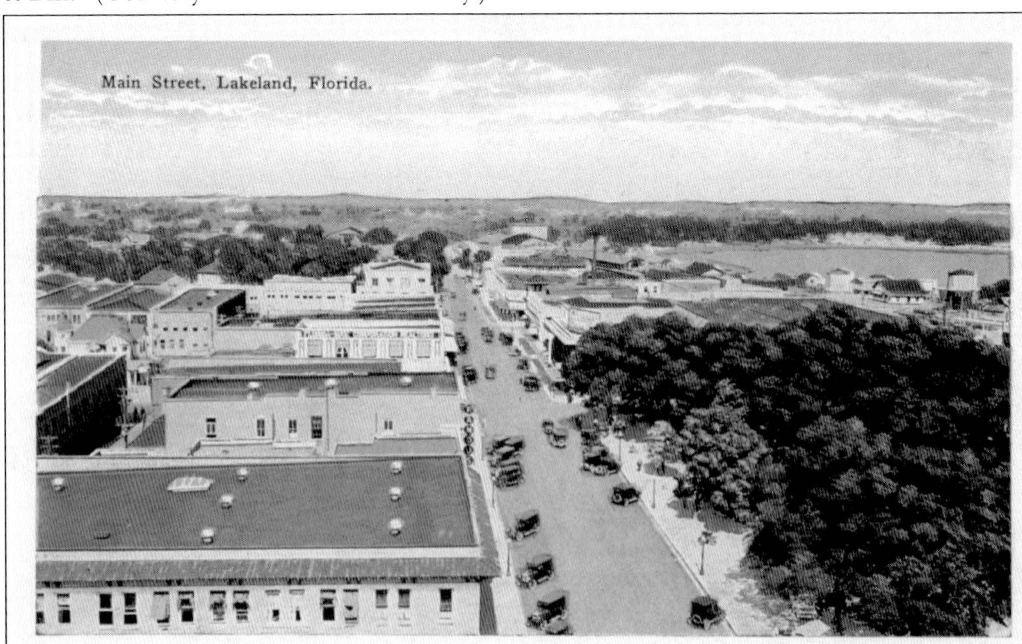

MAIN STREET, LAKELAND, FLORIDA. This view was taken from atop the Hotel Lakeland Terrace and looks westward toward Tampa. The 1920s postcard promoted the city: "At the right is Munn Park, a familiar resting place for Lakeland visitors. In the distance at the right can be seen Lake Wire, where the city has recently constructed an extensive public bathing dock." (Courtesy Lakeland Public Library.)

Three

LAKES

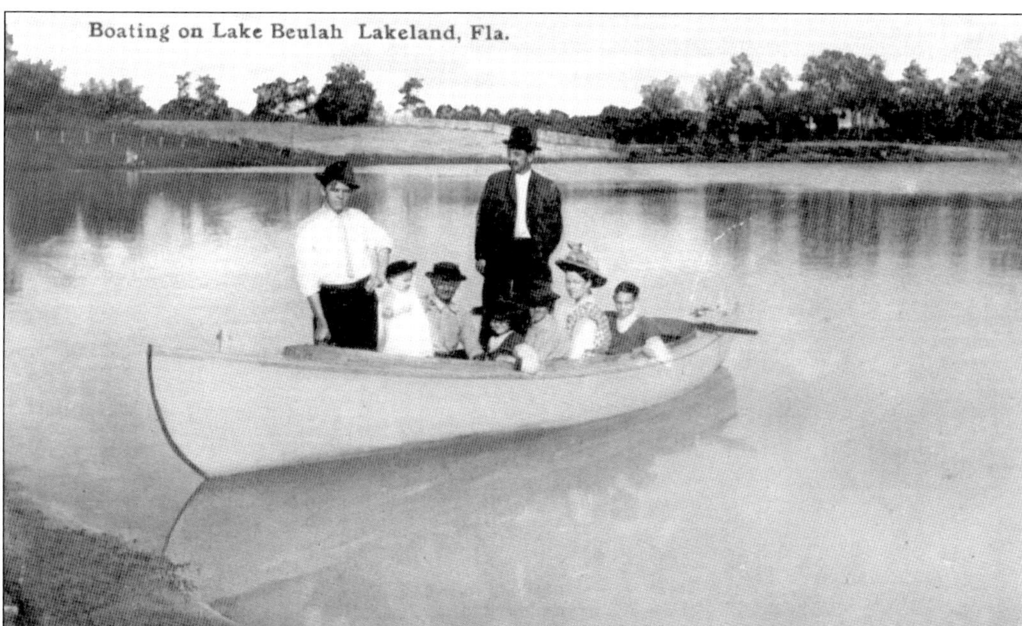

BOATING ON LAKE BEULAH, LAKELAND, FLA. What's in a name? Lakeland provides a hint of the landscape Lakelanders enjoy. There are lakes and plenty of them. Family entertainment in the 1910s included boating on the local lakes. The city limits encompassed at least a dozen named lakes during the early period, and this number has increased as the city grows. Lake Beulah is west of downtown. (Courtesy Lakeland Public Library.)

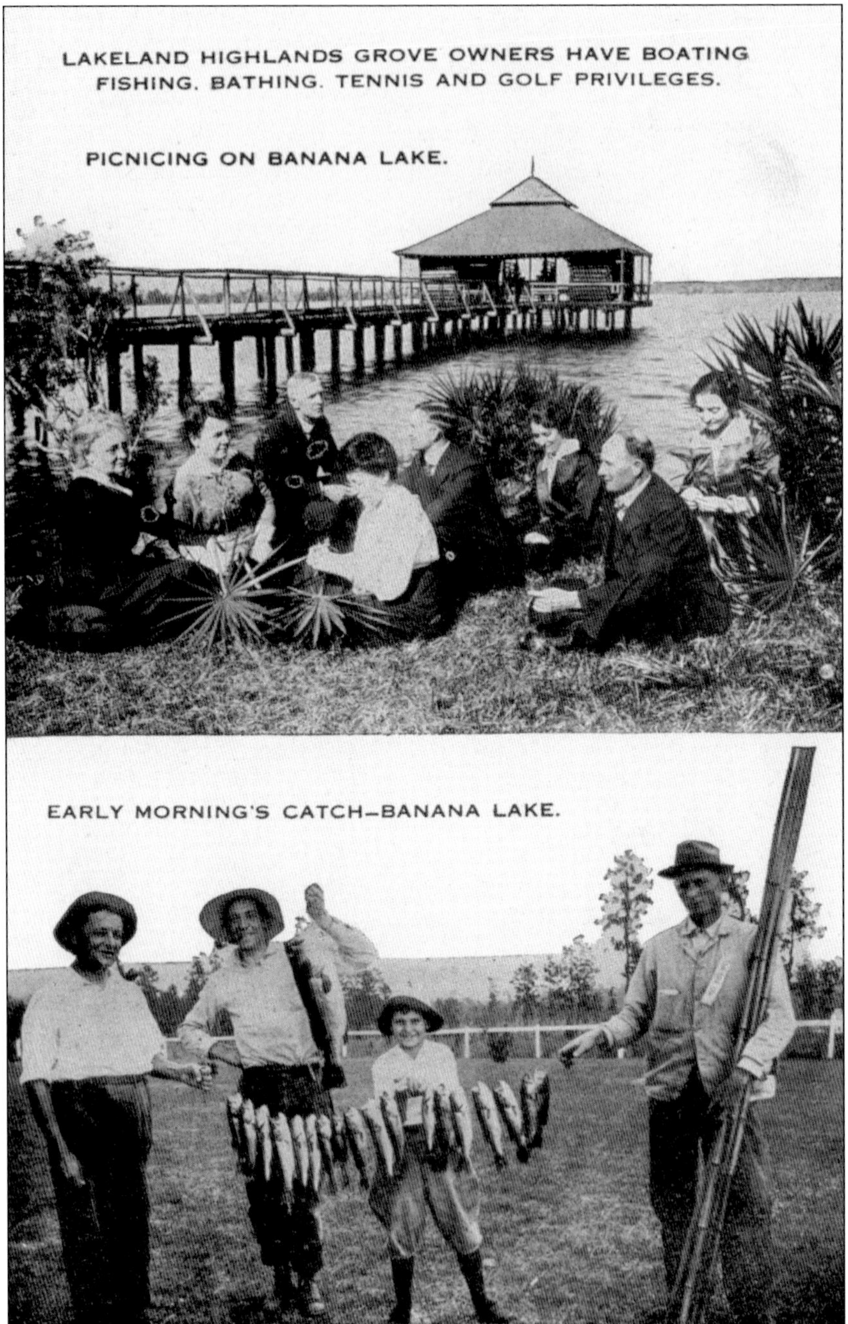

BANANA LAKE IN LAKELAND HIGHLANDS. This is one of a series of late 1910s postcards designed to promote development of the 13,000 acre Lakeland Highlands area. Banana Lake was south of the early Lakeland city limits. The images are quite enchanting, showing lakeside picnickers in formal attire and a group of fishermen, and the card promotes water activities, tennis, and golf. The centerpiece of the development was the lakeland Highlands Country Club, both promoted by W. E. Hallam until his death in 1920; afterward, the venture languished. (Courtesy Lakeland Public Library.)

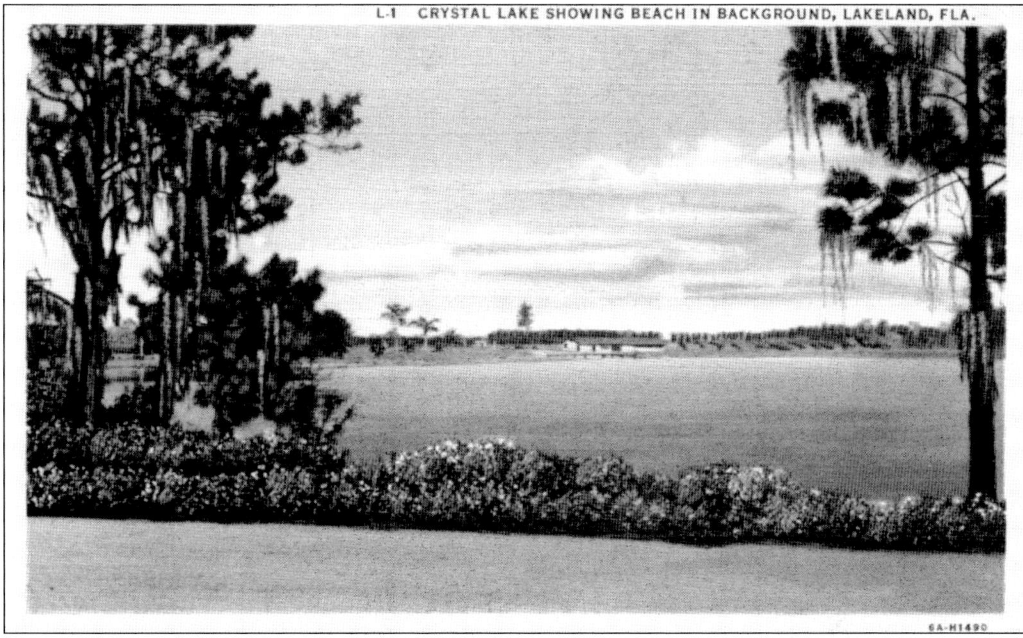

Crystal Lake Showing Beach in Background, Lakeland, Fla. The eastern edge of town was near Crystal Lake in April 1937 when this postcard was mailed. A vacationer wrote to a friend in Michigan: "April 13. Dear Florence, Arrived here last Sat. Weather is fine. We have the same apartment we had last year. Mrs. Crawford gave me my shot all right. She and her mother wished to be remembered to you. They are very pleasant. Irene N." (Courtesy Lakeland Public Library.)

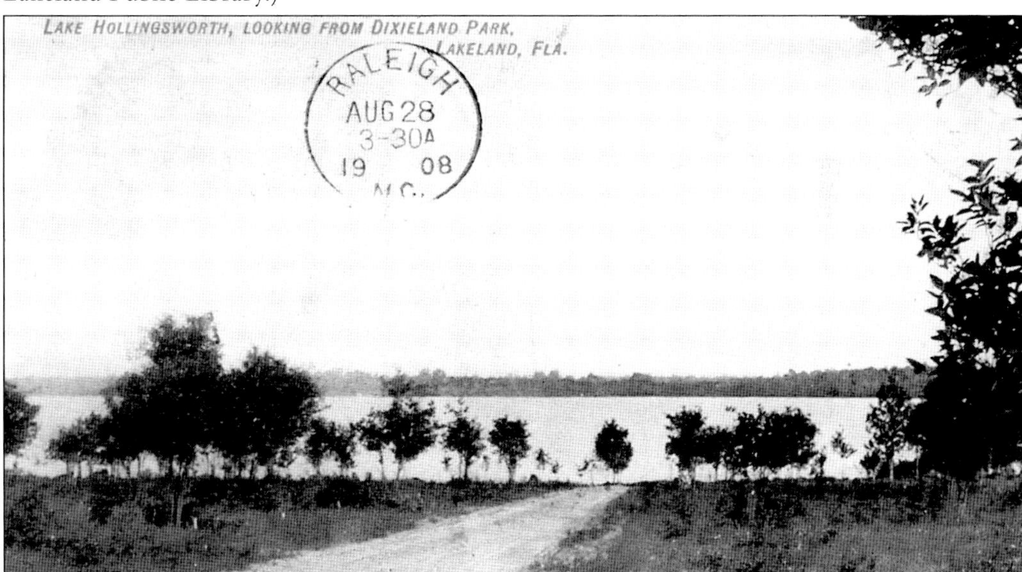

Lake Hollingsworth, Looking from Dixieland Park, Lakeland, Fla. The first phase of the Dixieland subdivision was generally between Lake Morton and Lake Hollingsworth east of South Florida Avenue; this area is now known as the Lake Morton Historic District. The second phase of the Dixieland subdivision was on the west side of South Florida Avenue to Lake Hunter. This postcard was mailed in August 1908. (Courtesy Larry Gray.)

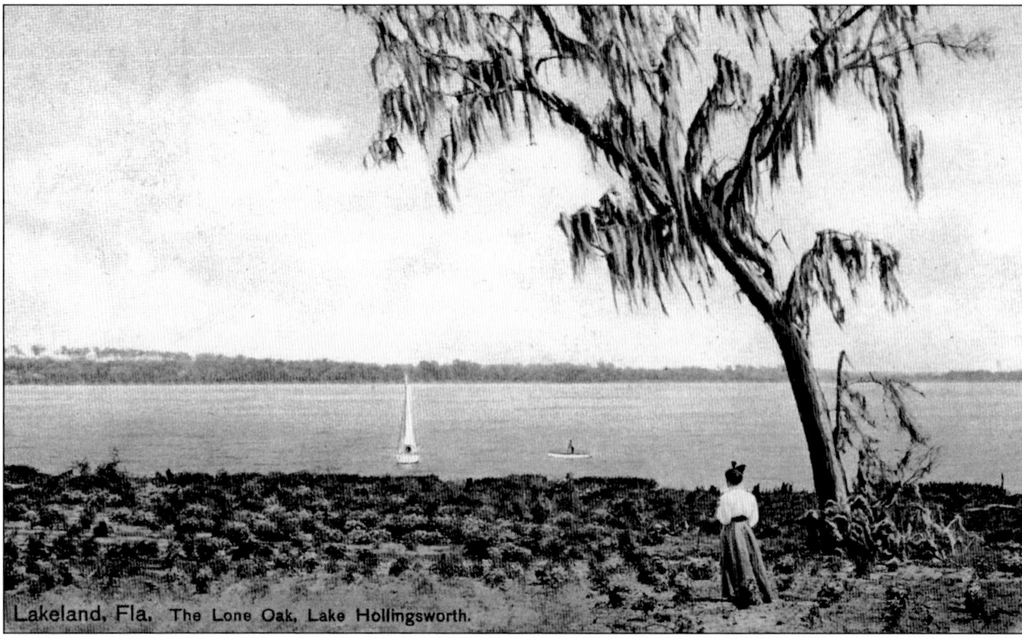

LAKELAND, FLA. THE LONE OAK, LAKE HOLLINGSWORTH. Who could have predicted how popular Lake Hollingsworth would become for walkers and bicycle riders? This view surely impressed the Beckley, West Virginia, recipient. Postmarked from Lakeland October 2, 1909, it reads: "I have been having a good time. I have been three weeks on the road. Will start to school Monday. From Thedford." (Courtesy Lakeland Public Library.)

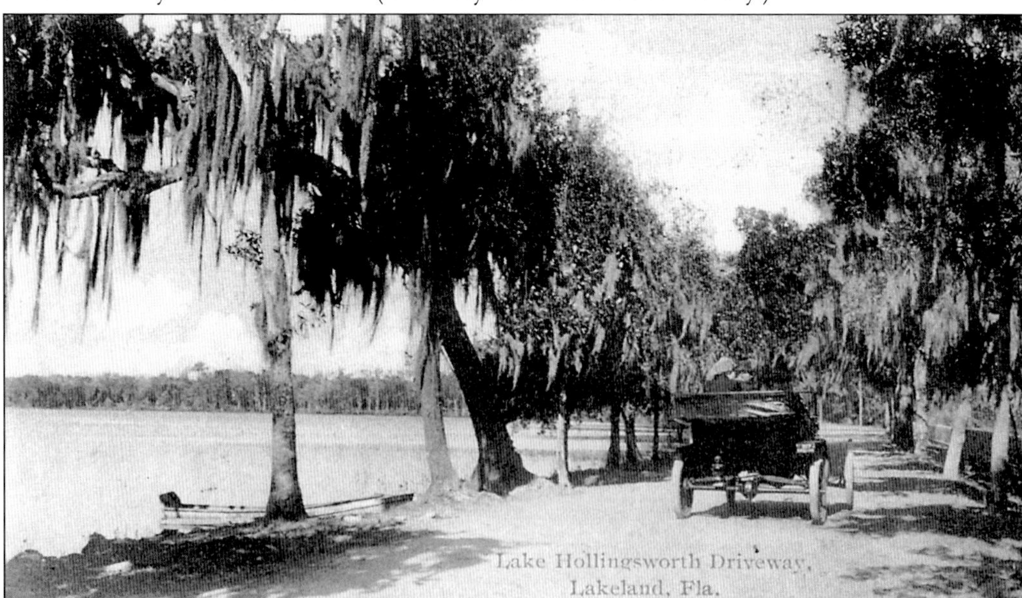

LAKE HOLLINGSWORTH DRIVEWAY, LAKELAND, FLA. Many of Lakeland's most prestigious properties face Lake Hollingsworth. Several 1910s postcards showed automobiles along this popular lakeside roadway. This was mailed in December 1915, carrying news home to Kahoka, Missouri: "Dear Mother—I'm sending you a small box of oranges by express. Be on the look out for them. Hope you are well & happy. Frances." (Courtesy Lakeland Public Library.)

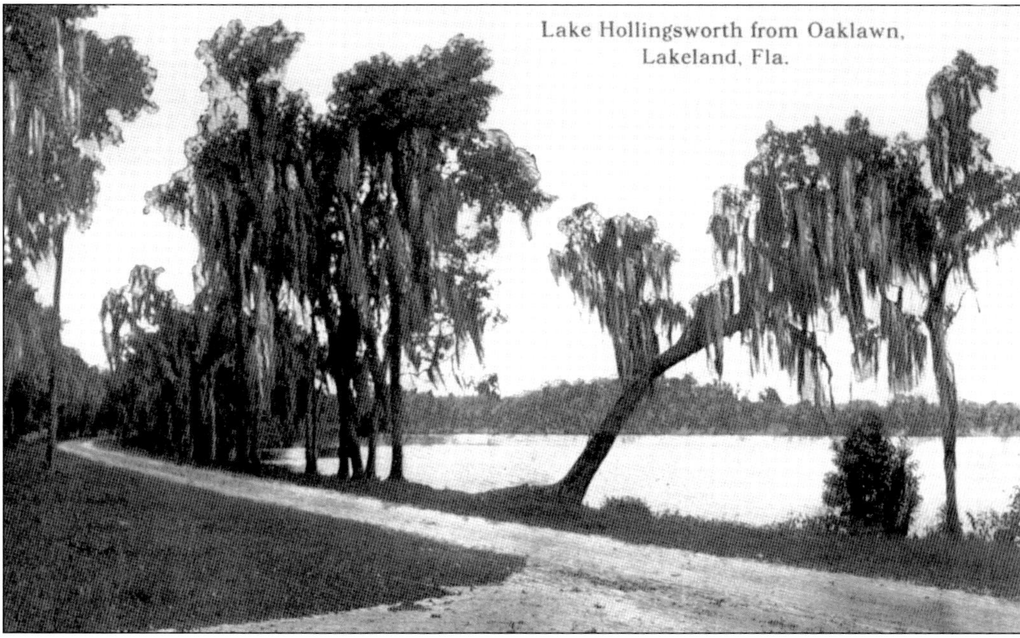

LAKE HOLLINGSWORTH FROM OAKLAWN, LAKELAND, FLA. Oaklawn, one of the early elegant residences, was on the east shore of Lake Hollingsworth. This postcards dates from about 1915. (Courtesy Lakeland Public Library.)

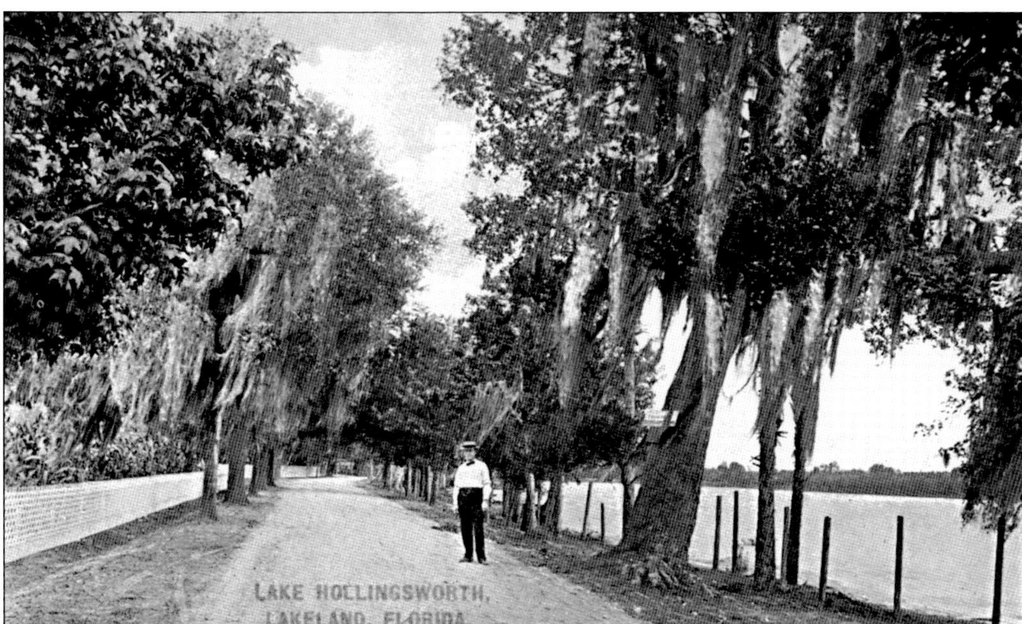

LAKE HOLLINGSWORTH, LAKELAND FLORIDA. A pre-1916 view shows Lake Hollingsworth and the rural residential area surrounding the lake. The unpaved road pre-dated modern Lake Hollingsworth Drive and today's busy, 2.8-mile walking path. Perhaps this gentleman was getting an early start. (Courtesy Lakeland Public Library.)

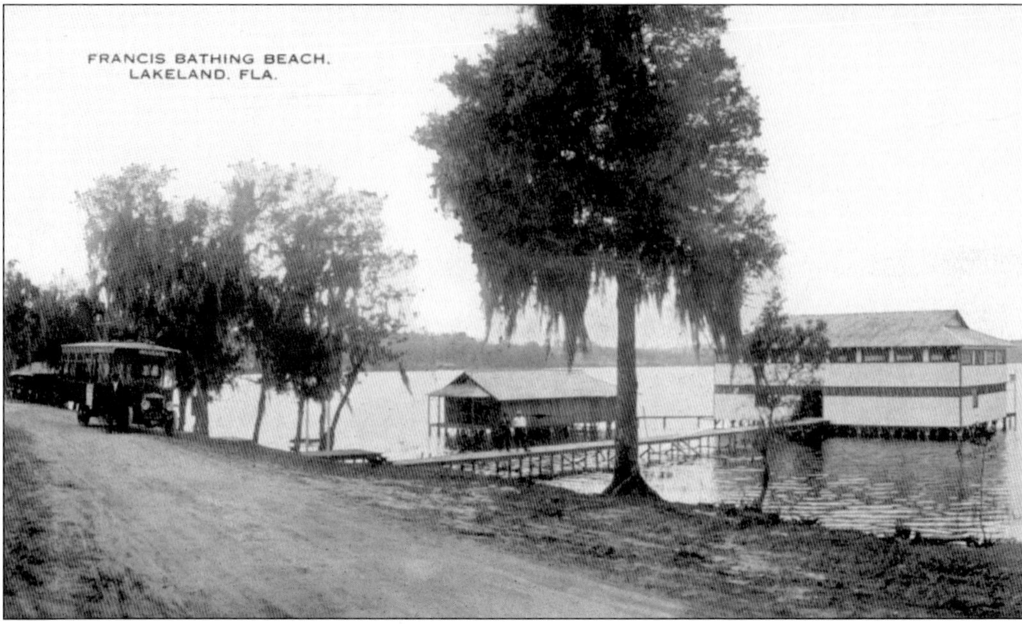

FRANCIS BATHING BEACH, LAKELAND, FLA. This promotional postcard published by J. L. Francis advertised Lakeland's first bathing and dancing pavilion and included a rare view of a Lakeland Interurban Line bus. Francis Beach opened in 1915 on the south shore of Lake Hollingsworth; it had a water slide and diving platform. A June 1922 *Lakeland Evening Telegram* article reports that a dozen nurses from Morrell Memorial Hospital were hosted by John L. and Alice P. Francis for a swimming party and watermelon cutting. (Courtesy Larry Gray.)

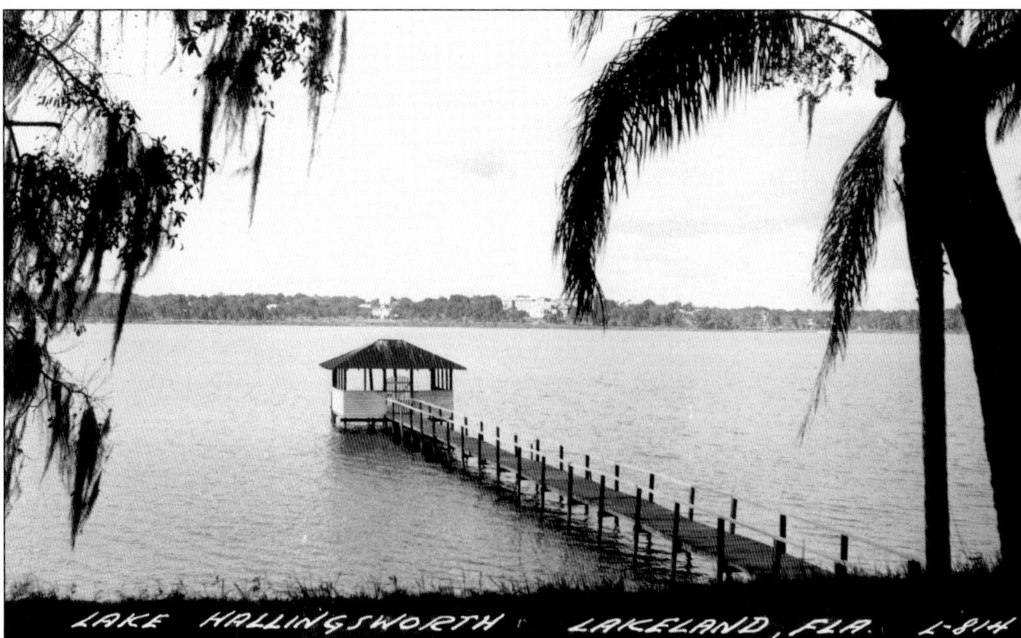

LAKE HOLLINGSWORTH, LAKELAND, FLA. A private dock graces the south shore of the lake across from Florida Southern College. (Courtesy Lakeland Public Library.)

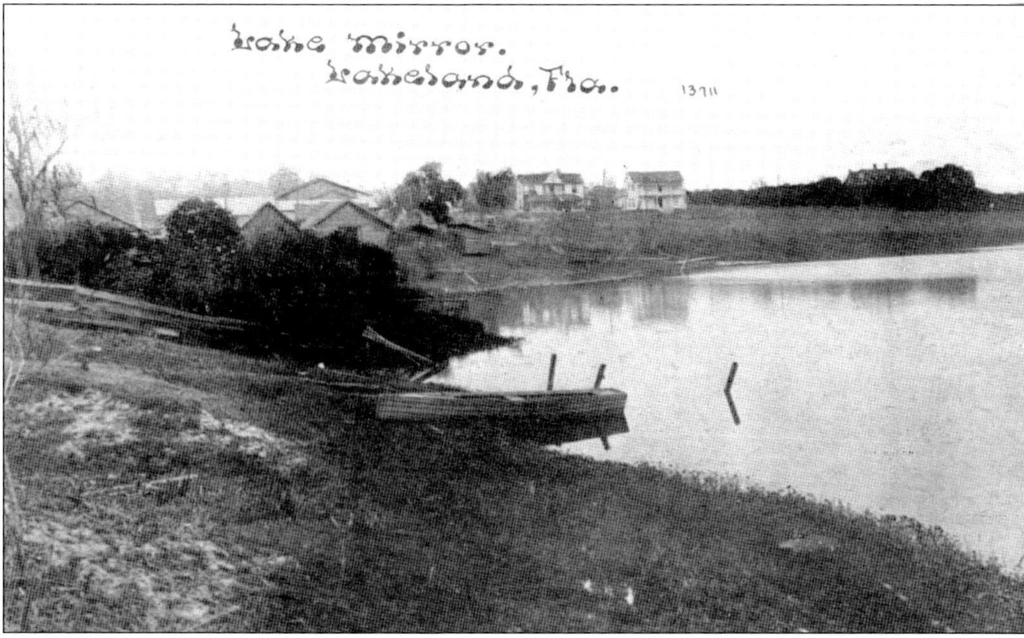

LAKE MIRROR, LAKELAND, FLA. This early postcard view of Lake Mirror was mailed from Auburndale in November 1911. Some 6,000 U.S. soldiers were encamped on Lakeland's shores in 1898 during the Spanish-American War. This large presence is believed to have positively influenced the young town's future, as former soldiers took up residence in Lakeland after the war. (Courtesy Larry Gray.)

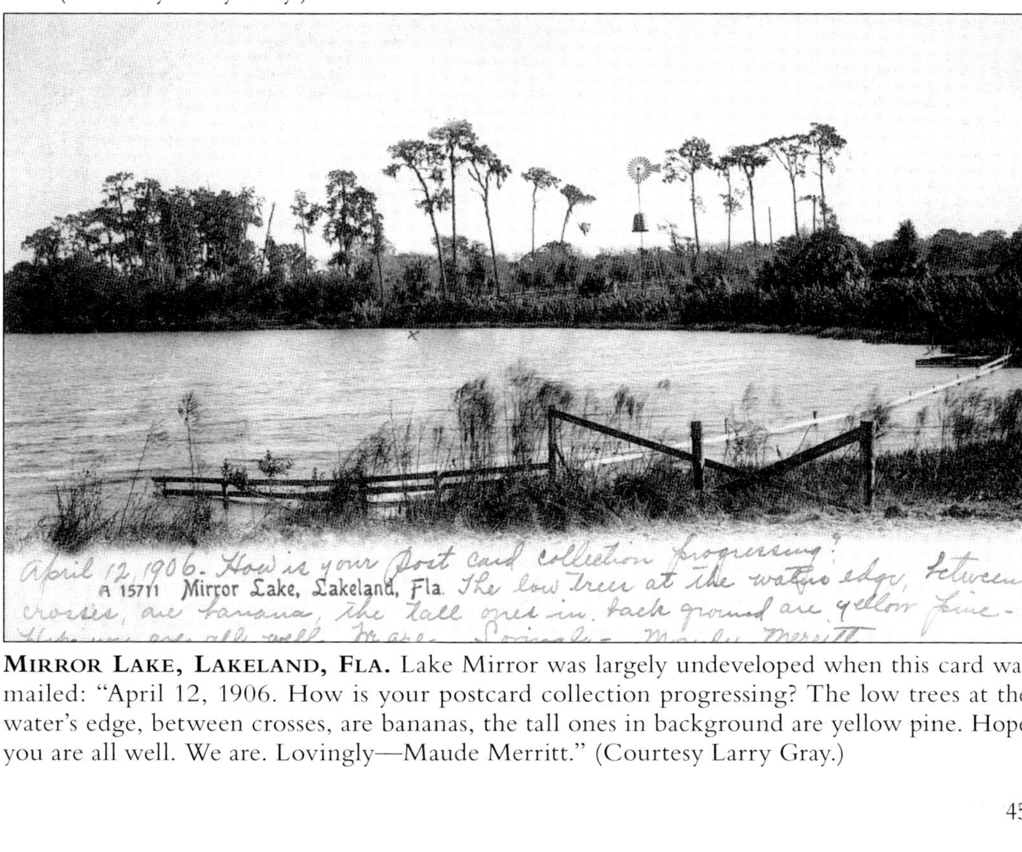

MIRROR LAKE, LAKELAND, FLA. Lake Mirror was largely undeveloped when this card was mailed: "April 12, 1906. How is your postcard collection progressing? The low trees at the water's edge, between crosses, are bananas, the tall ones in background are yellow pine. Hope you are all well. We are. Lovingly—Maude Merritt." (Courtesy Larry Gray.)

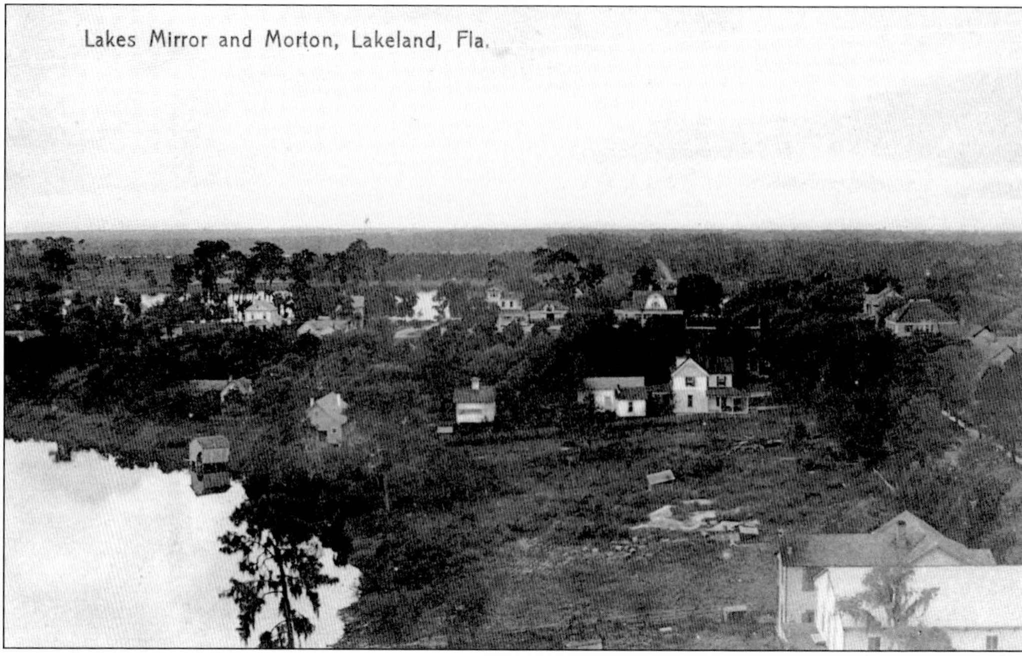

LAKES MIRROR AND MORTON, LAKELAND. FLA. The water tower afforded a magnificent southward view overlooking residences of mid-1910s Lakeland. Included is the home of Morris G. Munn, son of Lakeland's founder. (Courtesy Larry Gray.)

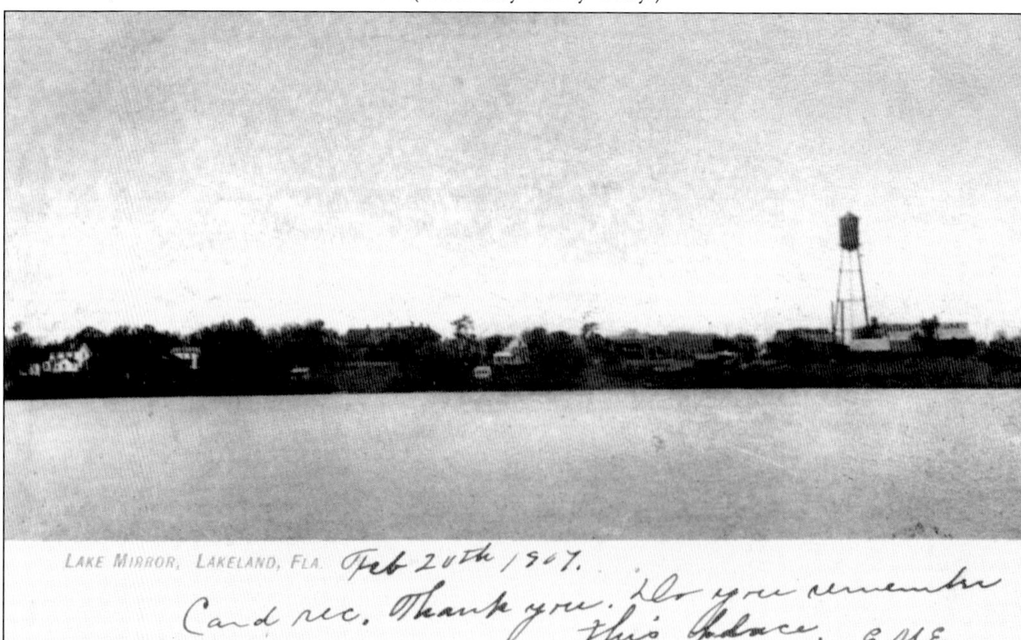

LAKE MIRROR, LAKELAND, FLA. Lakeland's light and water plant was at the southeast corner of Massachusetts Avenue and Cedar Street. The water tower from which early aerial postcard views were photographed is clearly visible; the plant was demolished in 1916. The message on the front reads: "Feb 20th 1907. Card rec. Thank you. Do you remember this place. EME" (Courtesy Lakeland Public Library.)

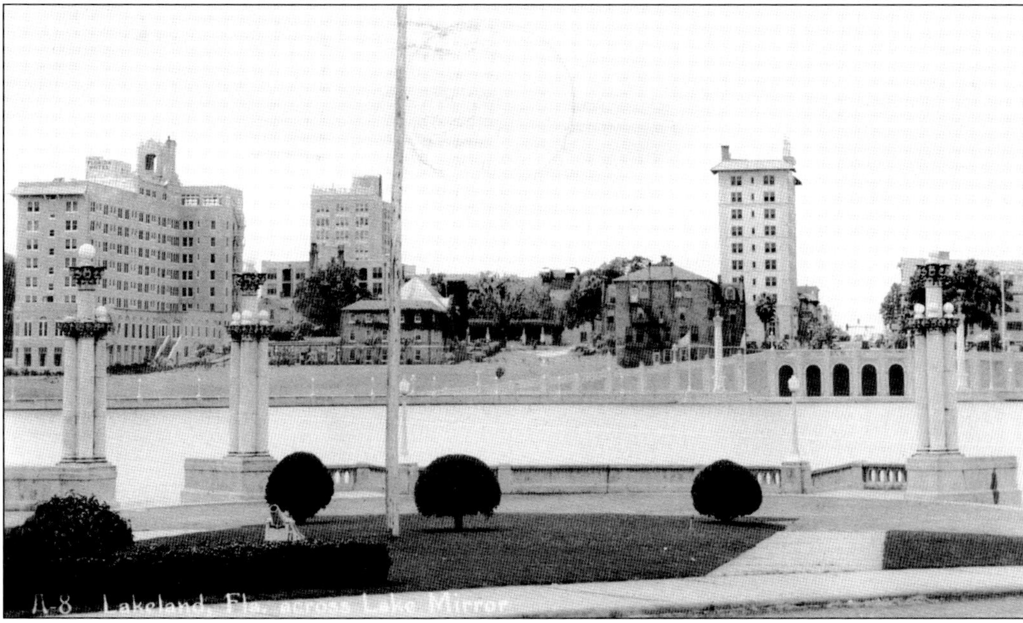

Lakeland, Fla. Across Lake Mirror. Looking west toward downtown, prominent buildings include from left to right the New Florida Hotel, the Marble Arcade, First Presbyterian Church, the Elks' Home, and the Hotel Lakeland Terrace. The loggia of the Frances Langford Promenade is visible just above the water. The January 1937 message reads: "Lakeland, Fla., Jan. 16–1938, Dear Friend, I thank you for your pretty Xmas greeting. My sister and I are spending the winter in Lakeland, Fla. It is a very pretty place. We are enjoying the warm sunshine, palm trees and flowers. Sincerely, Louise Elveser." (Courtesy Lakeland Public Library.)

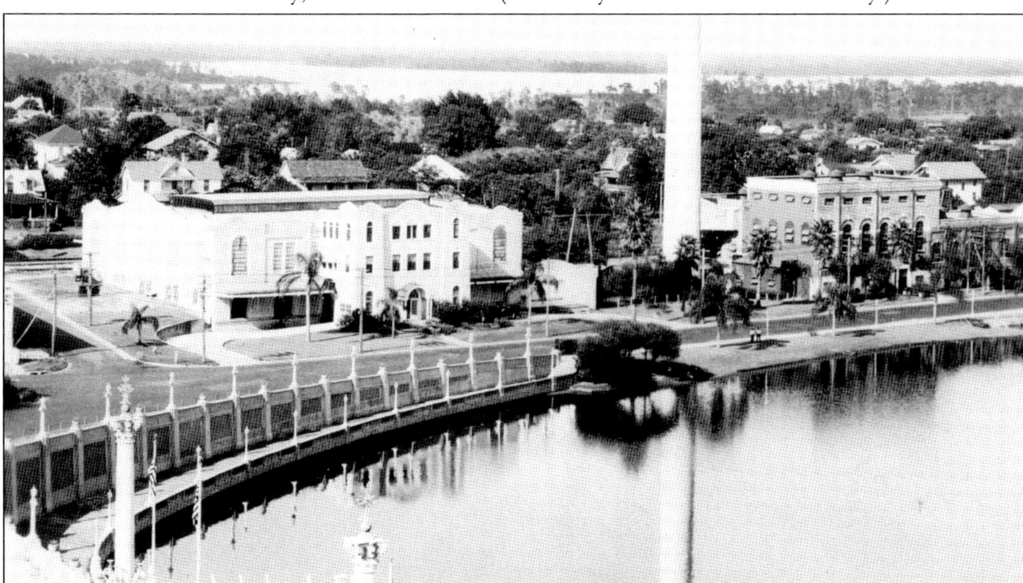

Skyline of Lakeland—Lakeland, Florida. A northeastern view from the Hotel Lakeland Terrace shows the Lakeland Cash Feed building and the Lake Mirror Power Plant (1916) on the north side of Lake Mirror. Lake Parker is visible on the horizon. (Courtesy Lakeland Public Library.)

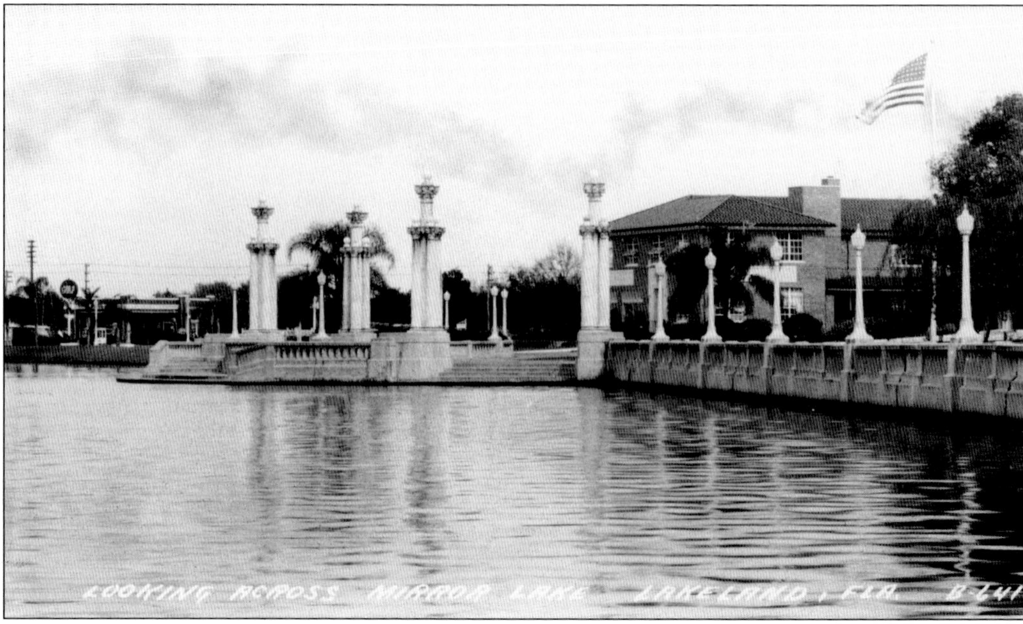

Looking across Mirror Lake, Lakeland, Fla. This real-photo postcard shows the northeast corner of the lake in front of the civic center, including the promenade near the 1937 Coca-Cola bottling plant. The Coca-Cola plant now houses Lakeland Fire Department administrative offices. (Courtesy Lakeland Public Library.)

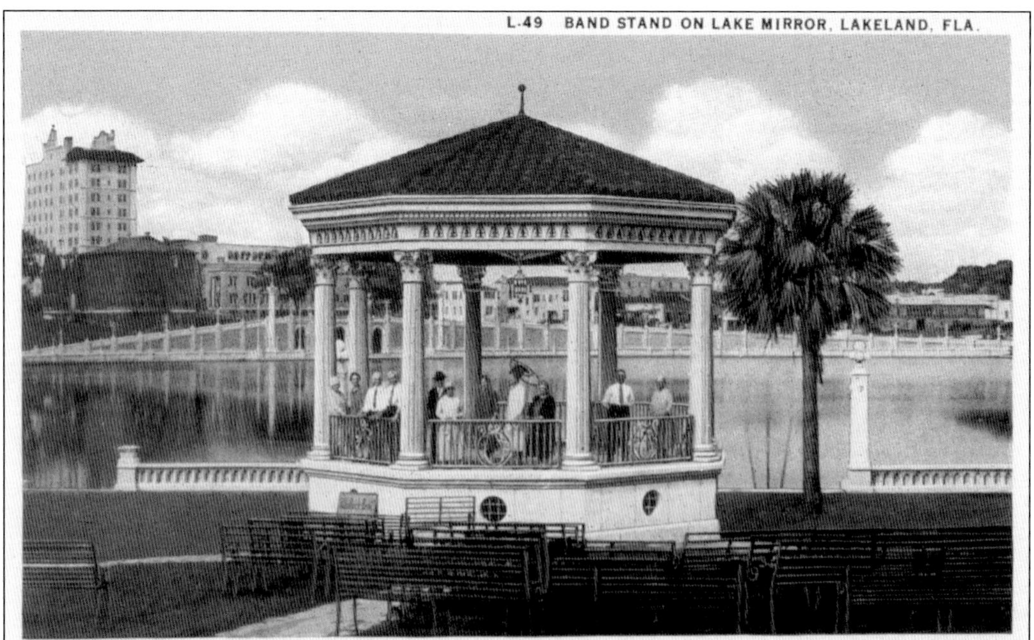

Band stand on Lake Mirror, Lakeland, Fla. The ornate bandstand was situated on the southeast corner of Lake Mirror, adjacent to the civic center. (Courtesy Lakeland Public Library.)

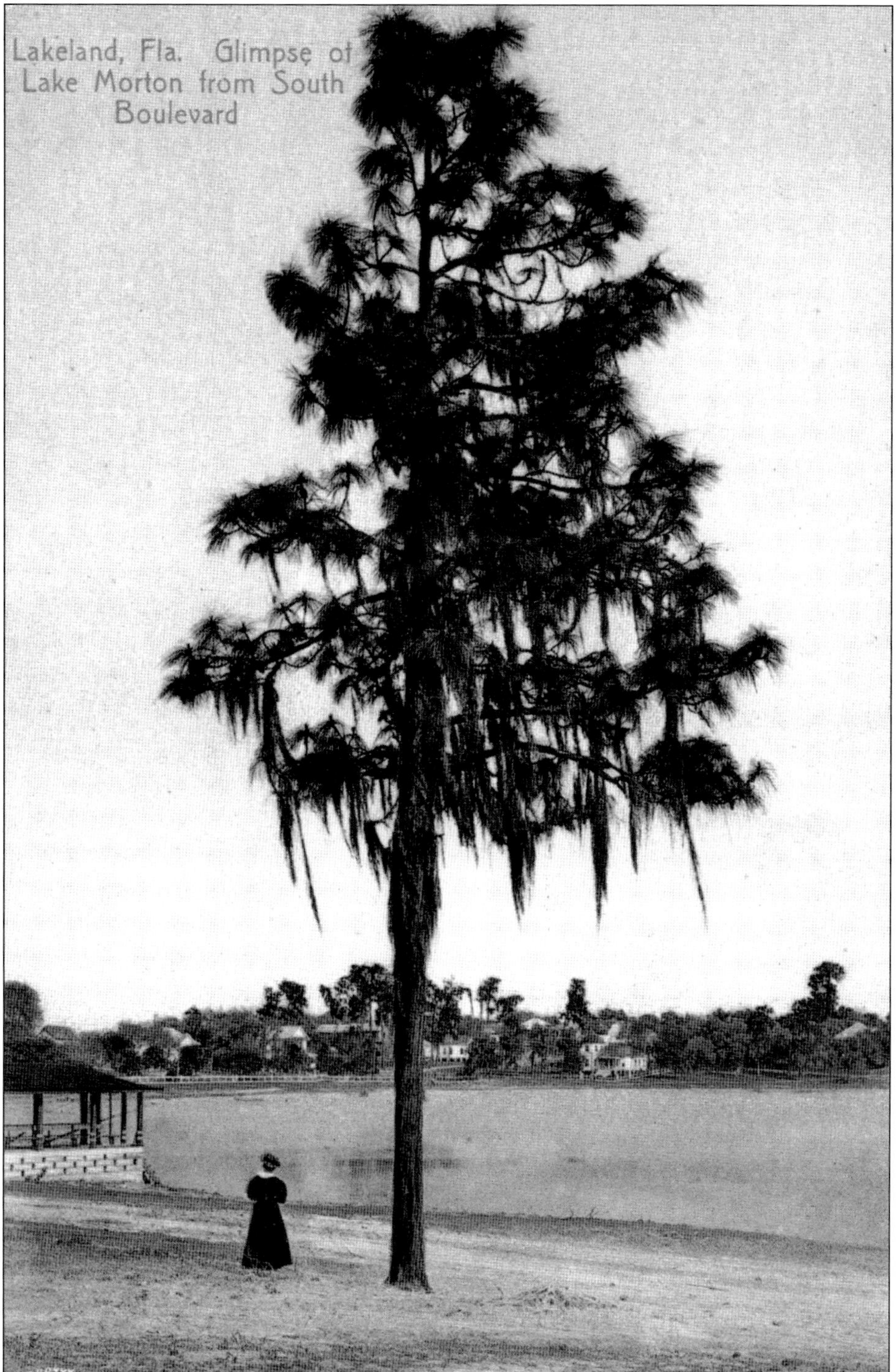

LAKELAND, FLA. GLIMPSE OF LAKE MORTON FROM SOUTH BOULEVARD. Downtown is across the lake; the north shore of Lake Morton marked the original southern edge of the town. (Courtesy Lakeland Public Library.)

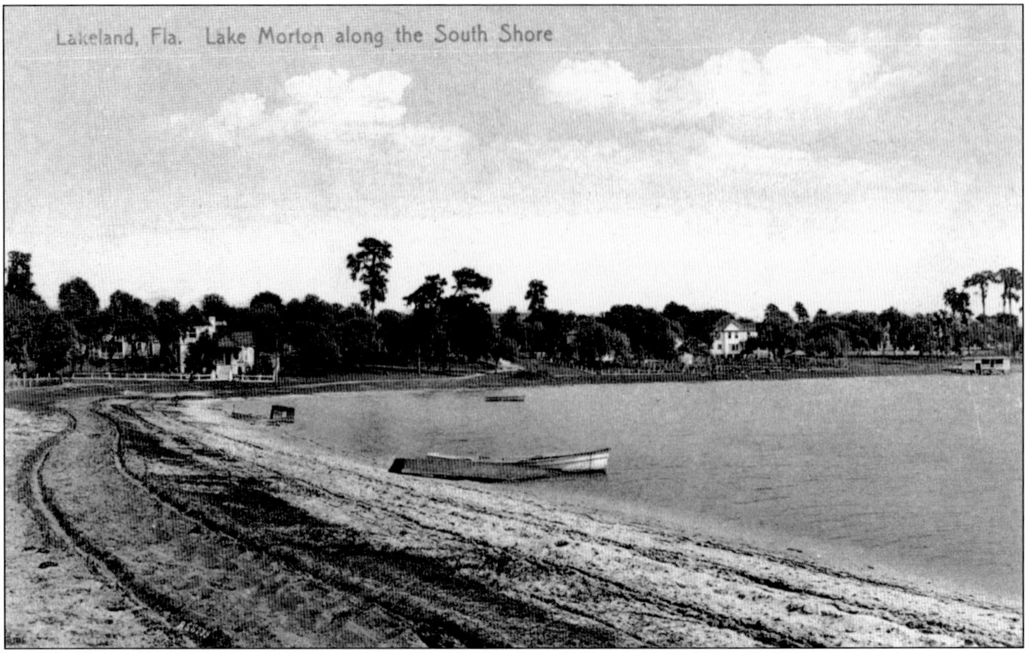

Lakeland, Fla. Lake Morton along the South Shore. Boating on local lakes provided both pleasure and sustenance. The sandy dirt path that became Lake Morton Drive was opened in the mid-1890s. (Courtesy Lakeland Public Library.)

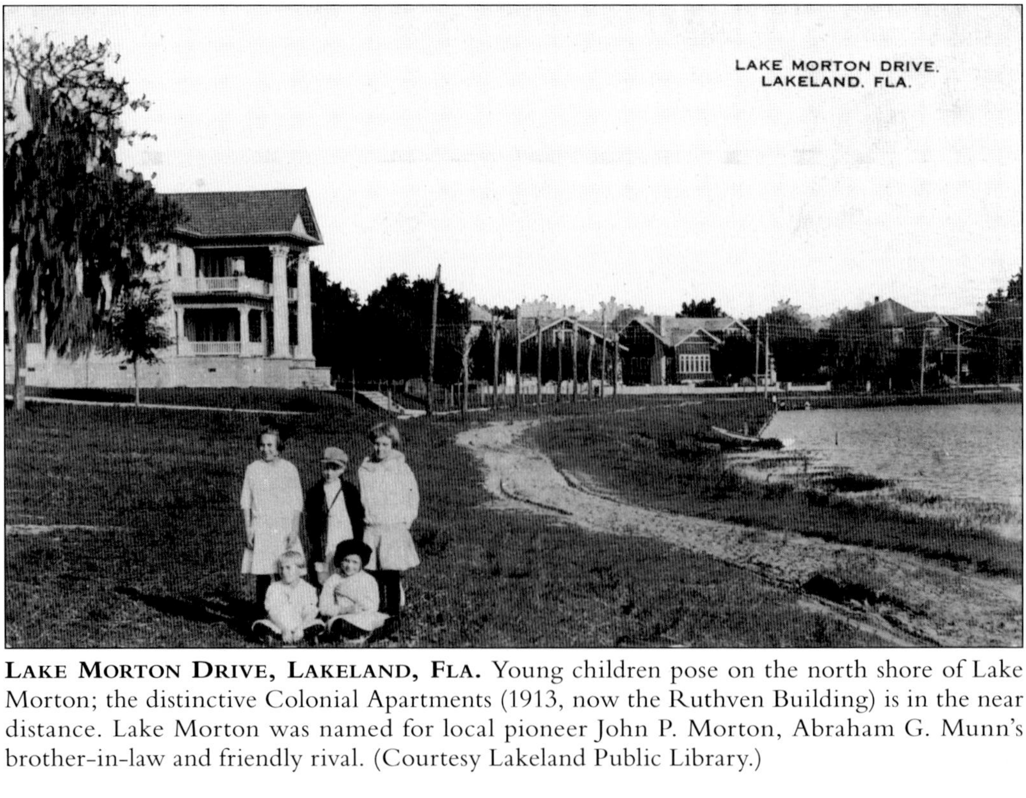

Lake Morton Drive, Lakeland, Fla. Young children pose on the north shore of Lake Morton; the distinctive Colonial Apartments (1913, now the Ruthven Building) is in the near distance. Lake Morton was named for local pioneer John P. Morton, Abraham G. Munn's brother-in-law and friendly rival. (Courtesy Lakeland Public Library.)

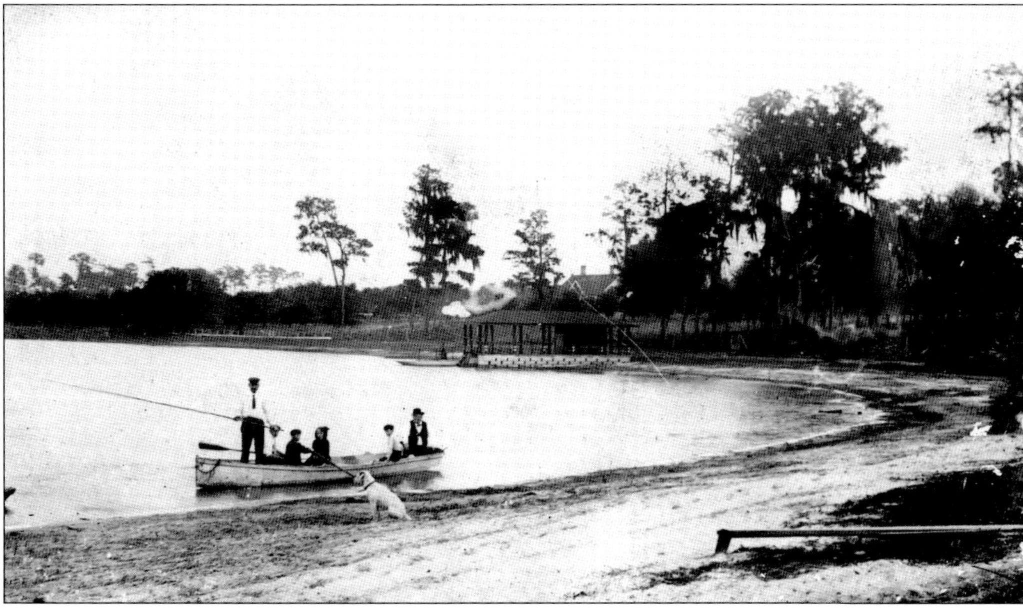

FISHING ON LAKE MORTON. A fisherman and his boatload of intrepid companions fish off the southwest shore of Lake Morton in this *c.* 1910 real-photo postcard. Orange groves are visible on the far shore, and the Mosswood boathouse is featured prominently. (Courtesy Lakeland Public Library.)

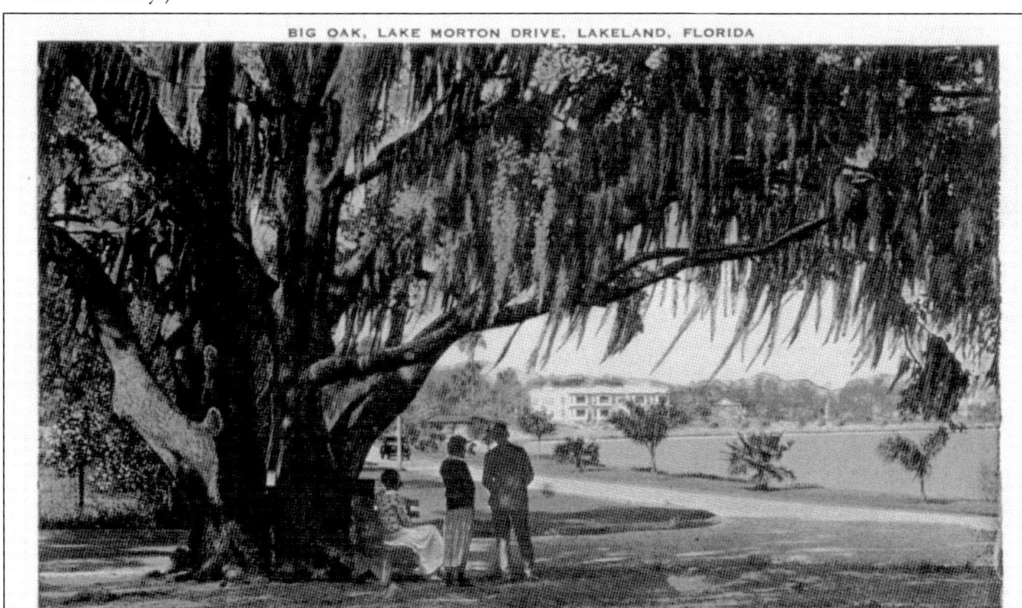

BIG OAK, LAKE MORTON DRIVE, LAKELAND, FLORIDA. Mann Patterson Riggins cleared 80 acres for a citrus grove in the 1880s, but he spared this magnificent oak at what became the corner of Success Avenue and Lake Morton Drive. The oak was featured on several postcards and remains a local landmark. Harold R. wrote home in November 1926: "Dear Sister: We arrived here in Lakeland a week ago today. I am feeling fine and like it here although there isn't much work to be had here." (Courtesy Lakeland Public Library.)

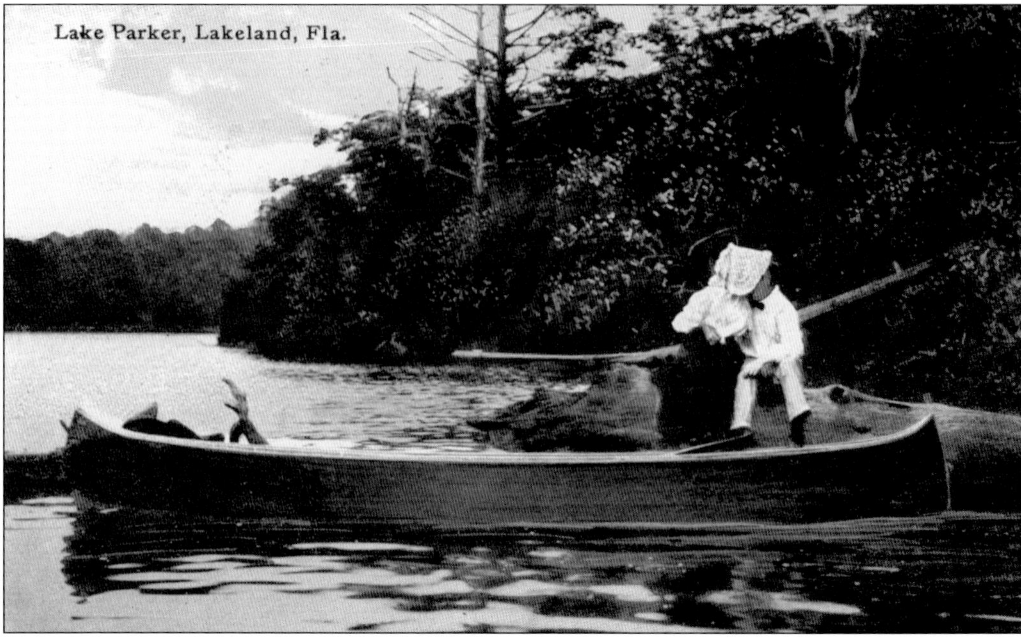

Lake Parker, Lakeland, Fla. A couple enjoys a little romance on Lake Parker. Boaters on this large lake were featured on many postcards, such as this one mailed in 1912. (Authors' Collection.)

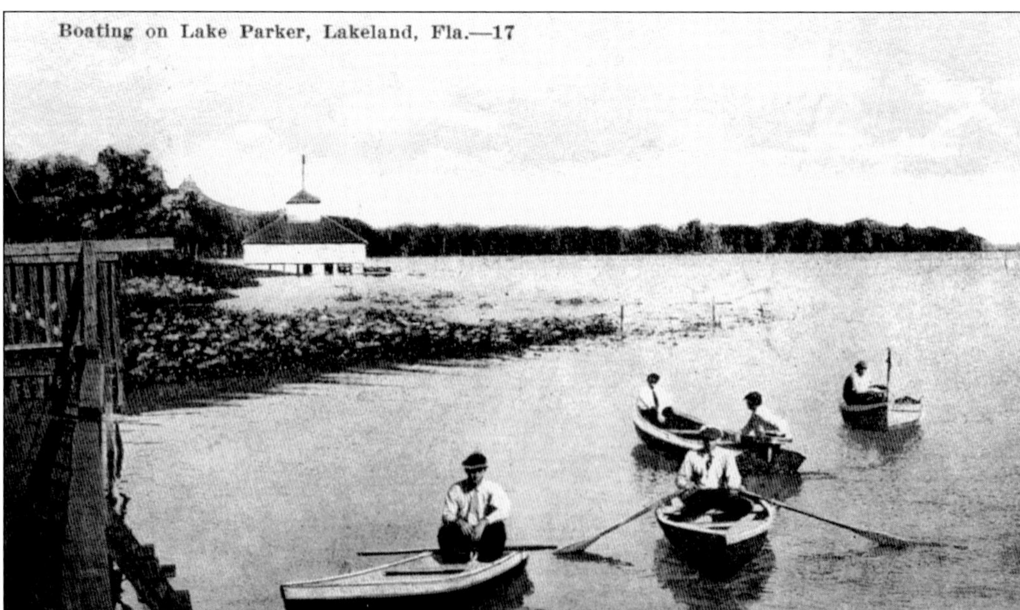

Boating on Lake Parker, Lakeland, Fla. Lake Parker is the largest body of water in Lakeland, named for early settler Streety Parker. The annual Sun 'n Fun Fly-in uses Lake Parker as a seaplane base. This postcard was mailed in 1921. (Courtesy Lakeland Public Library.)

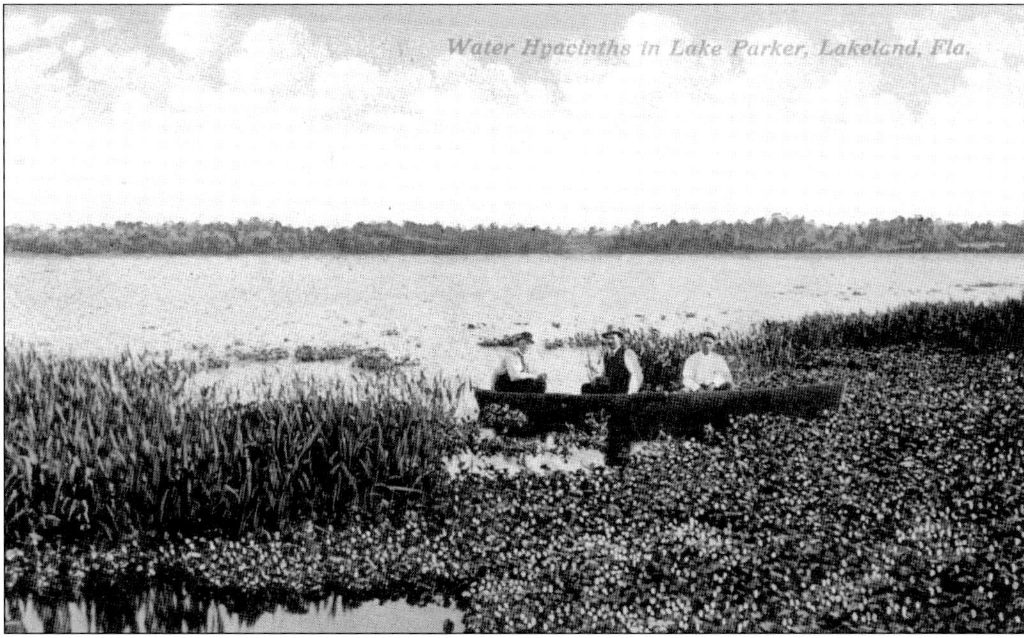

Water Hyacinths in Lake Parker, Lakeland, Fla. This pre-1916 postcard was published in Lakeland by R. E. Lufsey, an early Lakeland historian. (Courtesy Lakeland Public Library.)

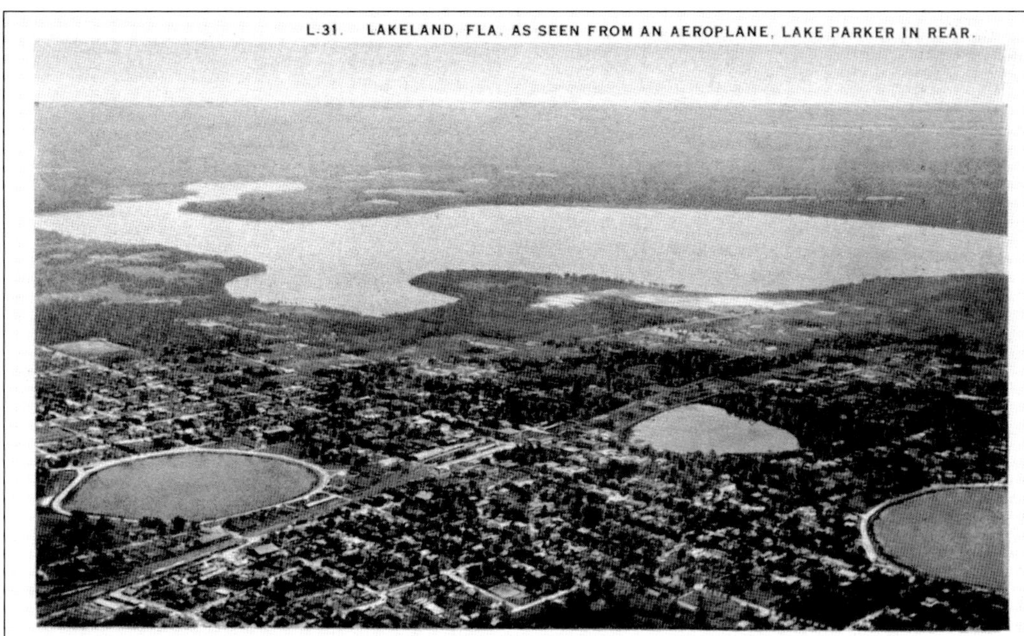

Lakeland, Fla. As Seen from an Aeroplane, Lake Parker in the Rear. Lakes Wire, Mirror, and Morton are from left to right in the foreground of this view toward the northeast. (Courtesy Lakeland Public Library.)

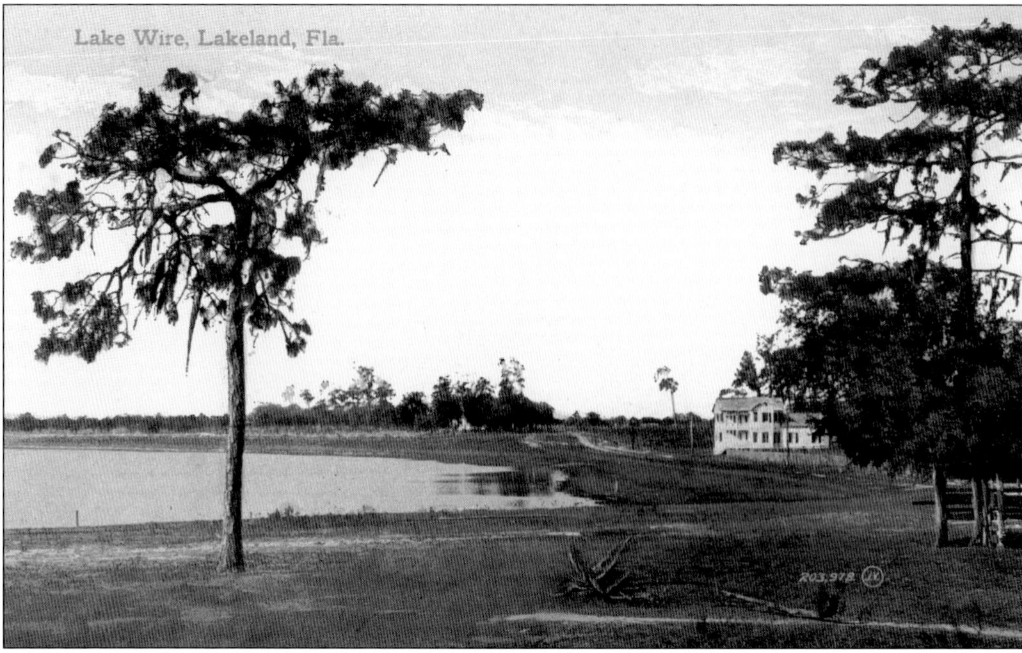

LAKE WIRE, LAKELAND, FLA. This card was postmarked January 29, 1908. Lake Wire was once on the outskirts but is now part of downtown and is bordered by Lawton Chiles Middle Academy, busy thoroughfares, and local industries. (Courtesy Lakeland Public Library.)

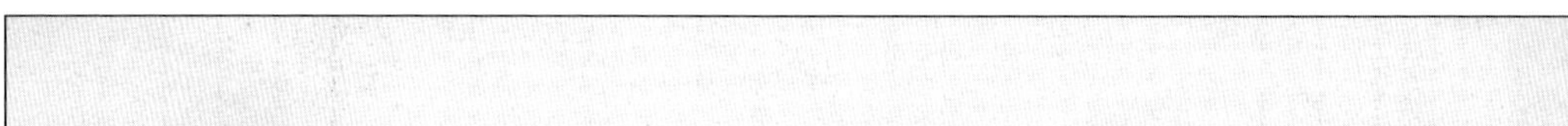

LAKE WIRE AND LAKELAND HIGH SCHOOL, LAKELAND, FLA. This view was taken from the northwest corner of Lake Wire toward downtown. The residences on the left side were along Peachtree Street, but most are no longer standing. This unsent postcard likely dates from the mid-1910s. (Courtesy Lakeland Public Library.)

Four

Schools

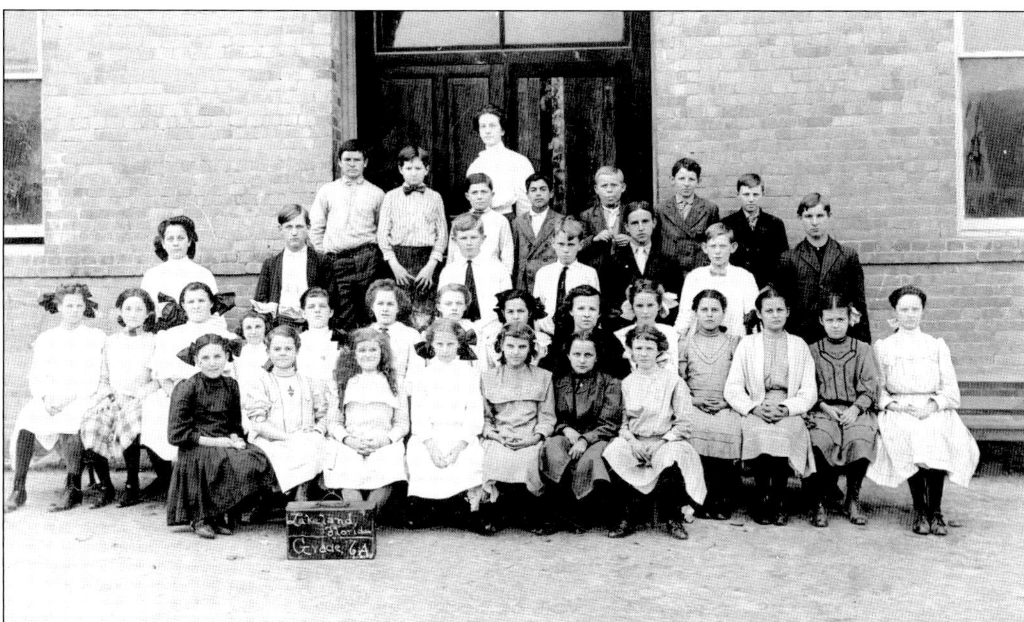

LAKELAND FLORIDA, GRADE 6A. GENUINE PHOTO BY C. U. WILLIAMS, BLOOMINGTON, ILL. Where there is settlement, sooner or later there are children who must be educated. There were several schools in Lakeland by the second decade of the 20th century, including Lakeland High School and the Lake Morton Grammar School. This real-photo postcard is believed to date from the 1920s. Only four of those pictured were identified on the back of the postcard: "Miss Allie Patton—teacher, 2nd row—Helen Schaffer, 3rd row—N. Glover, 4th row—A. Ramondo." (Courtesy Lakeland Public Library.)

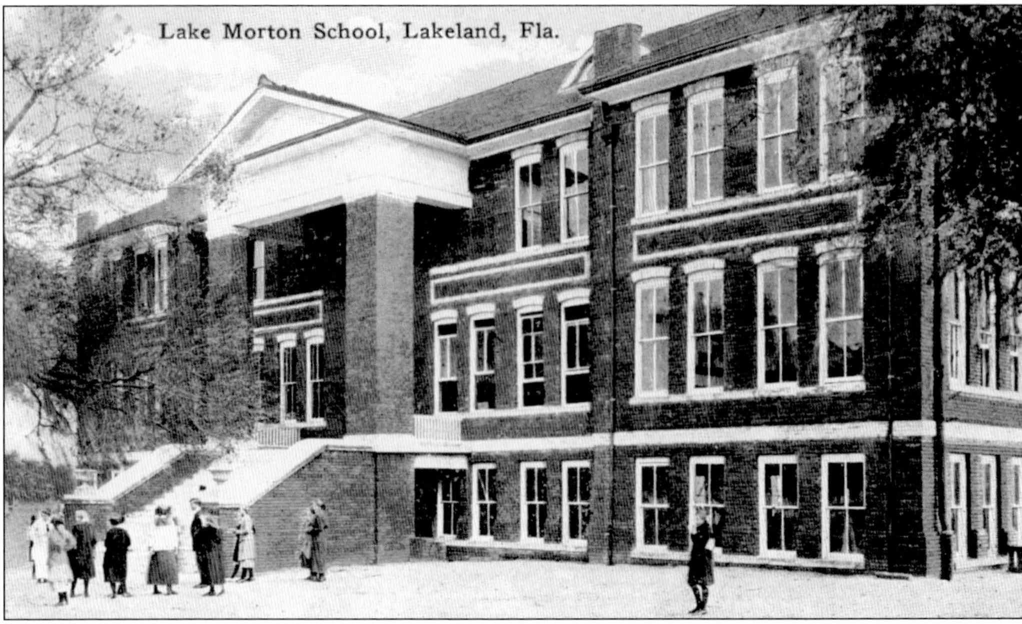

LAKE MORTON SCHOOL, LAKELAND, FLA. The school was located on Lake Morton Drive at East Palmetto Street on the site presently occupied by the Lakeland Public Library. Opened in January 1915, the school served until destroyed by fire in February 1963. (Courtesy Lakeland Public Library.)

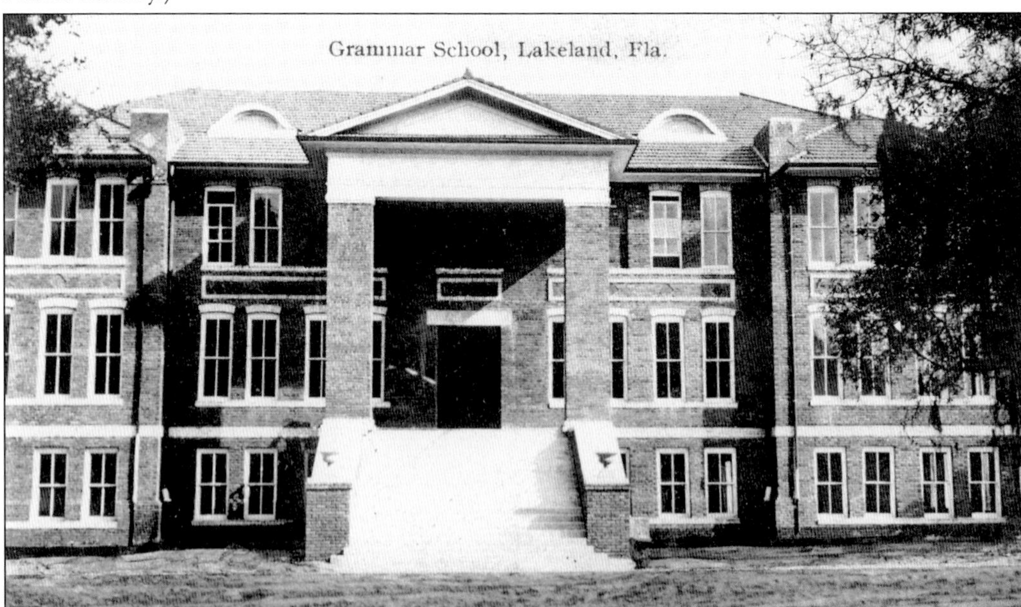

GRAMMAR SCHOOL, LAKELAND, FLA. This is the west façade of the Lake Morton Grammar School. The 1915 city directory reported that the schools were overcrowded. The major push for new classroom space came in the 1920s, as Lakeland was transformed by the Florida land boom. Dixieland Grammar School (1924), Webster Avenue School (1925), Central Avenue School (1926), John F. Cox Grammar School (1928), and Washington Park High School (1928) were among those constructed during this heady decade. (Courtesy Larry Gray.)

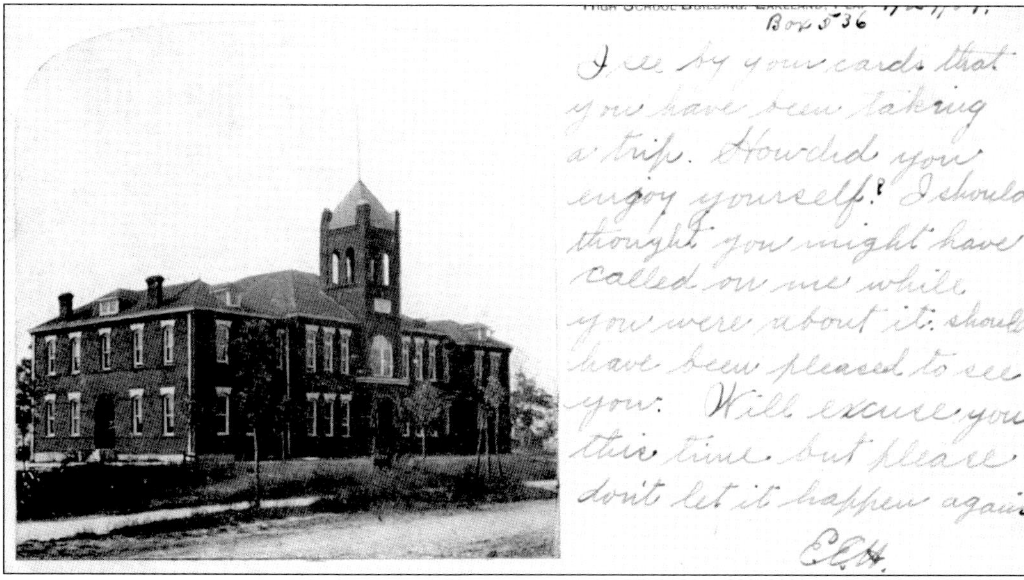

HIGH SCHOOL BUILDING, LAKELAND, FLA. The school opened in 1902, but this main building was destroyed by fire on June 9, 1927. Another building was constructed at the same North Florida Avenue location, close to downtown and uphill from Lake Wire. The message on the front reads: "1/24/07. I see by your cards that you have been taking a trip. How did you enjoy yourself? I should thought you might have called on me while you were about it. Should have been pleased to see you. Will excuse you this time but please don't let it happen again. E. I. H." (Courtesy Lakeland Public Library.)

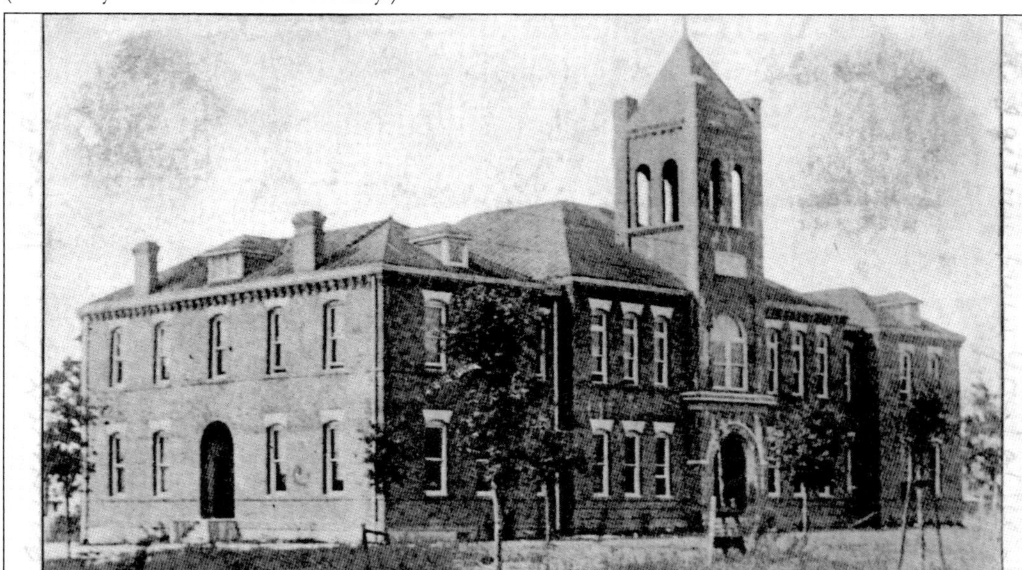

LAKELAND HIGH SCHOOL, LAKELAND, FLA. A local schoolgirl wrote her friend about her postcard collection in February 1908: "Hello Grace received your card today. This is the school house that I go to. I will send you a view of Lake Morton next time. I am getting collection of Post Cards and if you know of any one of the same mind Remember me. Would you like a scene of an orange tree. I will send you one, some time. I will mark the grade that I am in. Callie Phillips." (Courtesy Lakeland Public Library.)

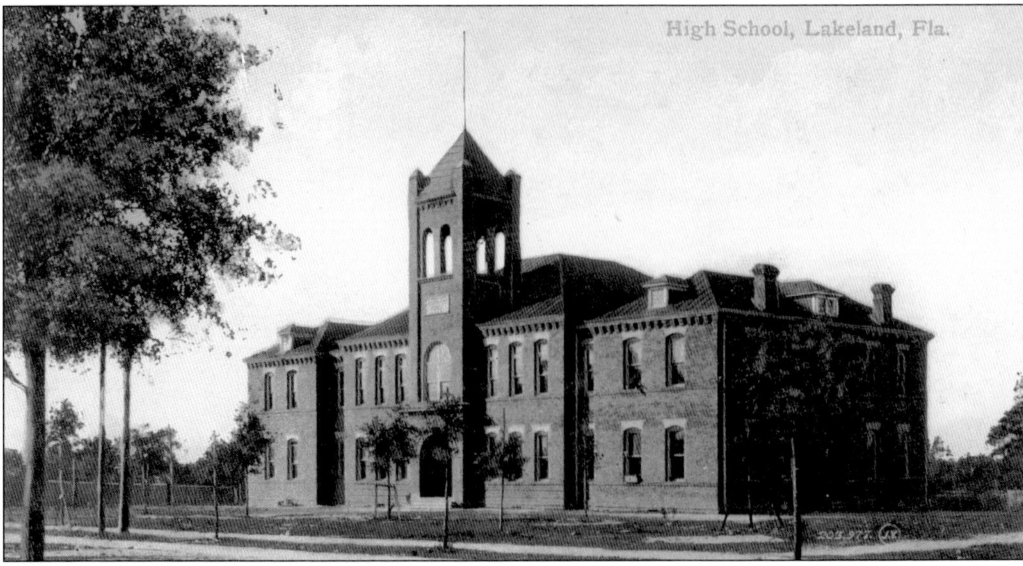

HIGH SCHOOL, LAKELAND, FLA., C. 1907. An earlier school known as the Academy existed in Lakeland and was located on property bordered by Orange and Lime Streets and Tennessee and Florida Avenues. The wood-frame building was constructed in 1884 and burned in 1897. The school was housed in temporary quarters until the high school was constructed in 1902. (Courtesy Lakeland Public Library.)

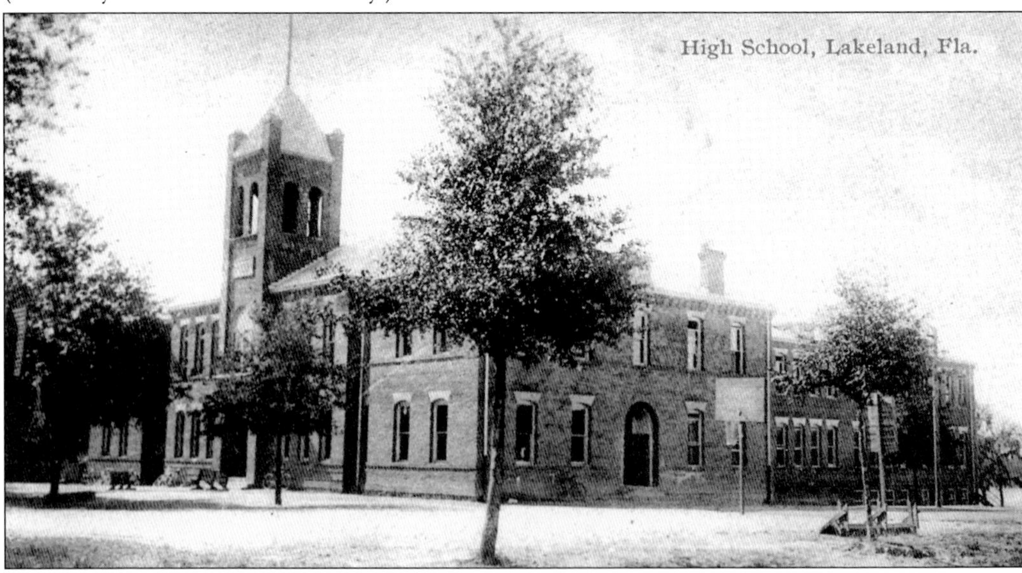

HIGH SCHOOL, LAKELAND, FLA. By the time this postcard was published, an addition to the west side had been erected. Although Lakeland had telephone service by 1902, postcards carried routine news of the day: "6/23/15 My very dear friend: was so glad to hear from you. Hope you are both real well & thoroughly rested. There is no appreciable change in any thing here since you left, except we have a new fence around our home which greatly enhances its looks. . . . Had a fine rain this morning. My vines and caladiums have grown so much. We missed you and your brother & the Bagleys. Oh how I would like one of your hugs! And how your laugh would cheer me! My health is no better—worse I think. Love Mrs. M." (Courtesy Lakeland Public Library.)

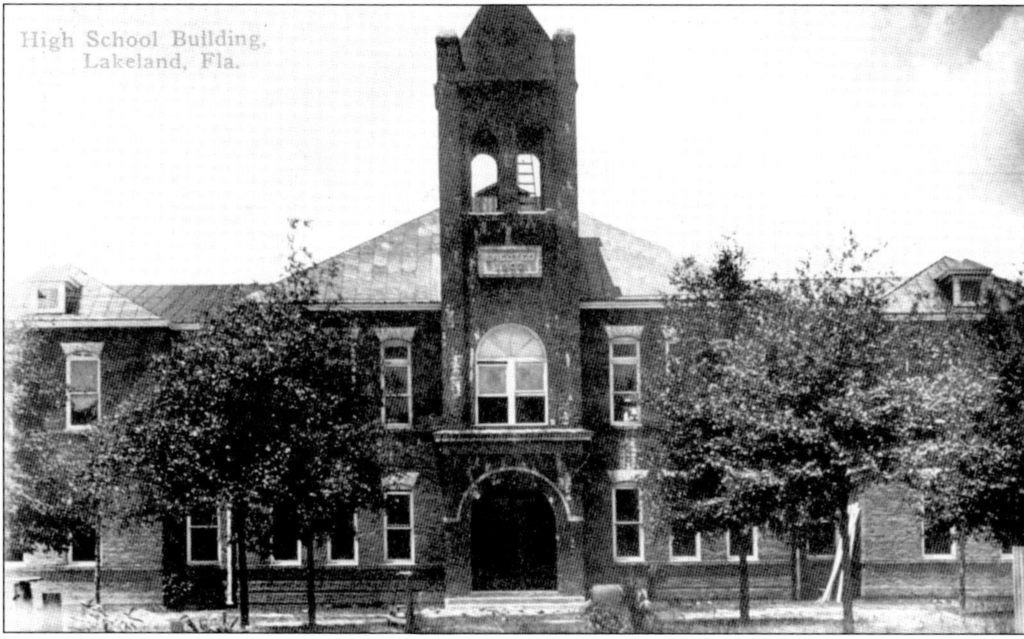

HIGH SCHOOL BUILDING, LAKELAND, FLA. This unusual and unsent postcard shows the high school building looking west across North Florida Avenue and likely dates from the mid-1910s. (Courtesy Larry Gray.)

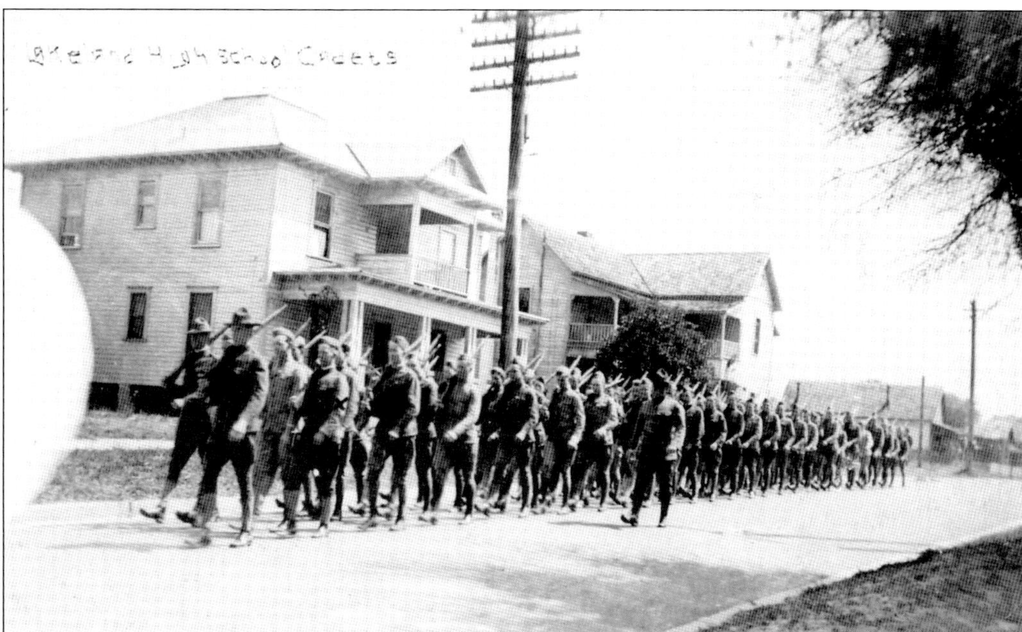

LAKELAND HIGH SCHOOL CADETS. World War I-era cadets from Lakeland High School are on a marching drill, possibly on Peachtree Street north of the high school. (Courtesy Lakeland Public Library.)

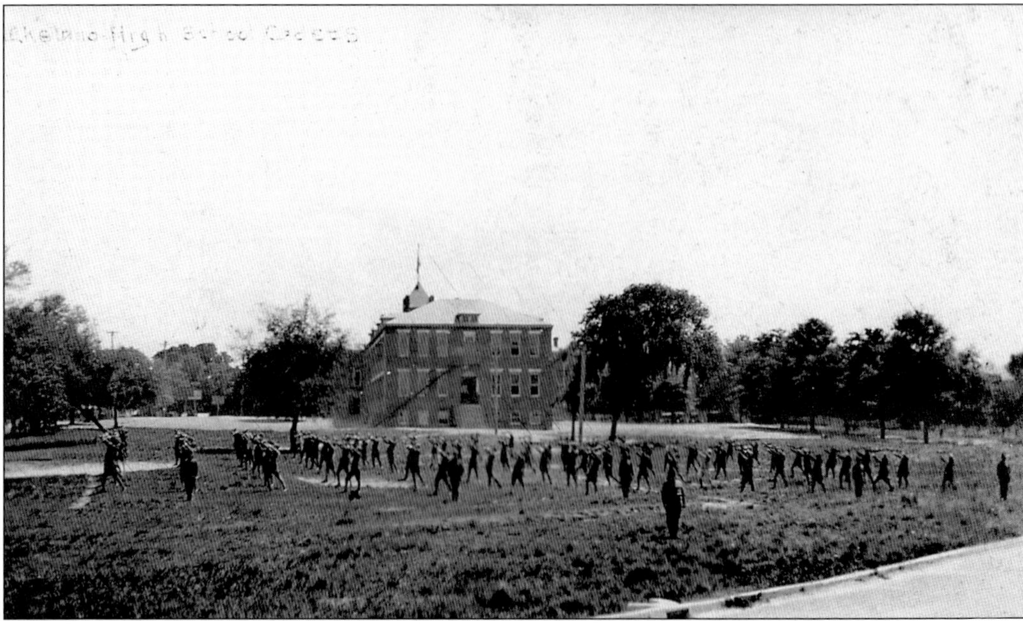

LAKELAND HIGH SCHOOL CADETS. The cadets work on their drills in back of Lakeland High School. This real-photo postcard and others showing the Lakeland High School cadets may have been produced by Miller's Studio or Miller and Bay, an early Lakeland photography studio and publisher of local postcards and photographs. (Courtesy Lakeland Public Library.)

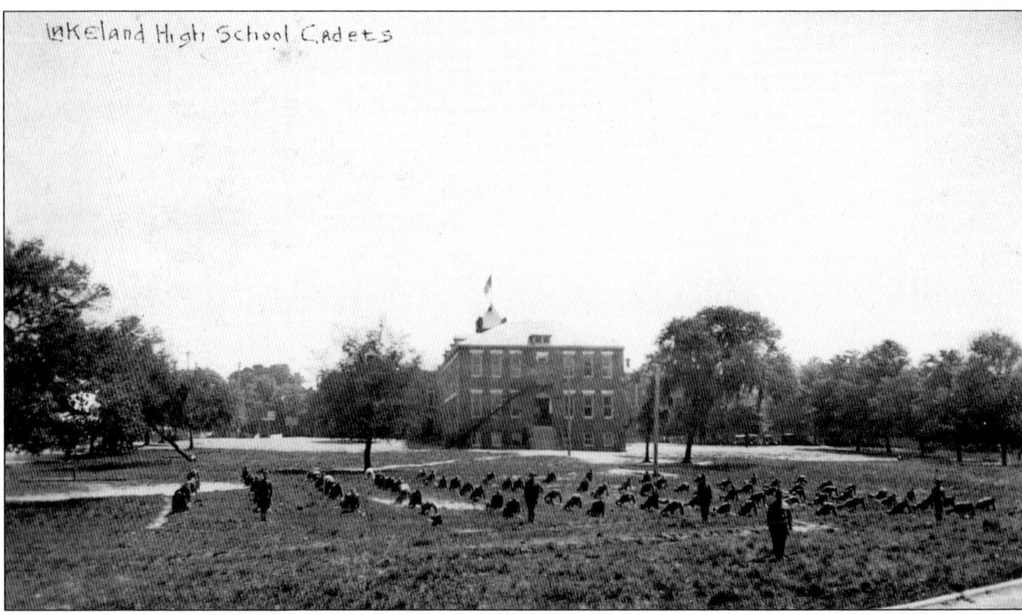

LAKELAND HIGH SCHOOL CADETS. Cadets perform calisthenics in back of the high school. (Courtesy Lakeland Public Library.)

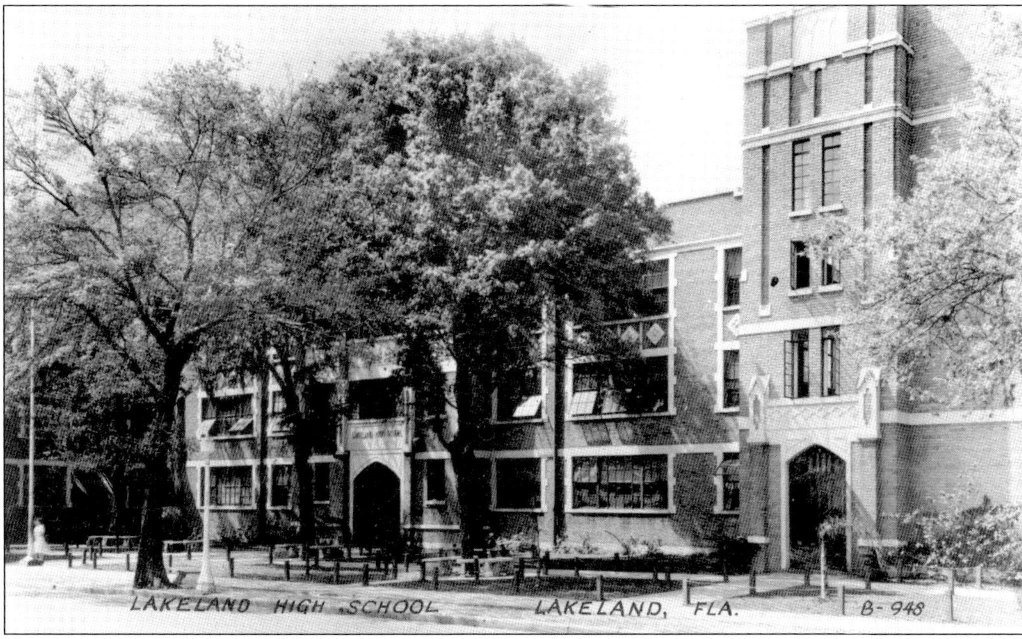

LAKELAND HIGH SCHOOL, LAKELAND, FLA. The 1927 Lakeland High School building was constructed on the same site as the 1902 school. This is a real-photo postcard of the high school's front façade. (Courtesy Larry Gray.)

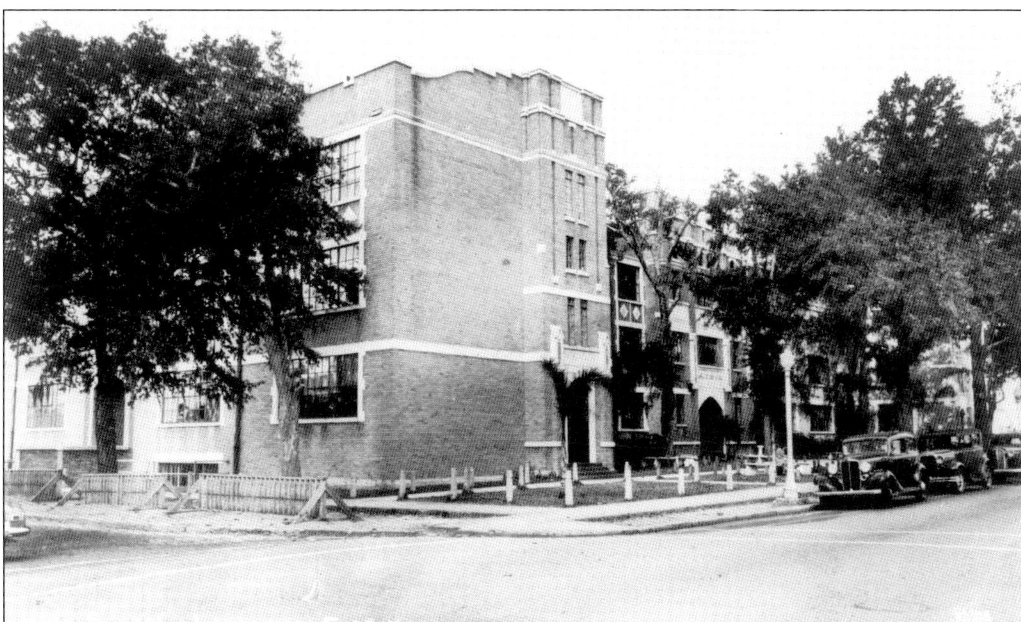

HIGH SCHOOL—LAKELAND, FLORIDA. Bicycle racks lined West Oak Streets, and cars parked along North Florida Avenue in this view of the southeast corner of the high school building. This building is presently the Lawton Chiles Middle Academy, named in honor of late U.S. senator and Florida governor "Walkin' " Lawton M. Chiles Jr., a 1948 Lakeland High School graduate. (Courtesy Lakeland Public Library.)

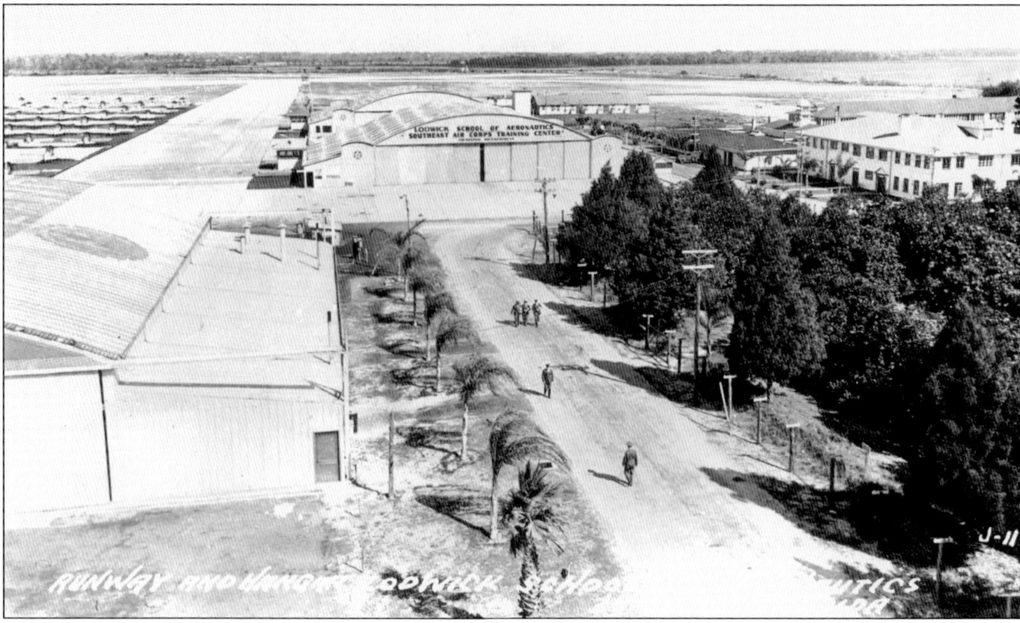

RUNWAY AND HANGER, LODWICK SCHOOL OF AERONAUTICS, LAKELAND, FLORIDA. The school was operated from 1940 to 1945 as a training site for military pilots by aviation businessman Albert I. Lodwick (1904–1961). This view looks north with Lake Parker to the right. The site is now known as the Tiger Town complex adjacent to Joker Marchant Stadium, home of the Detroit Tigers spring training camp and minor league Lakeland Tigers. (Courtesy Lakeland Public Library.)

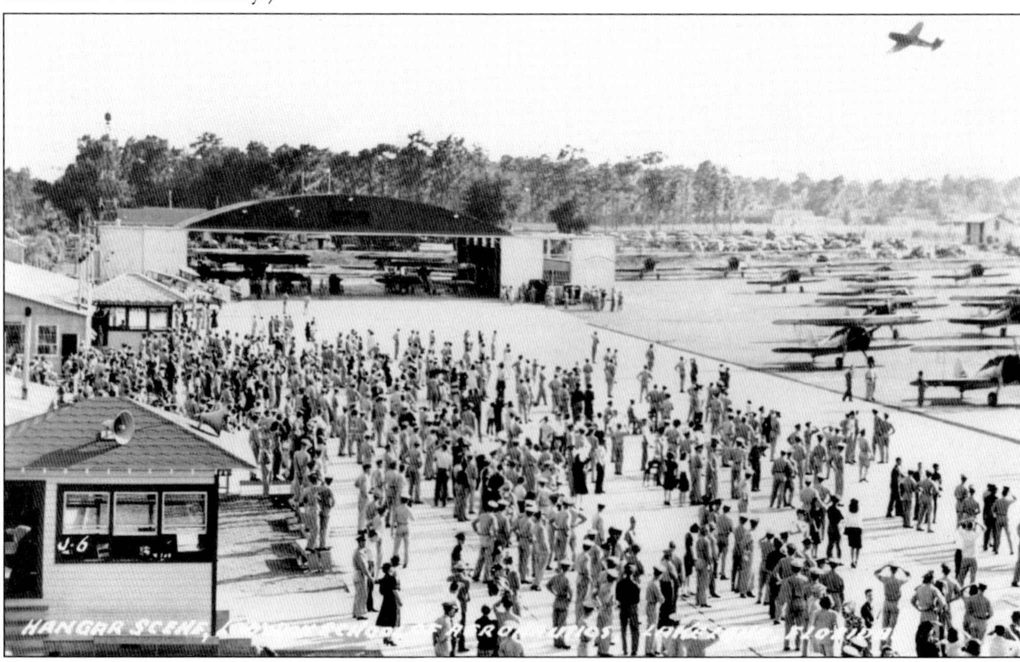

HANGER SCENE, LODWICK SCHOOL OF AERONAUTICS, LAKELAND, FLORIDA. The view is looking south. Airmen and guests celebrate a base open house in 1944. (Courtesy Lakeland Public Library.)

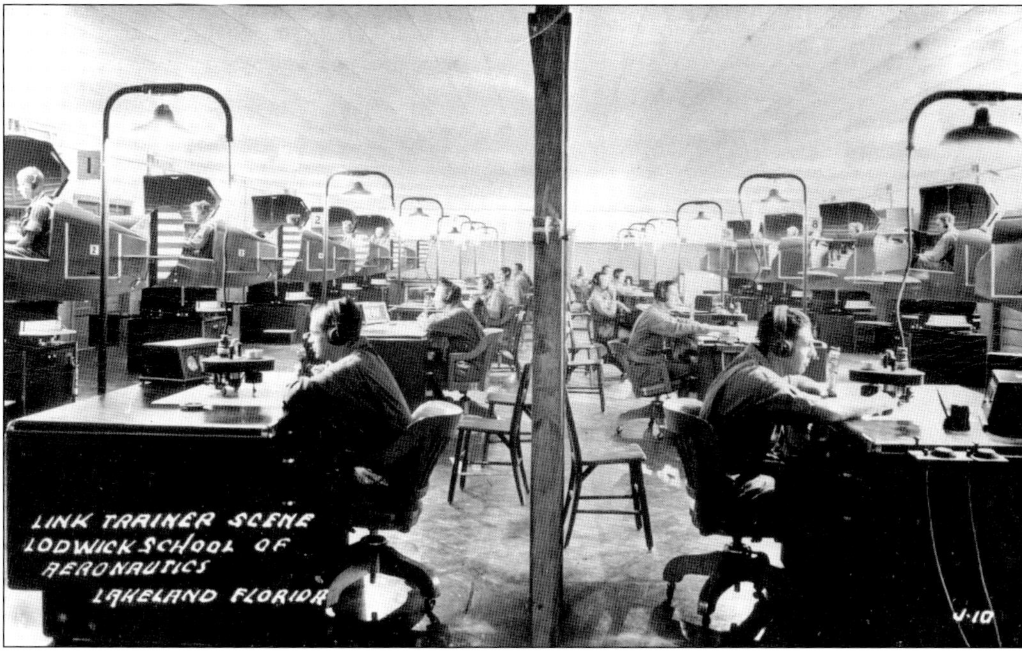

LINK TRAINER SCENE, LODWICK SCHOOL OF AERONAUTICS, LAKELAND, FLORIDA. This unusual view was described by a visitor to the school: "I'm surprised at number of Link Trainers. Completely manned by non-com military. Sgt Cooper—1st position on right was in charge—each cadet got some limited training instrument instruction. Civilian pilots were included in program. Picture probably early 1944." (Courtesy Lakeland Public Library.)

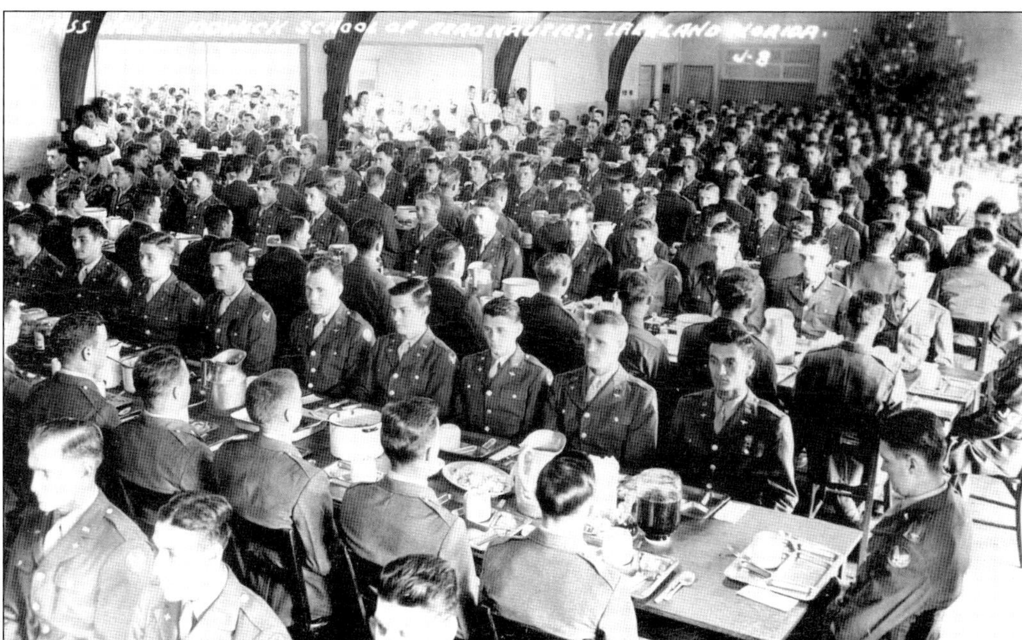

MESS HALL, LODWICK SCHOOL OF AERONAUTICS, LAKELAND, FLORIDA. Scores of airmen prepare to dine during the Christmas season. (Courtesy Lakeland Public Library.)

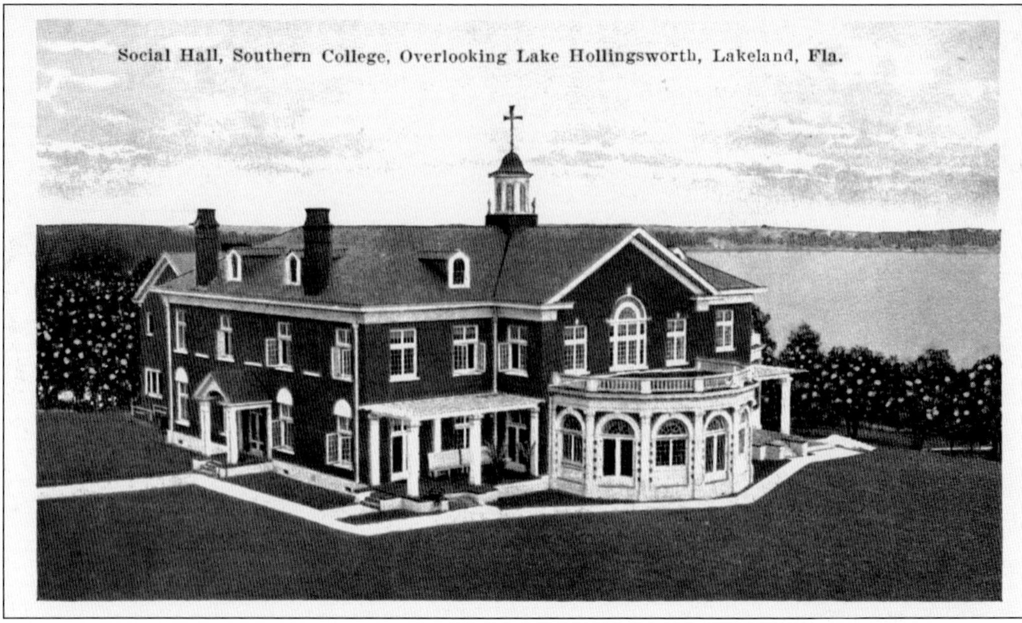

SOCIAL HALL, SOUTHERN COLLEGE, OVERLOOKING LAKE HOLLINGSWORTH, LAKELAND, FLA. Southern College moved to town in 1922, having experienced disastrous fires and hurricanes in both Sutherland (now Palm Harbor) and Clearwater. The Social Hall was one of the first two buildings constructed, and it housed the dining room, library, classrooms, and faculty offices. Other institutions of higher education presently call Lakeland home; South-Eastern Bible Institute (now Southeastern University) arrived in 1946 and moved to its Longfellow Boulevard campus in 1952. (Courtesy Florida Southern College Library.)

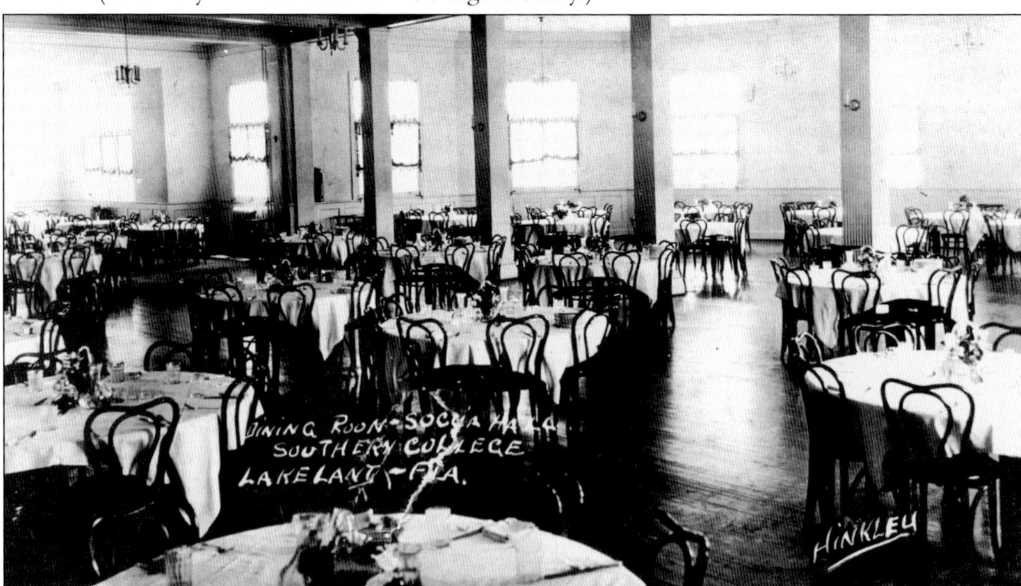

DINING ROOM & SOCIAL HALL, SOUTHERN COLLEGE, LAKELAND, FLA. A rare mid-1920s real-photo postcard shows the large dining room on the second floor of Social Hall. It was rededicated in 1935 as Edge Hall in memory of longtime trustee E. E. (Elliott Erastus) Edge of Groveland. (Courtesy Florida Southern College Library.)

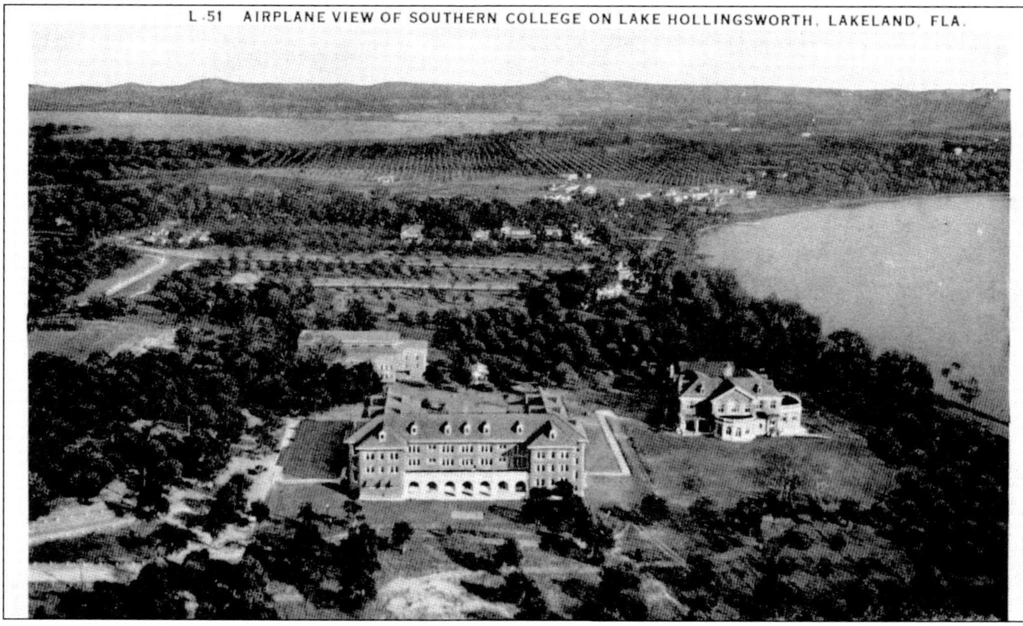

AIRPLANE VIEW OF SOUTHERN COLLEGE ON LAKE HOLLINGSWORTH, LAKELAND, FLA. Southern College was still a small college when this late-1920s eastward-facing postcard was published. The Dormitory for Women was centrally located in front of the original gymnasium. Social Hall is to the right toward Lake Hollingsworth. Acres of citrus are visible in the distance along with a fanciful low mountain range, the latter evidently added during production to enhance the view. (Courtesy Florida Southern College Library.)

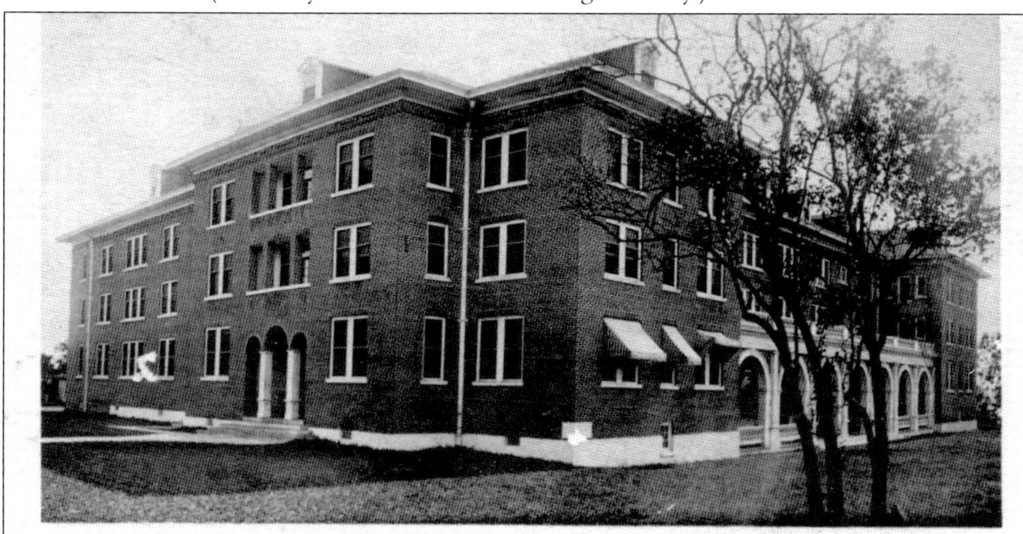

GIRLS DORMITORY, FRONT VIEW. SOUTHERN COLLEGE, LAKELAND, FLORIDA. The card shows the northwest corner of the Dormitory for Women (1922). The hall was advertised by the college as the "most beautiful women's dormitory in America." The Dormitory for Women was renamed Joseph-Reynolds Hall, honoring the late Cordyon S. and Louise R. Joseph and Mrs. Joseph's mother, the late Mrs. Louise Reynolds, who had contributed quite generously to the college for many years. (Courtesy Florida Southern College Library.)

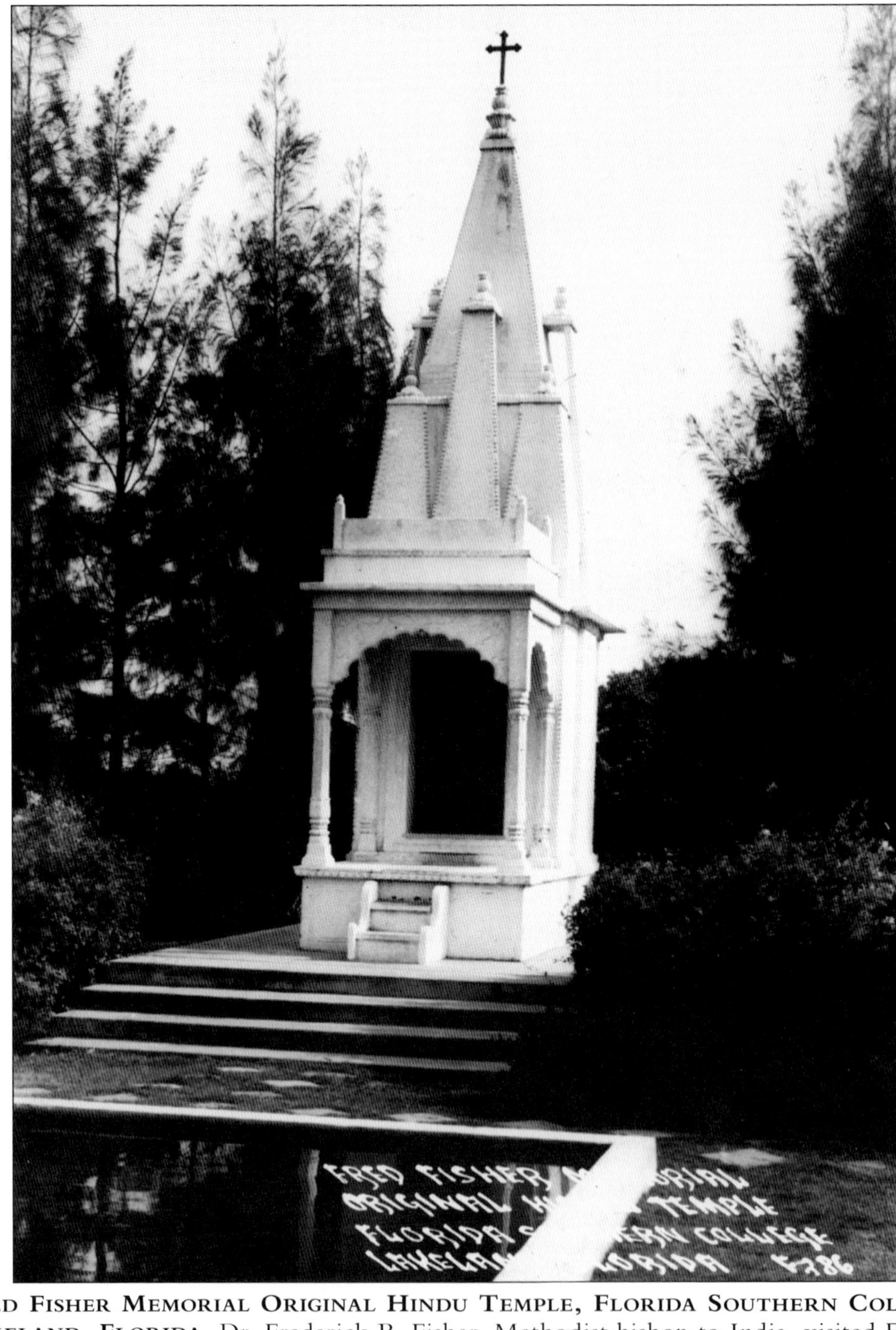

Fred Fisher Memorial Original Hindu Temple, Florida Southern College, Lakeland, Florida. Dr. Frederick B. Fisher, Methodist bishop to India, visited Florida Southern College in 1938 and was impressed with the spirit of the institution. He offered to donate a 239-piece, hand-carved, red sandstone Indian temple to the school to form the foundation of a campus garden. Dr. Fisher died suddenly, and it was left to his widow, Welthy Honsinger Fisher, to carry out his plans. The beautiful temple was erected near Edge Hall (Social Hall) during the summer of 1938 and was surrounded by a garden of meditation. (Courtesy Florida Southern College Library.)

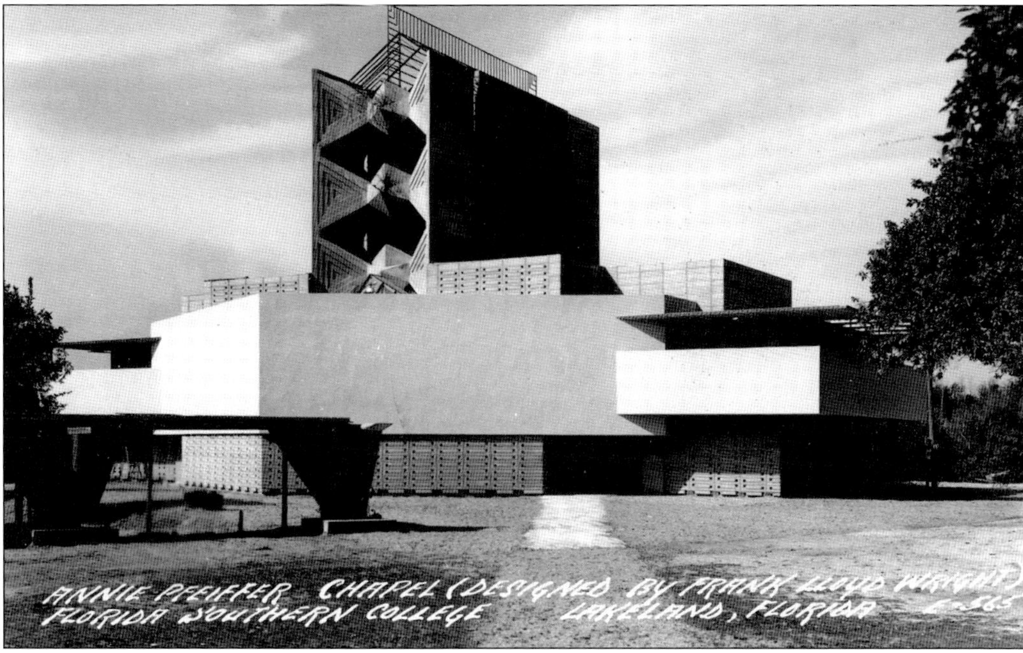

ANNIE PFEIFFER CHAPEL, FLORIDA SOUTHERN COLLEGE. Seen from the northeast, this real-photo postcard shows the Frank Lloyd Wright-designed chapel nearing completion; the esplanades in the left foreground were under construction. The chapel was constructed primarily using student labor between 1938 and 1941 and served as a centerpiece of Wright's "Child of the Sun" campus. (Courtesy Florida Southern College Library.)

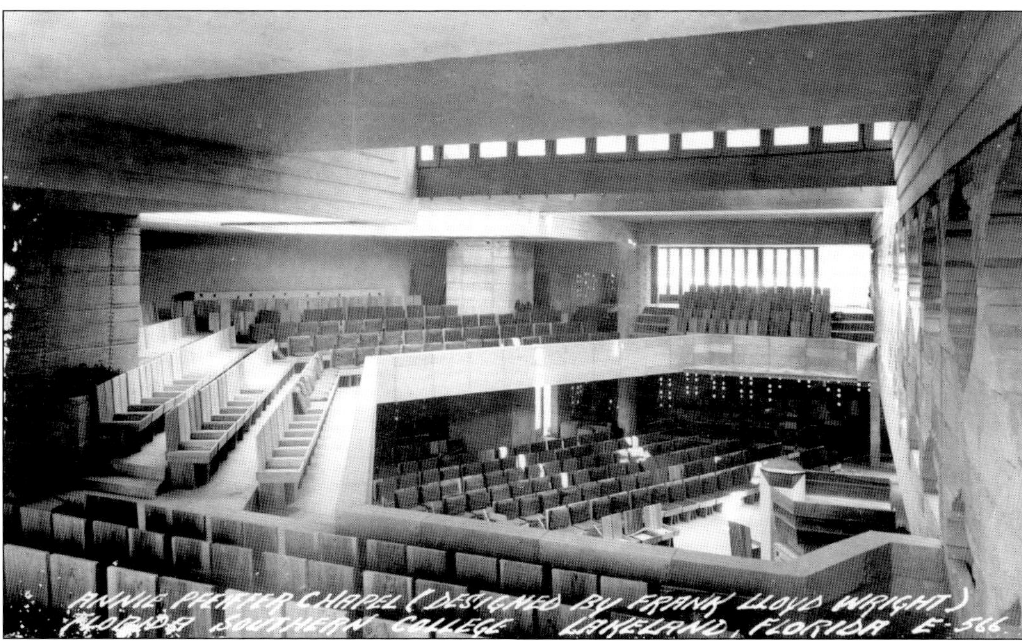

ANNIE PFEIFFER CHAPEL. An interior image of the chapel shows the seating nearing completion and the "ship's prow pulpit" on the right. The chapel was designed so that no one would be more than 50 feet from the speaker. (Courtesy Florida Southern College Library.)

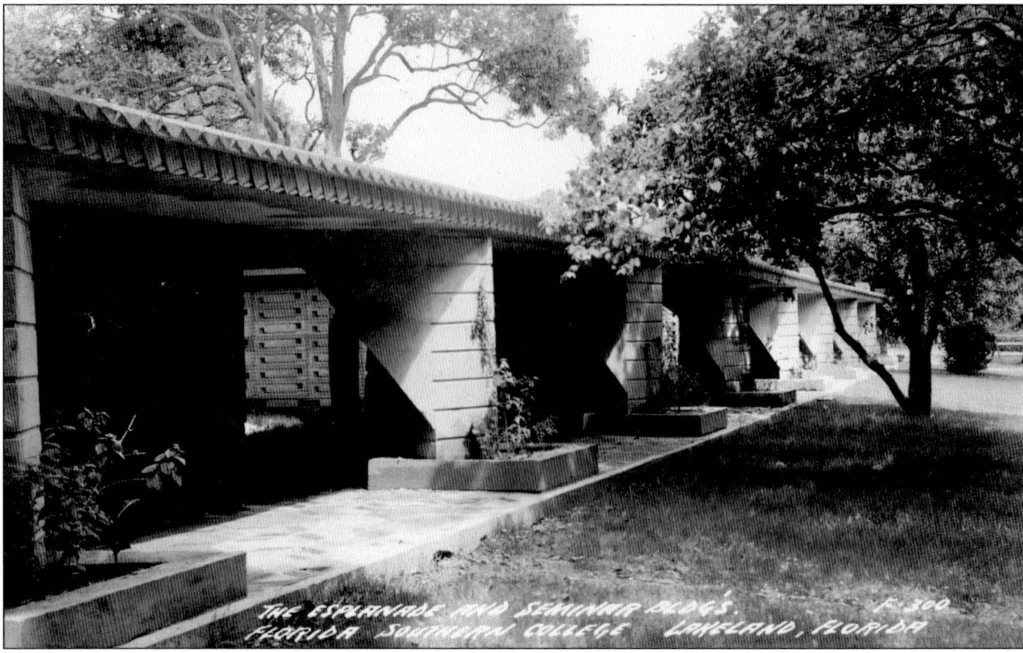

THE ESPLANADE AND SEMINAR BLDGS. FLORIDA SOUTHERN COLLEGE, LAKELAND, FLORIDA. The three Seminar Buildings were completed in 1941 and housed classrooms, faculty offices, and the office of Pres. Ludd M. Spivey. (Courtesy Florida Southern College Library.)

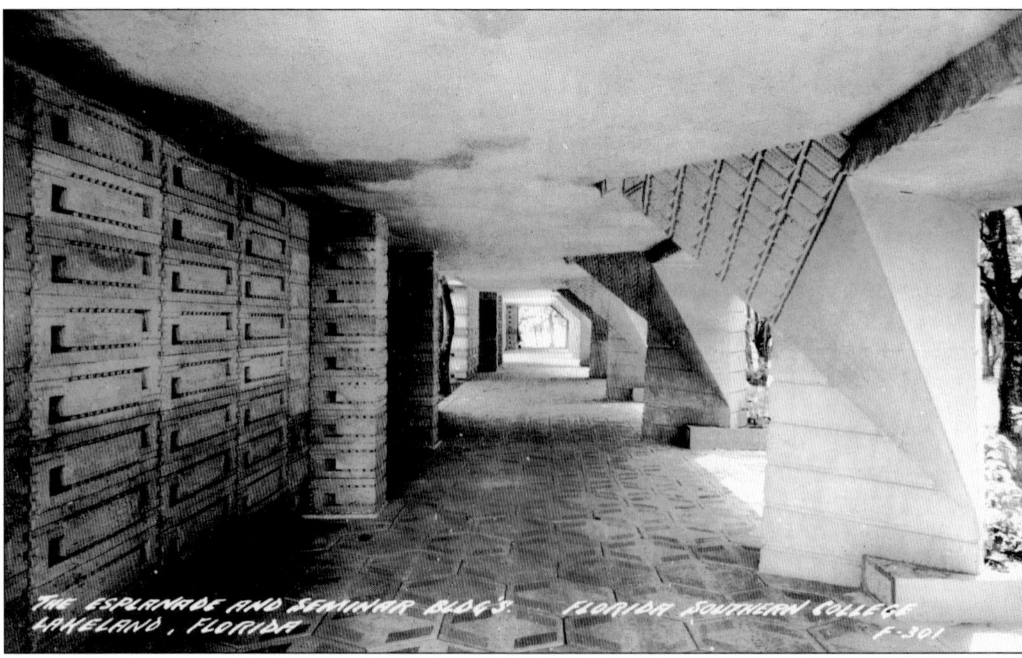

THE ESPLANADE AND SEMINAR BLDGS. FLORIDA SOUTHERN COLLEGE, LAKELAND, FLORIDA. This view looks east along the walkway in front of the Seminar Buildings. The hexagonal pavers were donated by friends of the college and were individually inscribed. (Courtesy Florida Southern College Library.)

Five

Churches

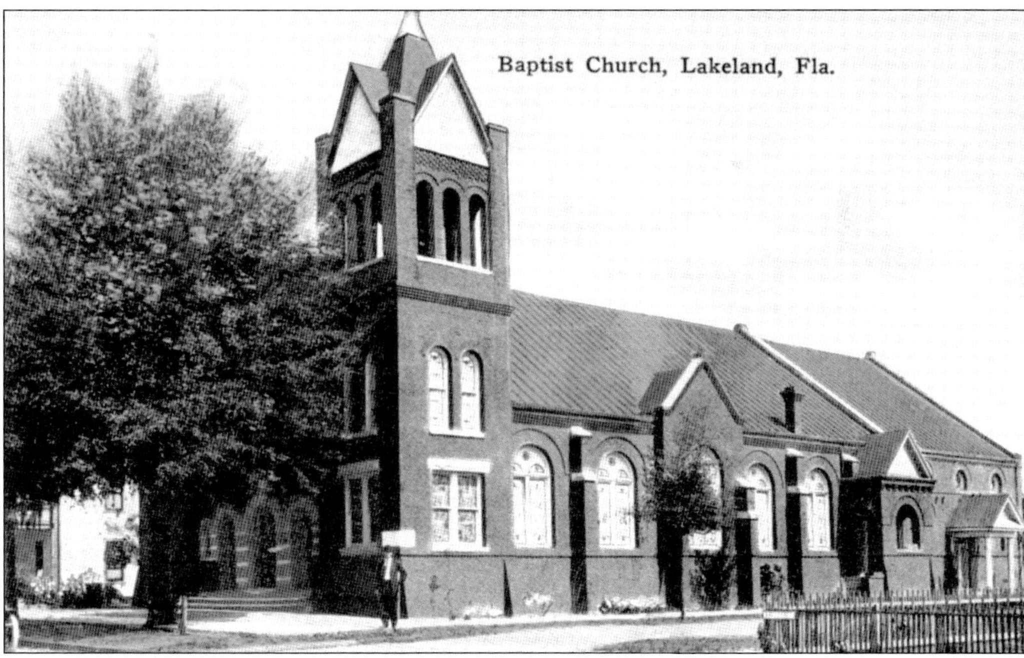

Baptist Church, Lakeland, Fla. This brick sanctuary was constructed in 1904 and seated 400 people. The total cost including furnishings was $11,000. It was subsequently replaced by another sanctuary at the same location. (Courtesy Lakeland Public Library.)

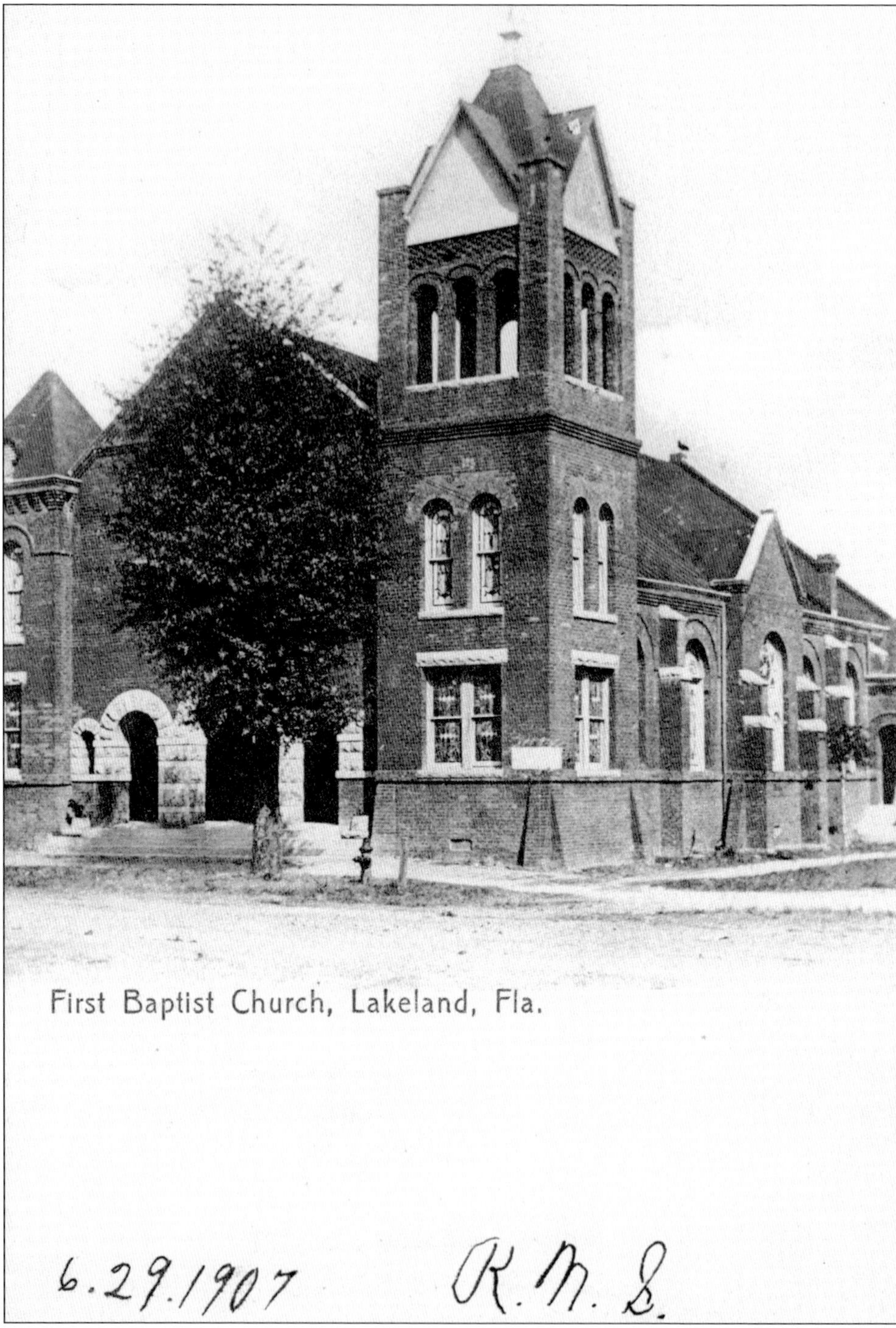

FIRST BAPTIST CHURCH, LAKELAND, FLA. This distinctive edifice is shown in this early unsent postcard dated June 29, 1907. By the 1920s, Lakeland had nearly 20 organized churches, although only the largest churches were represented on postcards. Churches published postcards to advertise and recruit, to announce meetings, and to welcome visitors. (Courtesy Lakeland Public Library.)

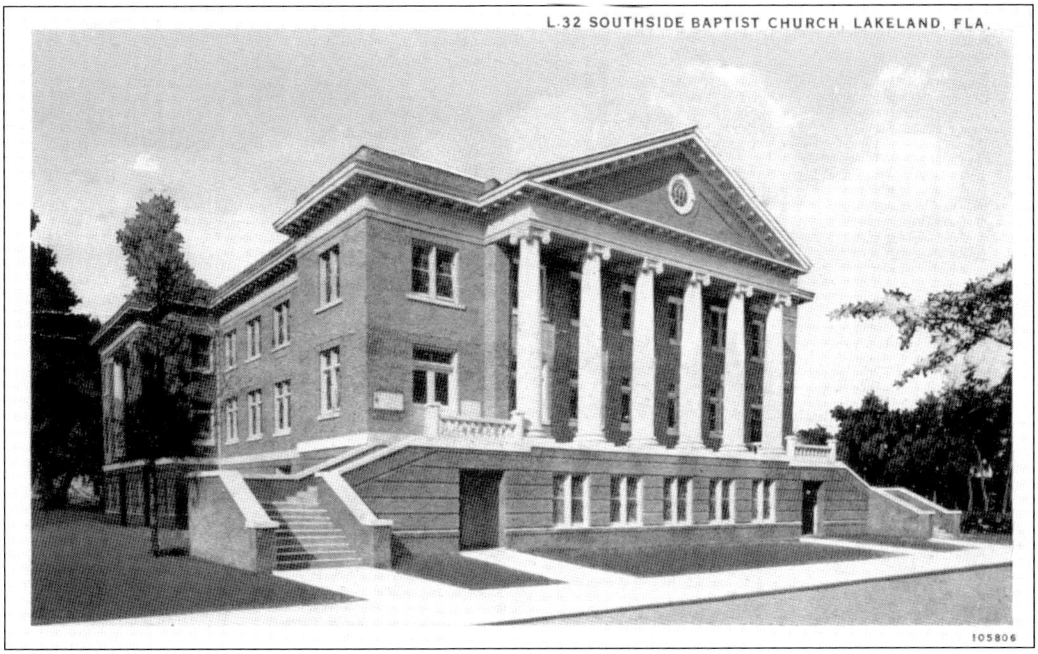

SOUTHSIDE BAPTIST CHURCH, LAKELAND, FLA. This sanctuary was constructed at 310 McDonald Street in 1924 and served the church until 1967. The congregation now worships in a larger sanctuary at the same address. This grand building was demolished in the late 1970s. (Courtesy Lakeland Public Library.)

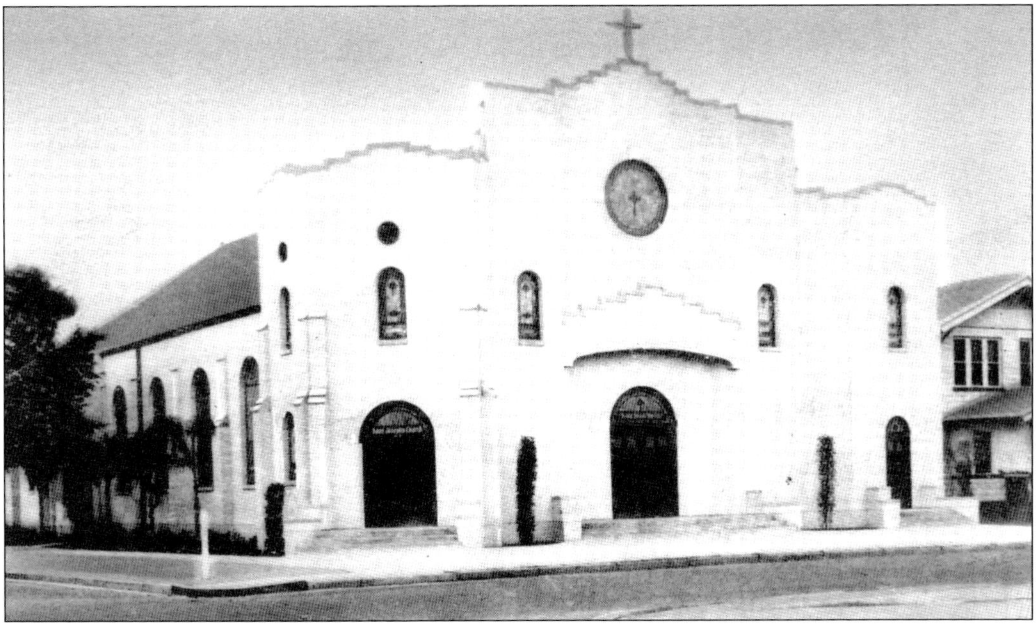

ST. JOSEPH'S CATHOLIC CHURCH, LAKELAND, FLORIDA. Catholic services in Lakeland date back to the late 1880s. St. Joseph's Catholic Church was the first Catholic church in Lakeland, constructed in 1936 and designed to seat 500 people. The church is located at 210 West Lemon Street. This view is from the northeast showing the front of the church. (Courtesy Lakeland Public Library.)

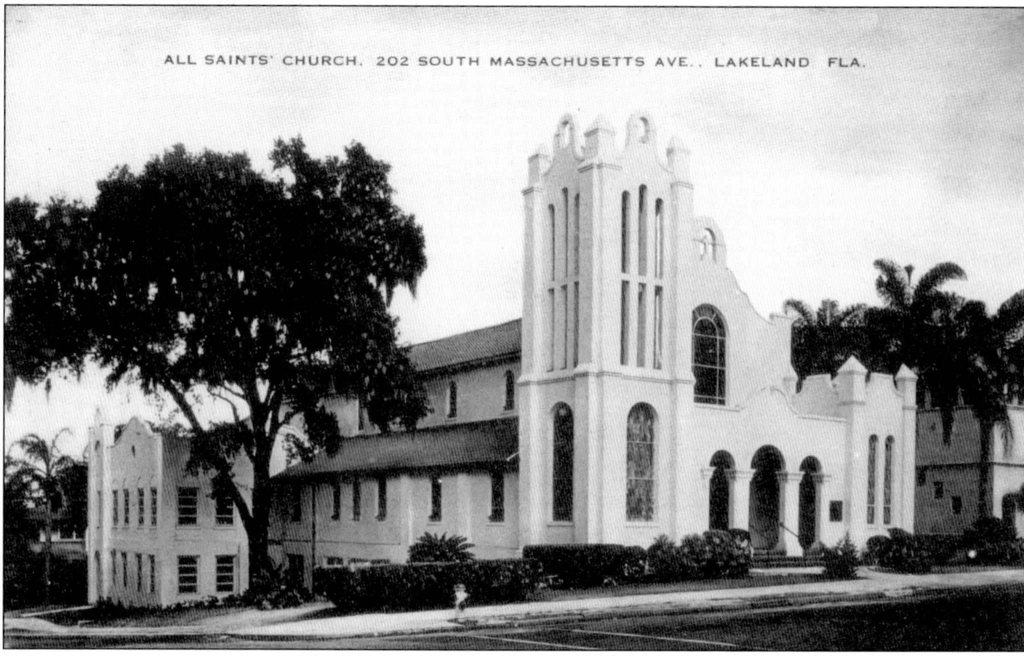

ALL SAINTS' CHURCH, 202 SOUTH MASSACHUSETTS AVE., LAKELAND, FLA. All Saints Episcopal Church began in the community of Acton, which failed after the freeze of 1890. Under the leadership of the Reverend John H. Weddell, the church relocated to Lakeland in 1892, where the present building was constructed in 1924 at South Massachusetts Avenue and East Lemon Street. (Courtesy Lakeland Public Library.)

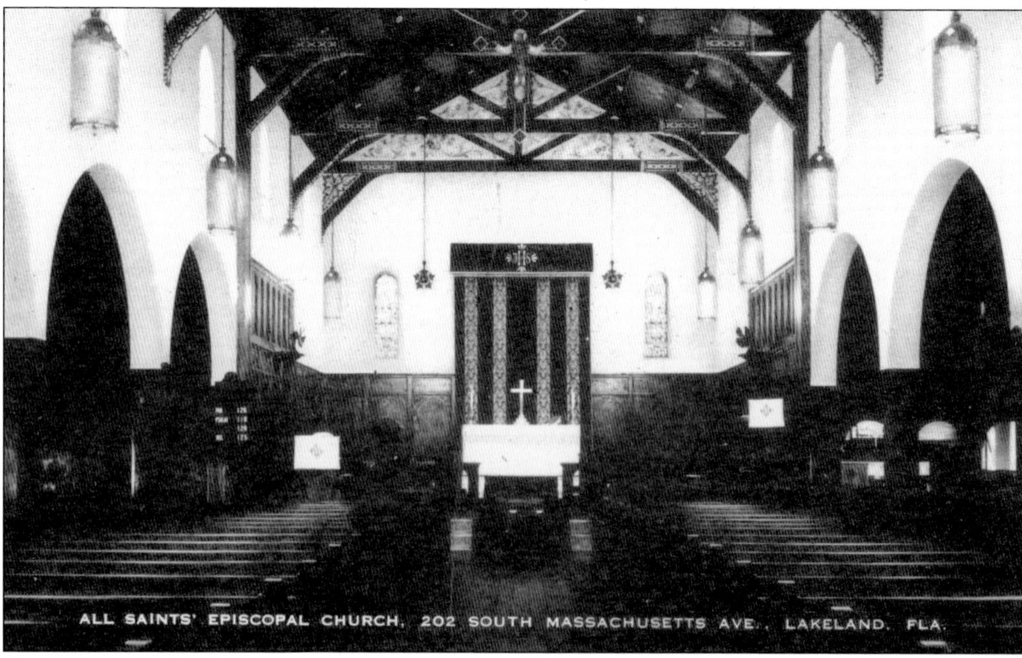

ALL SAINTS' EPISCOPAL CHURCH, 202 SOUTH MASSACHUSETTS AVE., LAKELAND, FLA. The church was designed by local architect Herbert Mendenhall. This view of the sanctuary dates from the 1920s. (Courtesy Lakeland Public Library.)

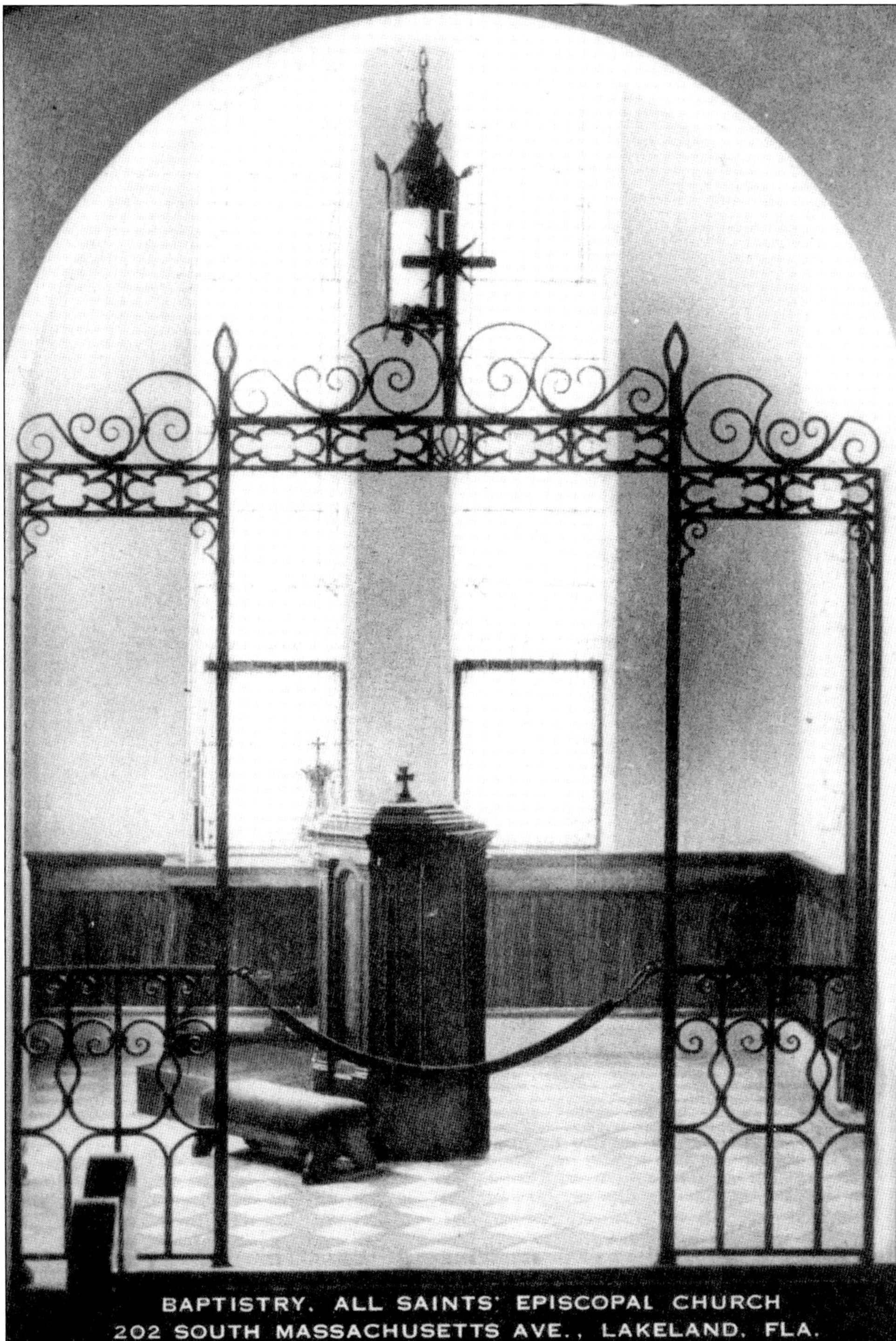

BAPTISTRY. ALL SAINTS' EPISCOPAL CHURCH, 202 SOUTH MASSACHUSETTS AVE., LAKELAND, FLA. This card was likely published by the church as a souvenir for its members and guests in the 1920s. (Courtesy Lakeland Public Library.)

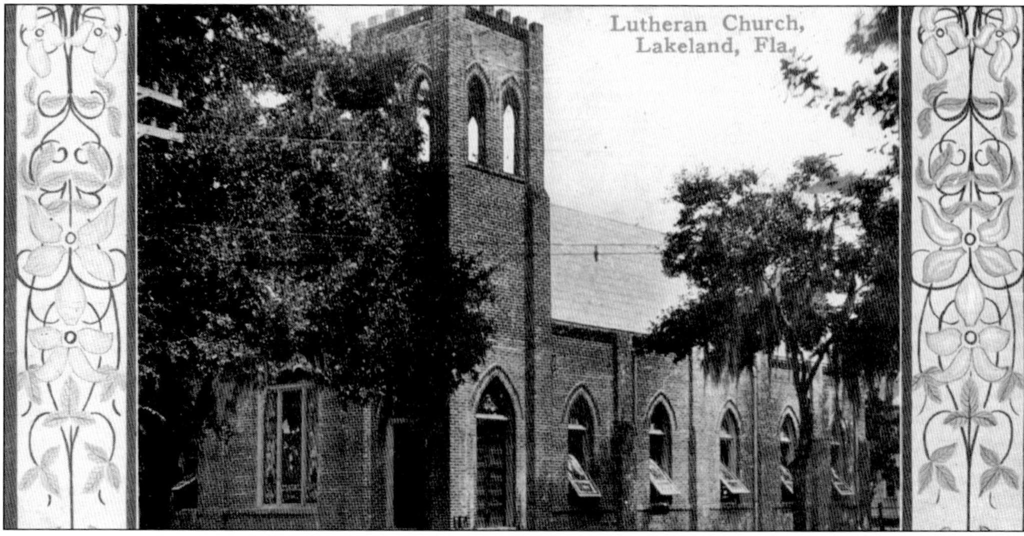

LUTHERAN CHURCH, LAKELAND, FLA. The church building was located at the corner of East Orange Street and Tennessee Avenue and was sold in 1955 to the First Federal Savings and Loan Association for $75,000 to make way for a new office building. The reverse of this postcard carries printed information about the young church: "December 7, 1912. Dear Brother: You doubtless are aware that we have a church at this place organized about 3 years ago. Our membership is small, notwithstanding we have built a handsome church and have exhausted our means and are handicapped by not being able to seat the church. Will you not ask your church to aid us to the amount of one collection? Please help us, and God will bless you all." (Courtesy Lakeland Public Library.)

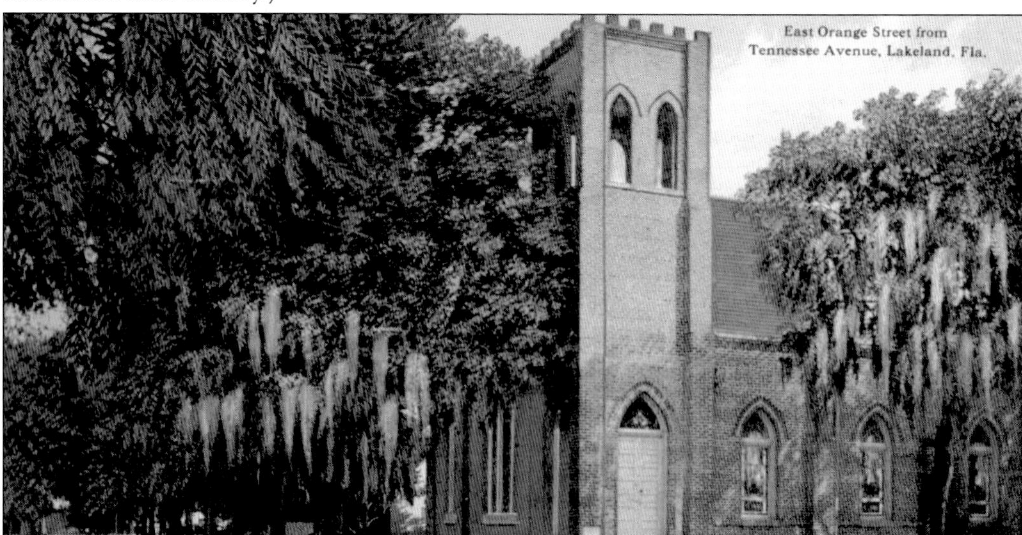

EAST ORANGE STREET FROM TENNESSEE AVENUE, LAKELAND, FLA. In 1908, a small group led by Valentine Van Huss organized a Lutheran church, which met in the Van Huss Opera House. The church organized on February 28, 1909, and in October, it welcomed its first regular pastor, H. J. Mathias. In 1911, ground was broken for the first sanctuary, and the cornerstone was laid on October 31, 1912—the 395th anniversary of the Reformation. This postcard was postmarked in Lakeland in 1917. (Courtesy Lakeland Public Library.)

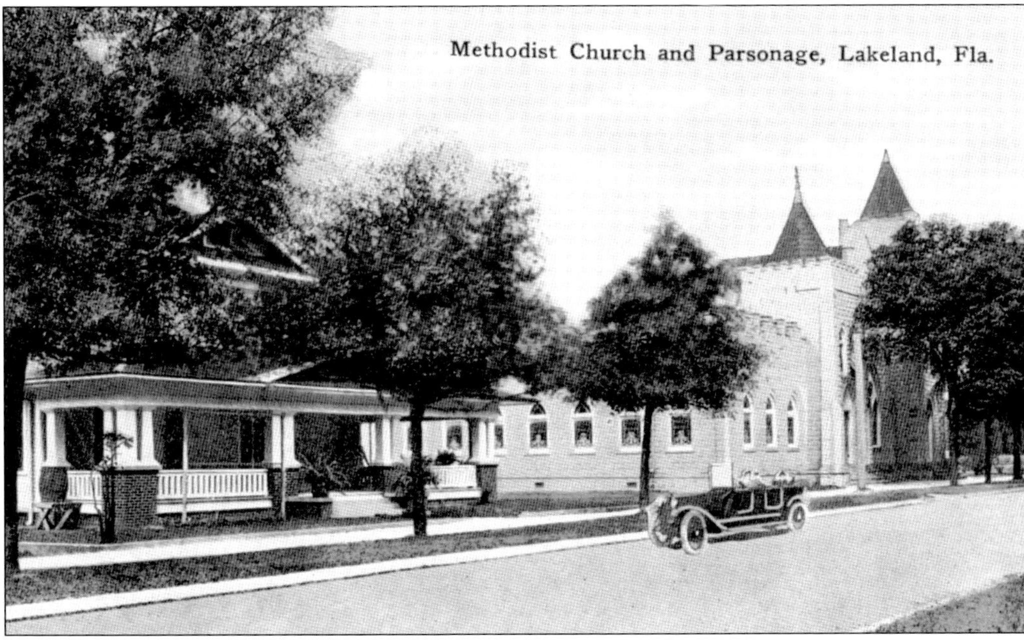

METHODIST CHURCH AND PARSONAGE, LAKELAND, FLA. This unique sanctuary was constructed in 1906 on the east side of South Kentucky Avenue. The church had a distinctive castle-like appearance and was a Lakeland landmark for some 60 years. (Courtesy Lakeland Public Library.)

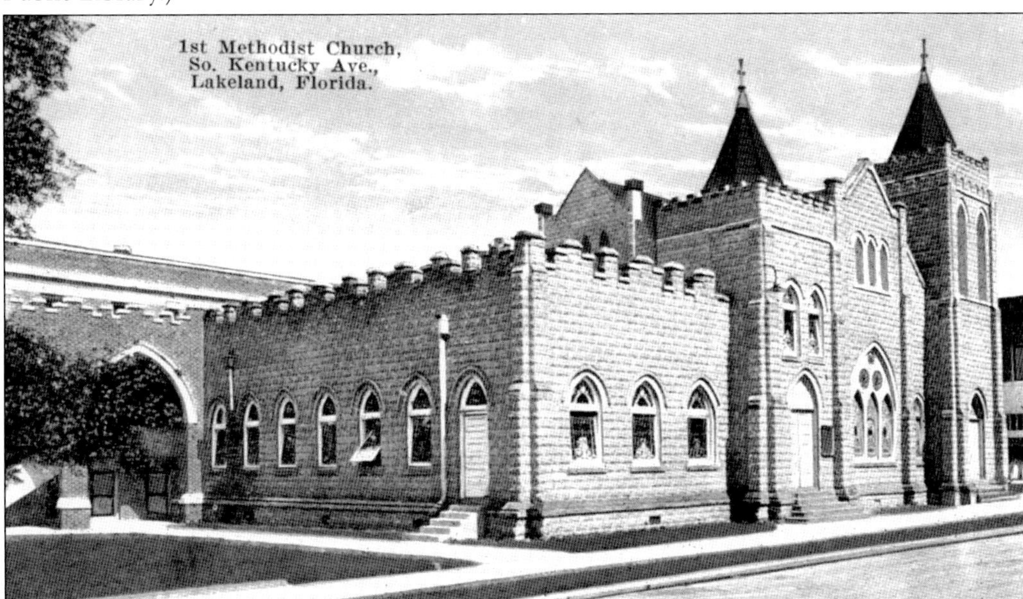

FIRST METHODIST CHURCH, SO. KENTUCKY AVE., LAKELAND, FLORIDA. First United Methodist moved to a new location at 72 Lake Morton Drive in 1955, and this building was purchased by Bible Presbyterian Church. Most of the oldest churches in town were formed downtown, and several still meet there. It is possible and interesting to retrace the movement of congregations from one sanctuary to another. Although most of the earliest church buildings have been replaced by newer structures, a few remain. (Courtesy Lakeland Public Library.)

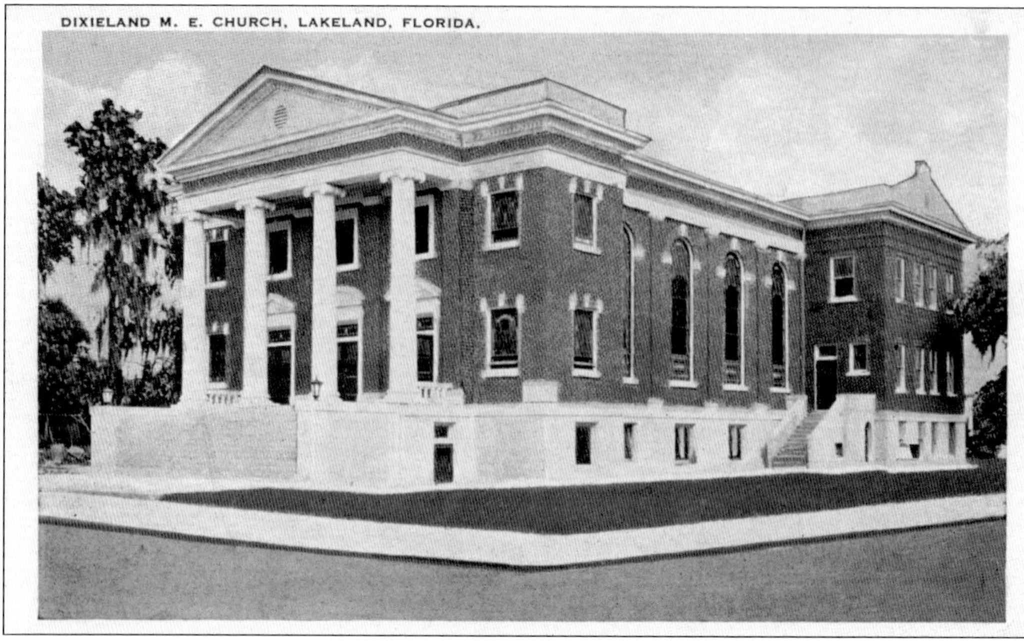

DIXIELAND M. E. CHURCH, LAKELAND, FLORIDA. The first church on this site—a small wood-frame structure—was built in a single day on June 17, 1912. Construction of this sanctuary at 942 South Boulevard took considerably longer, lasting from 1922 to 1924. The name was changed to College Heights Methodist Church in 1926, and the church remains active. (Courtesy Lakeland Public Library.)

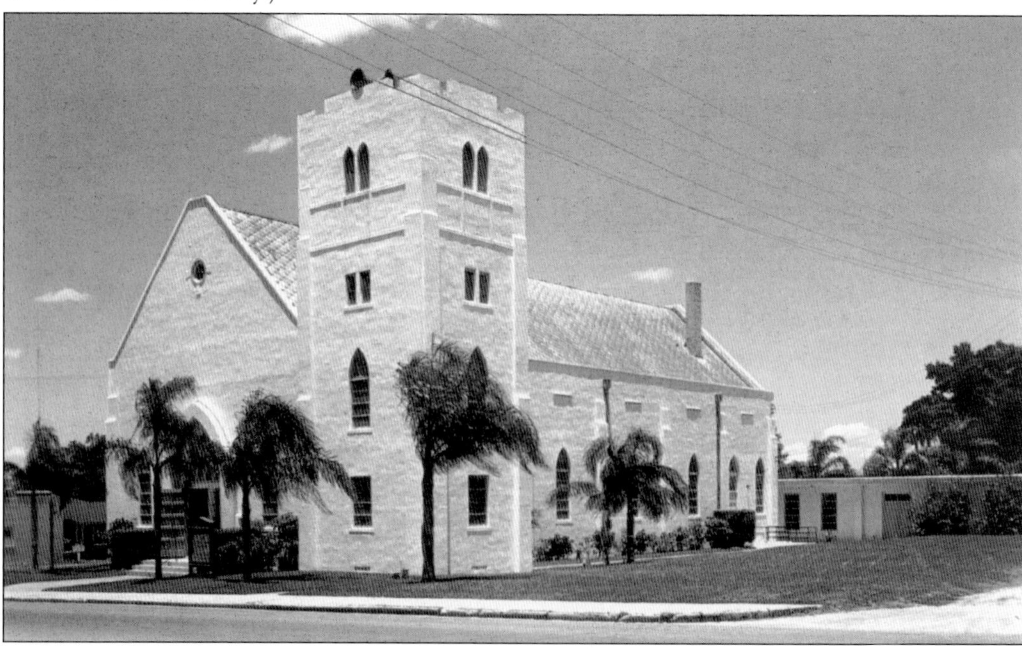

THE WESLEY MEMORIAL METHODIST CHURCH, NORTH MASSACHUSETTS AND PARKER STREETS, LAKELAND, FLA. This church was organized in 1913 as the Myrtle Street Methodist Church and is located just north of the downtown area. Wesley Memorial first held services in June 1949 and remains active at this location. (Courtesy Lakeland Public Library.)

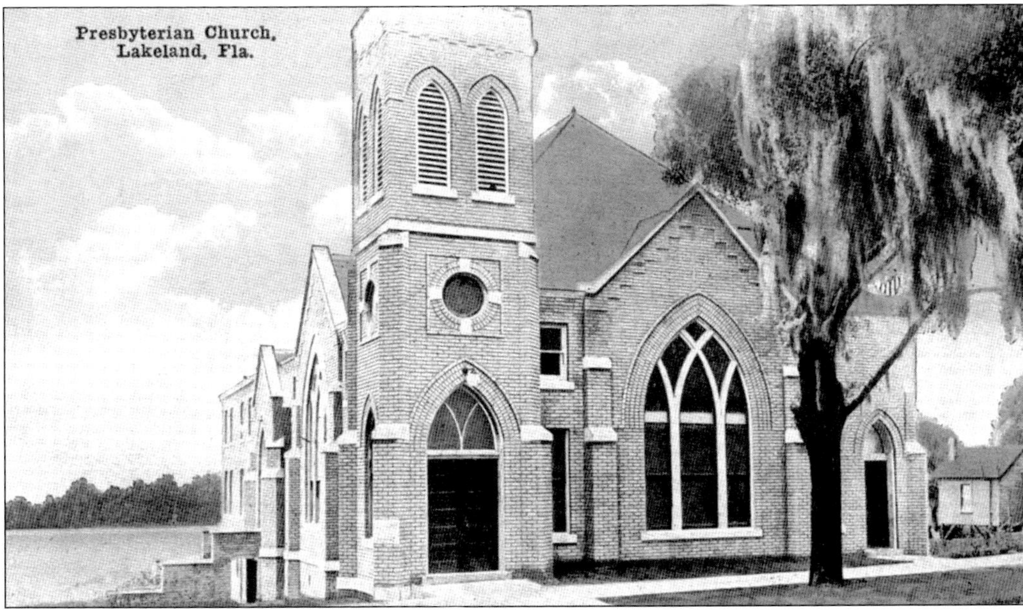

PRESBYTERIAN CHURCH, LAKELAND, FLA. The Presbyterians were the first to build a church home in Lakeland in the 1880s. Constructed in 1918, this sanctuary was on Massachusetts Avenue above the west shore of Lake Mirror, between the Elks' Home and the New Florida Hotel. (Courtesy Lakeland Public Library.)

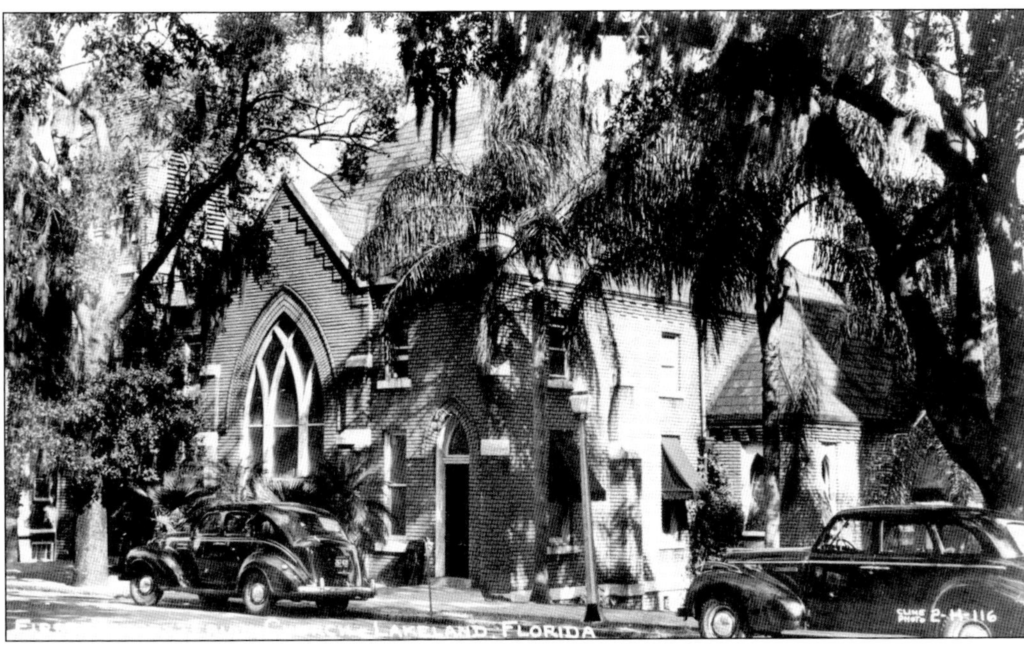

FIRST PRESBYTERIAN CHURCH, LAKELAND, FLORIDA. This beautiful sanctuary was replaced by a larger one in the mid-1950s, and the church relocated to the east shore of Lake Hollingsworth in 1978. (Courtesy Lakeland Public Library.)

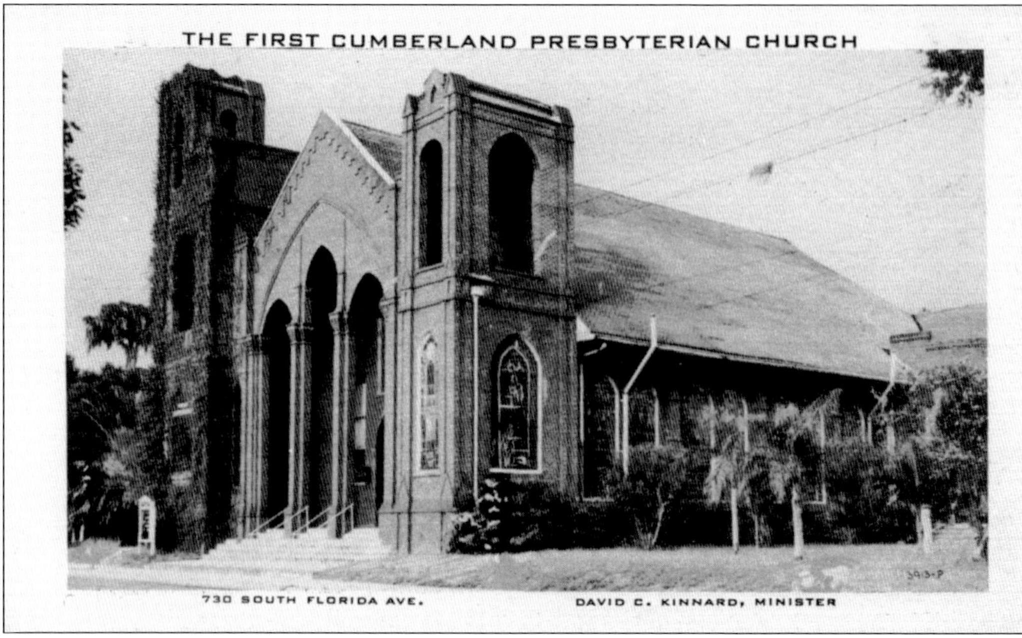

THE FIRST CUMBERLAND PRESBYTERIAN CHURCH, 730 SOUTH FLORIDA AVENUE, DAVID C. KINNARD, MINISTER. Construction of this sanctuary was completed in 1925, and the church was renamed Westminster Presbyterian Church in 1942. This church is still active. The ecumenical movement has always been strong in Lakeland, evidenced in the early years by the generosity of First Cumberland Presbyterian Church, who offered their sanctuary as a temporary church home for several denominations. (Courtesy Lakeland Public Library.)

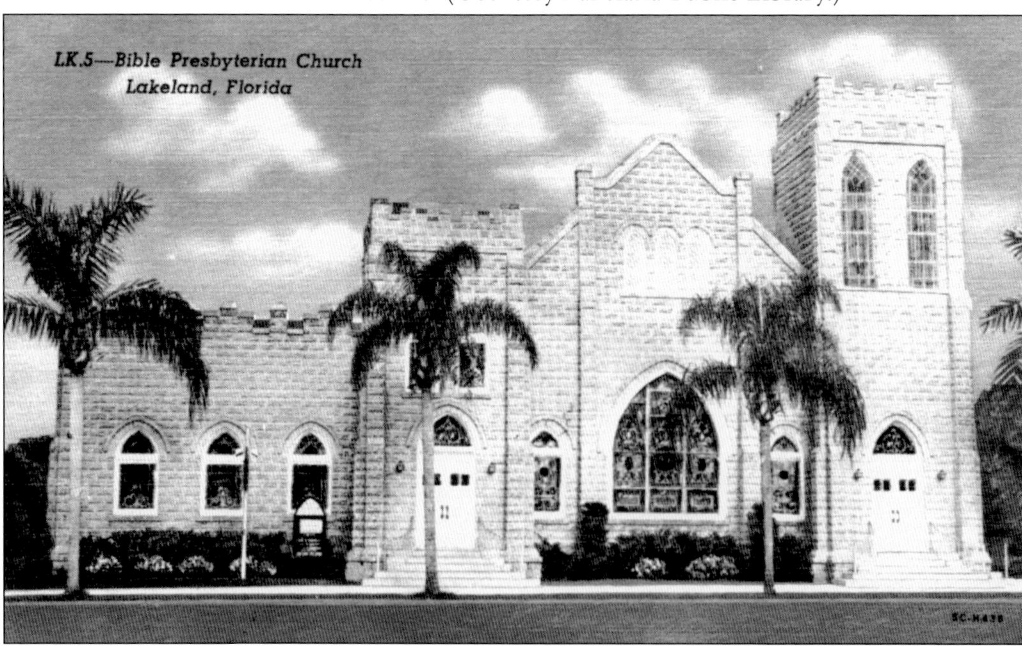

BIBLE PRESBYTERIAN CHURCH, LAKELAND, FLORIDA. The Presbyterians gave new life to a magnificent old church. First United Methodist Church relocated from this South Kentucky edifice in 1955, and Bible Presbyterian Church moved in. (Courtesy Lakeland Public Library.)

Six

Homes and Neighborhoods

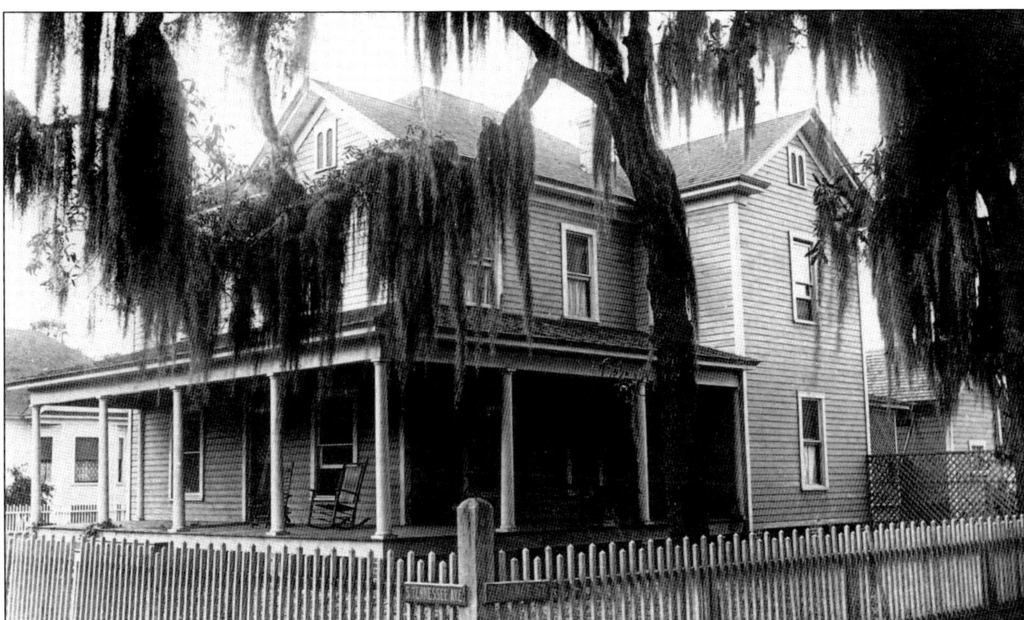

Miss. Manona Herron's Home. R. R. Herron established a business in Lakeland in 1899, and in 1908, he built a two-story brick building on Main Street. His store was on the lower floor, and the upper floor was called Herron's Opera House. After R. R. Herron's death, Manona Herron had a millinery shop, and her brother had a clock repair shop in the building. By 1922, the Herron home at the corner of Orange Street and Tennessee Avenue was remodeled into an 18-room apartment house. (Courtesy Lakeland Public Library.)

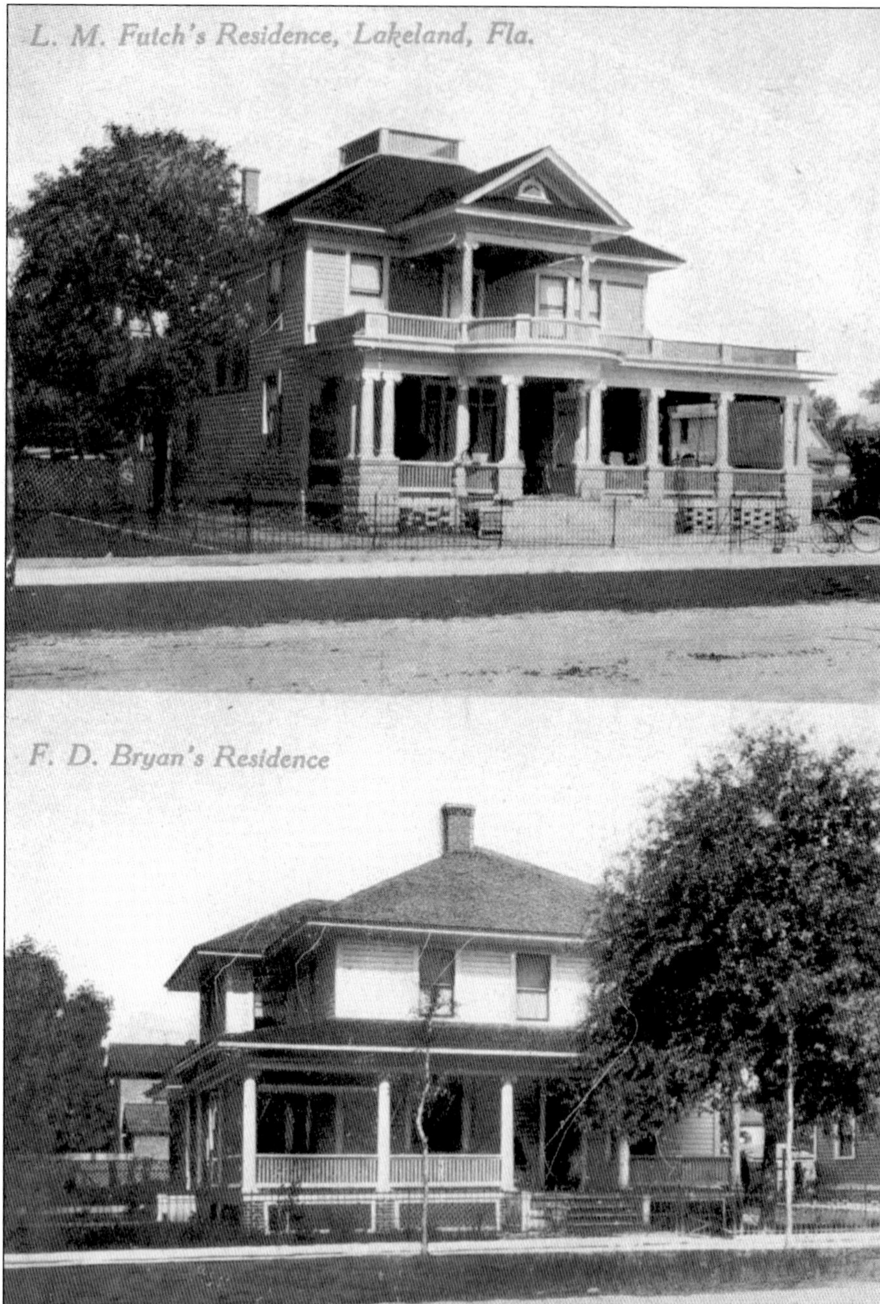

L. M. Futch's Residence, Lakeland, Fla.; F. D. Bryan's Residence. Lawrence Millard and Fannie Futch lived at 406 South Florida Avenue. Lawrence M. Futch was affiliated with Gentry Undertaking Company; the Futch and Gentry Building was at 120 1/2 East Main Street. Fenton D. Bryan lived at 402 South Florida Avenue and was proprietor of Lake Pharmacy. This postcard was written by someone who foresaw good things for Lakeland: "Lakeland, Fla., Jan. 28–1912. Dear Herman: Alice and I are enjoying our trip very much and both of us are much better. This is a fine little city with a big business future." (Courtesy Lakeland Public Library.)

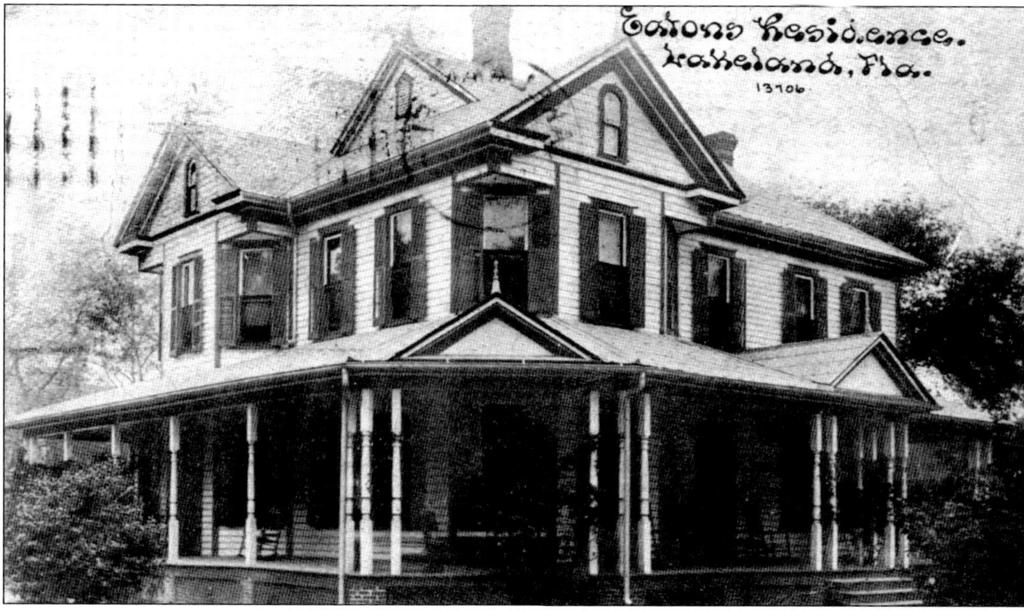

EATONS' RESIDENCE, LAKELAND, FLA. In 1913, the Eaton family lived at 409 South Massachusetts Avenue. Not surprisingly, the residential centers of Lakeland moved from downtown toward the suburbs over time. Only a few old single-family homes remain close to the center of town. Businesses seeking a downtown address purchased homes for conversion to office space, and many of those had been razed by the 1970s. (Courtesy Larry Gray.)

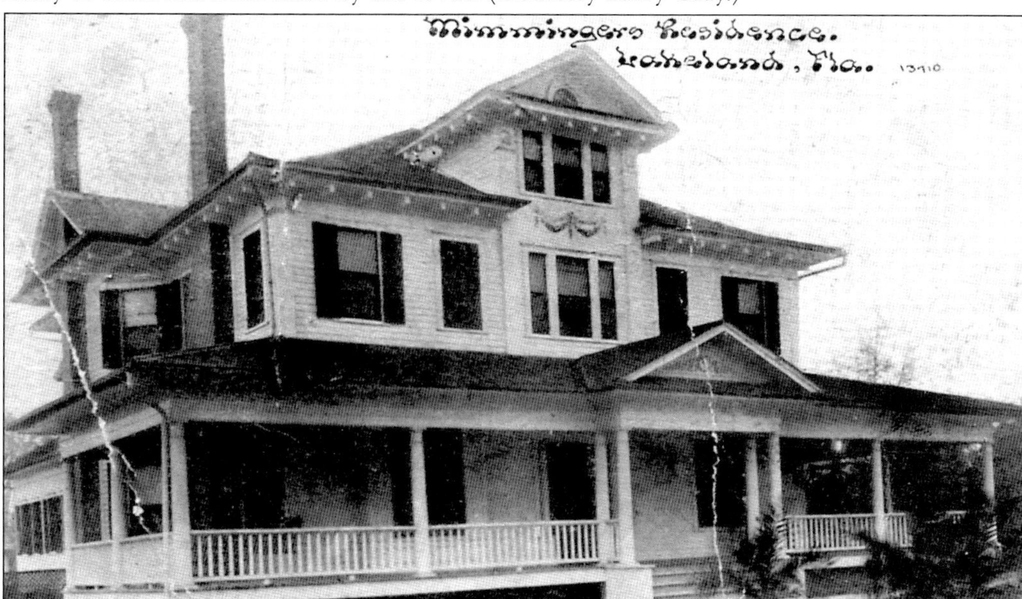

MIMMINGERS RESIDENCE, LAKELAND, FLA. This was the home of the C. G. Memminger family. Facing East Orange Street at the southwest corner of Iowa Avenue, this residence was also known as "The Palms" for its extravagant collection of palm varieties. Mr. Memminger was manager of the Coronet Phosphate Company, which had downtown offices at 208 Drane Building, Main Street. This postcard was postmarked from Lakeland in September 1911. (Courtesy Lakeland Public Library.)

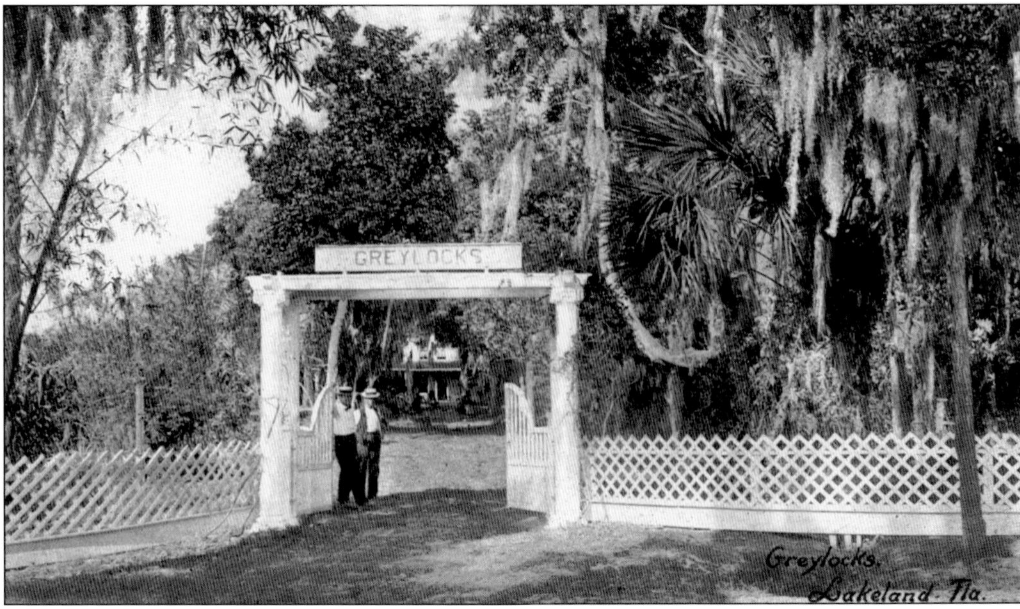

GREYLOCKS, LAKELAND, FLA. Greylocks (*c.* 1885) at 218 Lake Hollingsworth Drive, on the east shore, was the home of Lakeland pioneer Spence Minor Stephens. Galas and dances were frequent events at Greylocks, and the home was known for its beautiful gardens and majestic appearance. The home was later owned by long-serving U.S. senator Park Trammell (1876–1936), who served as Florida's governor from 1913 to 1917, and later by James L. Raulerson. The home was extensively damaged by fire in 1965 and razed in 1967. The site is currently occupied by Lake Hollingsworth Villa Apartments. (Courtesy Lakeland Public Library.)

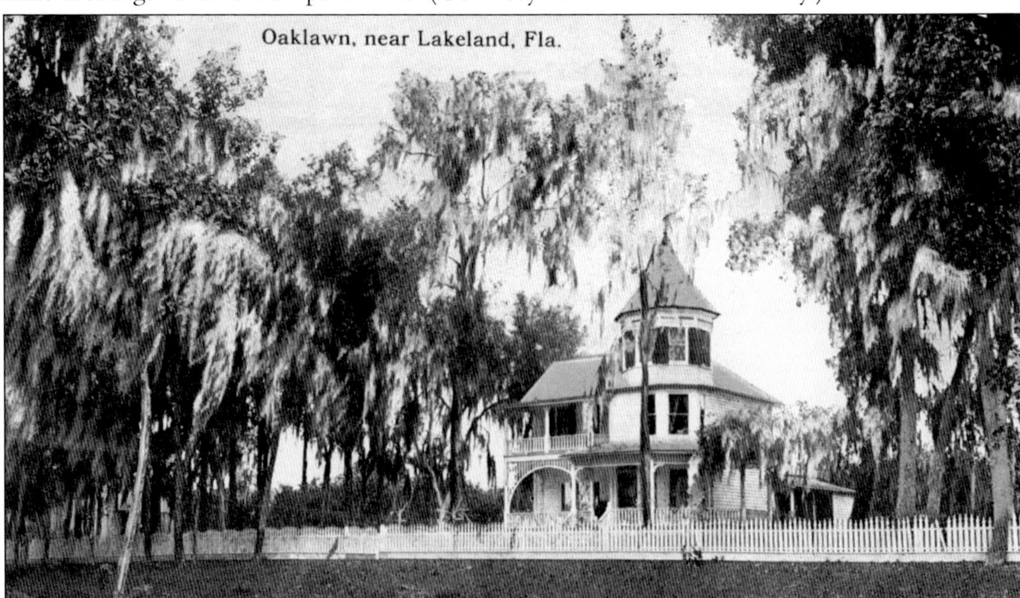

OAKLAWN, NEAR LAKELAND, FLA. Oaklawn was a stately mansion located on the east side of Lake Hollingsworth. Together with Greylocks and Mosswood, Oaklawn was one of the famed residences of early Lakeland. The postcard was postmarked in Lakeland in July 1914. (Courtesy Lakeland Public Library.)

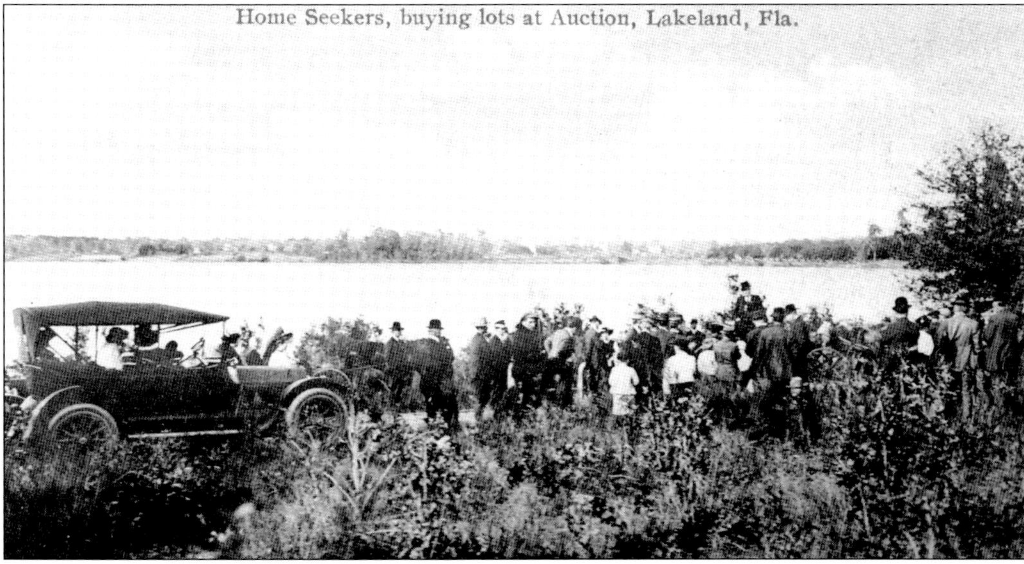

HOME SEEKERS, BUYING LOTS AT AUCTION, LAKELAND, FLA. This early postcard image was probably taken at Lake Hollingsworth during the height of the Florida land boom. (Courtesy Larry Gray.)

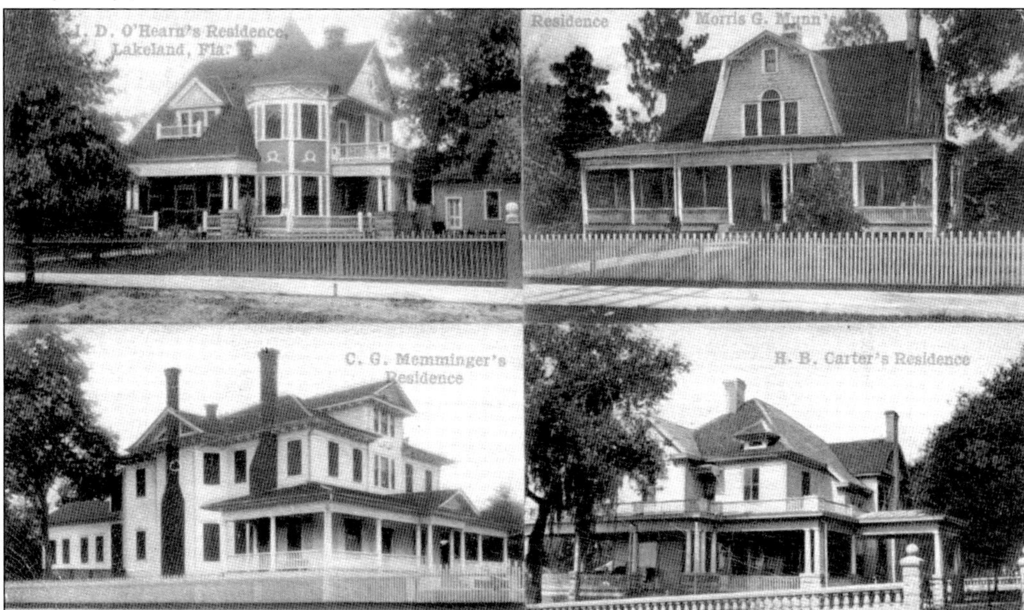

J. D. O'HEARN'S RESIDENCE, LAKELAND, FLA.; MORRIS G. MUNN'S RESIDENCE; C. G. MEMMINGER'S RESIDENCE; H. B. CARTER'S RESIDENCE. J. D. O'Hearn was a traveling salesman. He and Alice A. O'Hearn made their home at 401 South Massachusetts Avenue. Morris G. and Anna Belle Munn lived at 412 East Orange Street. Mr. Munn was in real estate. C. G. Memminger's home was adjacent to the Munns' at the southwest corner of East Orange Street and Iowa Avenue. Henry B. Carter was a lumberman; he and Lula S. Carter lived at 501 South Massachusetts Avenue and operated the Hotel Thelma for many years. The Carter residence was eventually moved to the southern edge of modern Lakeland, where it was the home of country music stars Tammy Wynette and George Jones. (Courtesy Larry Gray.)

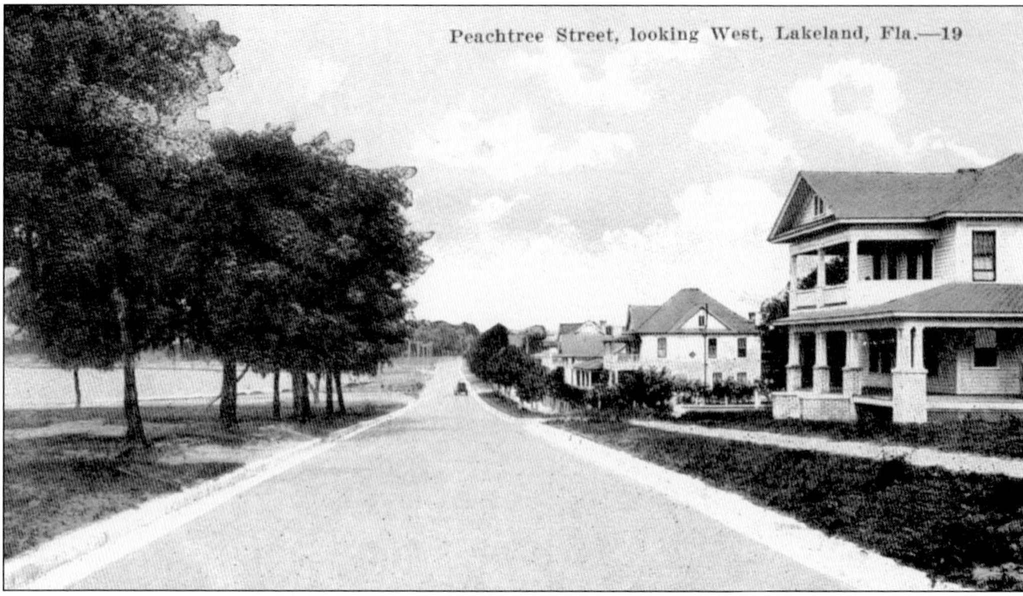

PEACHTREE STREET, LOOKING WEST, LAKELAND, FLA. A corner of the Lakeland High School grounds is at the far left of this 1920s view. (Courtesy Lakeland Public Library.)

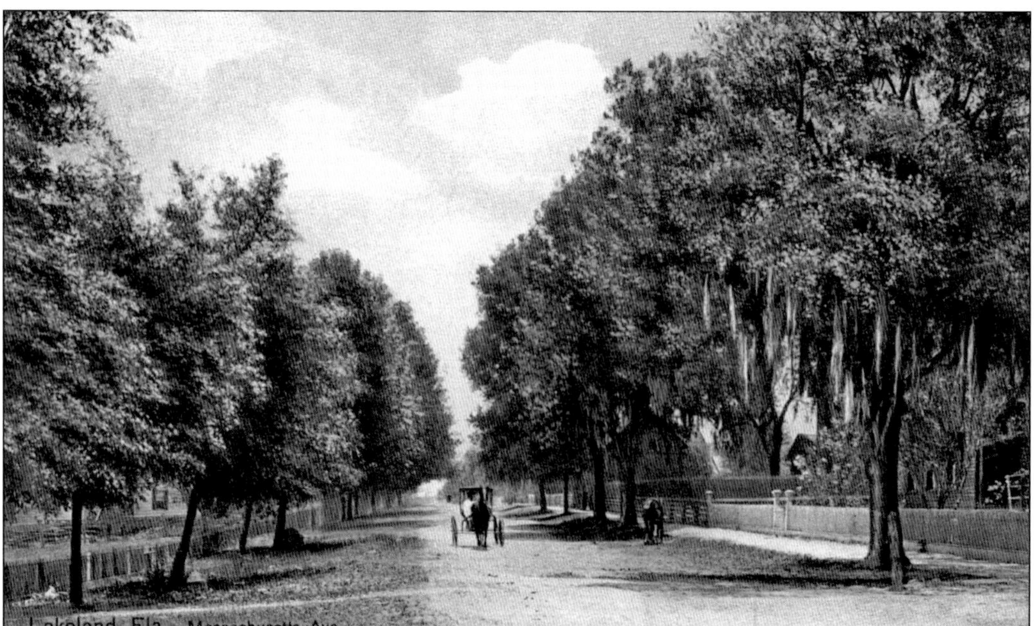

LAKELAND, FLA. MASSACHUSETTS AVE. This postcard was postmarked November 26, 1909. A horse and buggy pass through a rural landscape on the early dirt road that was Massachusetts Avenue. (Courtesy Lakeland Public Library.)

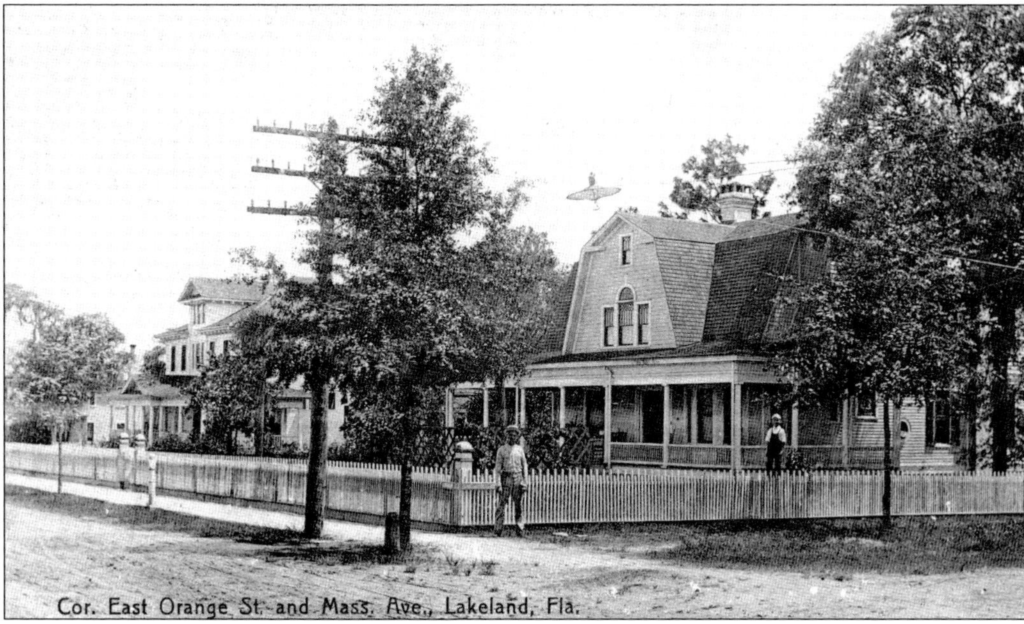

COR. EAST ORANGE ST. AND MASS. AVE., LAKELAND, FLA. The home on the corner belonged to Morris G. Munn, and the house visible on the left was the C. G. Memminger residence. The Florida Citrus Mutual building stands here today. (Courtesy Larry Gray.)

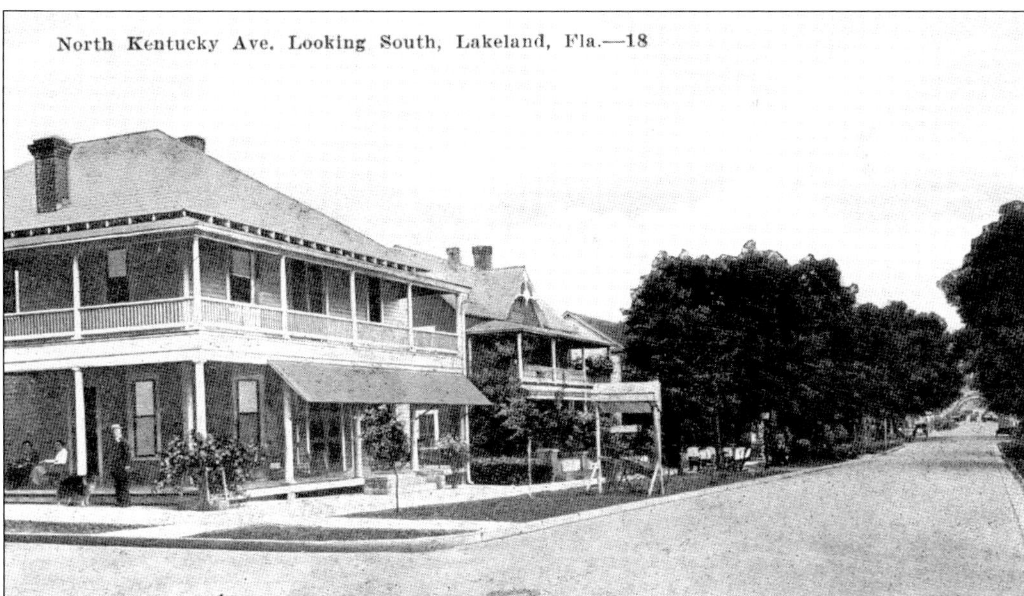

NORTH KENTUCKY AVE. LOOKING SOUTH, LAKELAND, FLA. These are Lakeland's fine residences just north of downtown. The Lakeland welcome arch is barely visible at the end of the street. (Courtesy Lakeland Public Library.)

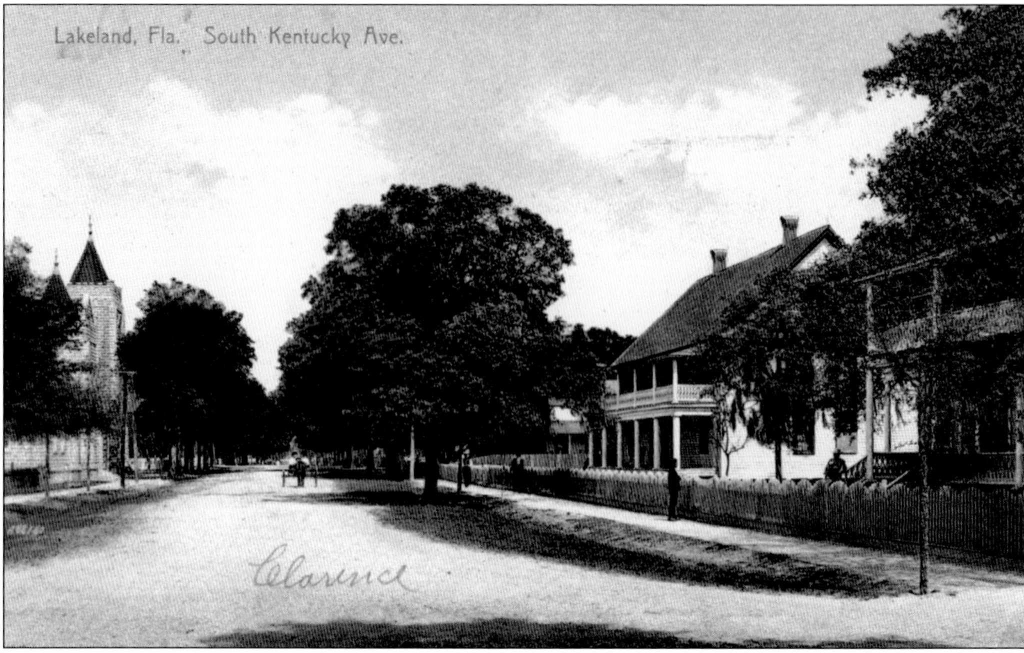

LAKELAND, FLA. SOUTH KENTUCKY AVE. When looking south, the First United Methodist Church is on the left. This message was mailed February 1911: "One of the street scenes in Florida where I spent the day Friday, Feb. 3/11 Very warm down here wearing straw hats. Hope you are all well. Clarence." (Courtesy Lakeland Public Library.)

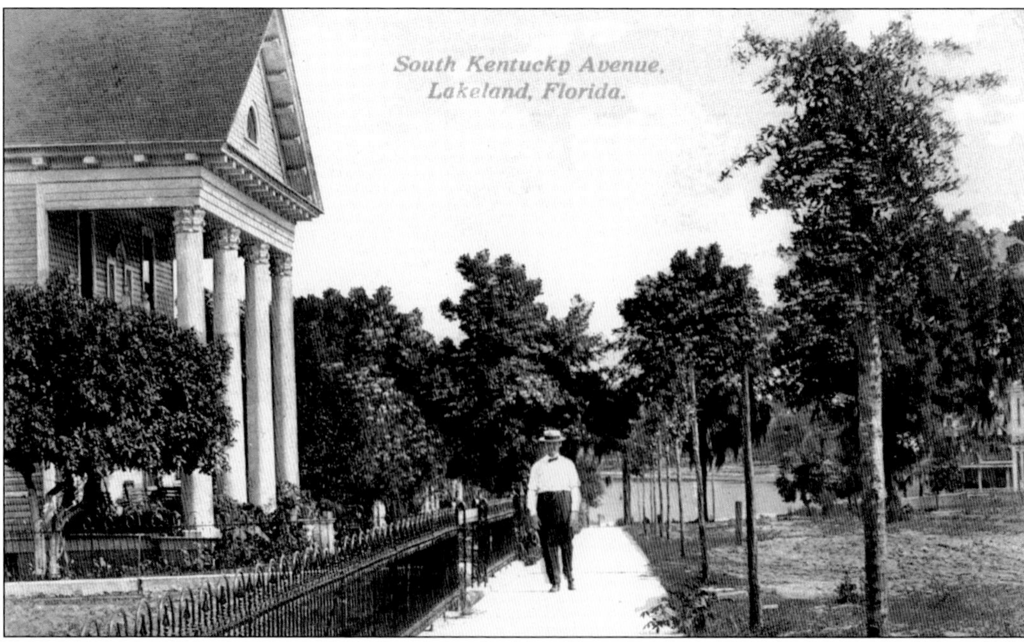

SOUTH KENTUCKY AVENUE, LAKELAND, FLORIDA. This card was mailed in January 1912 from Winter Haven to a Mrs. French at 308 New York Avenue in Lakeland. The view looks south with Lake Morton visible at the foot of the hill. (Courtesy Lakeland Public Library.)

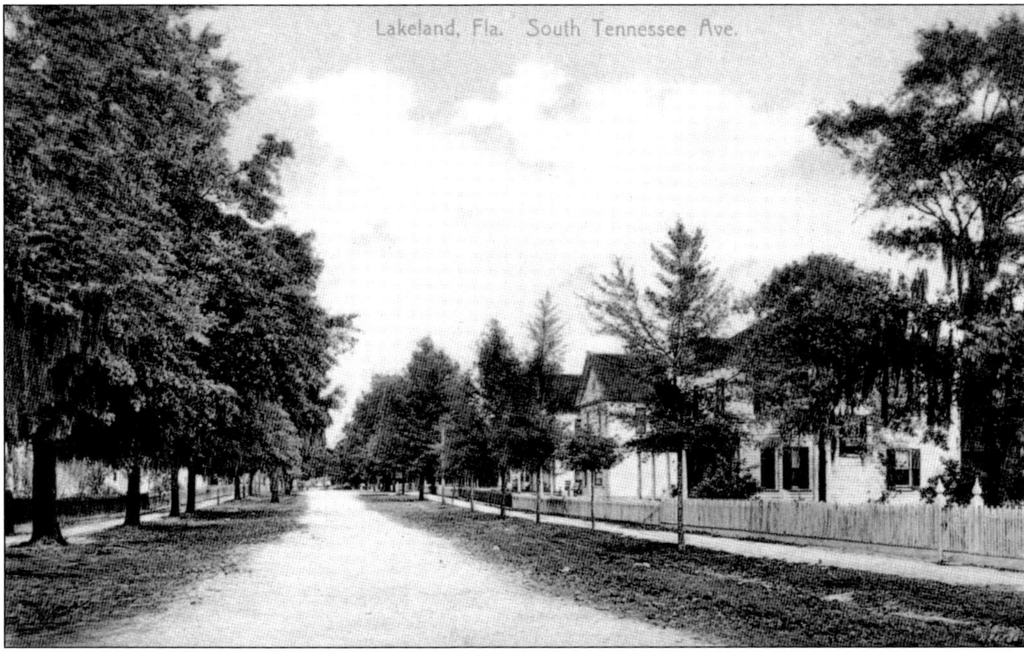

LAKELAND, FLA. SOUTH TENNESSEE AVE. Shown here is a comfortable mid-1910s Lakeland neighborhood, with beautiful tree-lined streets. Sadly many of these residences were demolished to make-way for downtown parking lots. (Courtesy Lakeland Public Library.)

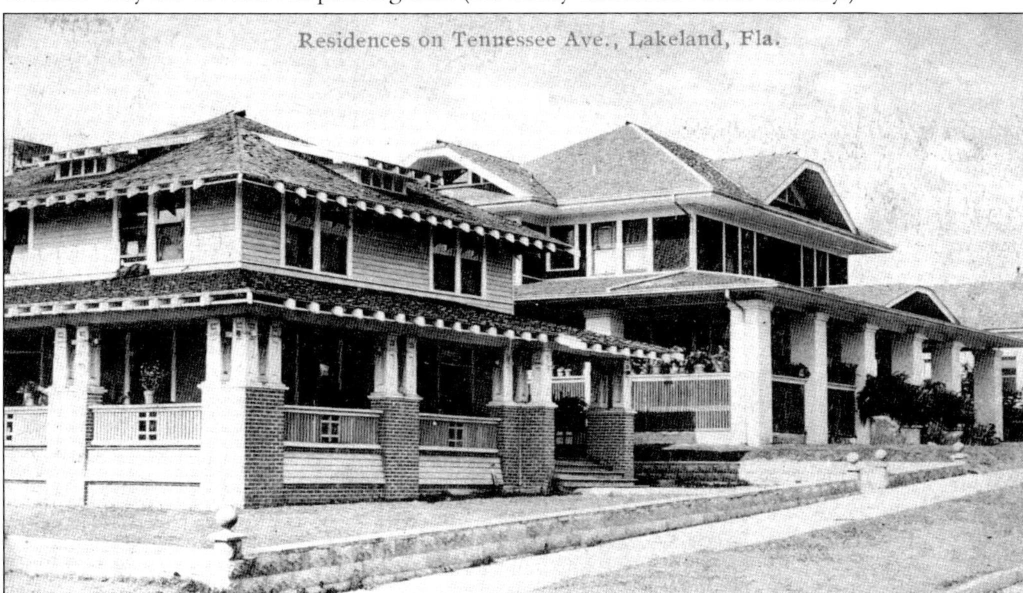

RESIDENCES ON TENNESSEE AVE., LAKELAND, FLA. These homes were on the west side of Tennessee Avenue, south of downtown. While many original homes have succumbed to the vicissitudes of time, fire, and storm, some have managed to survive. In the historic districts near downtown are Mediterranean, Renaissance, and Italianate influences and prairie-school homes, bungalows, and other classic American designs. Mansions, attractive homes of all shapes and sizes, and apartment buildings fill Lakeland's modern neighborhoods. (Courtesy Larry Gray.)

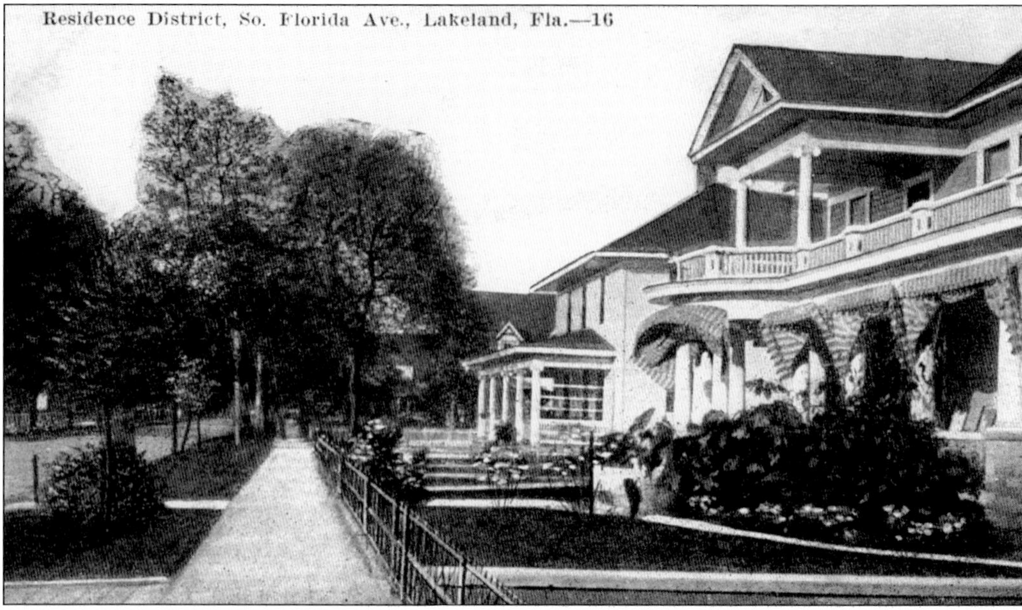

RESIDENCE DISTRICT, SO. FLORIDA AVE., LAKELAND, FLA. South Florida Avenue was an attractive residential street in the 1920s. It has evolved into the principal north-south business thoroughfare of modern Lakeland. (Courtesy Lakeland Public Library.)

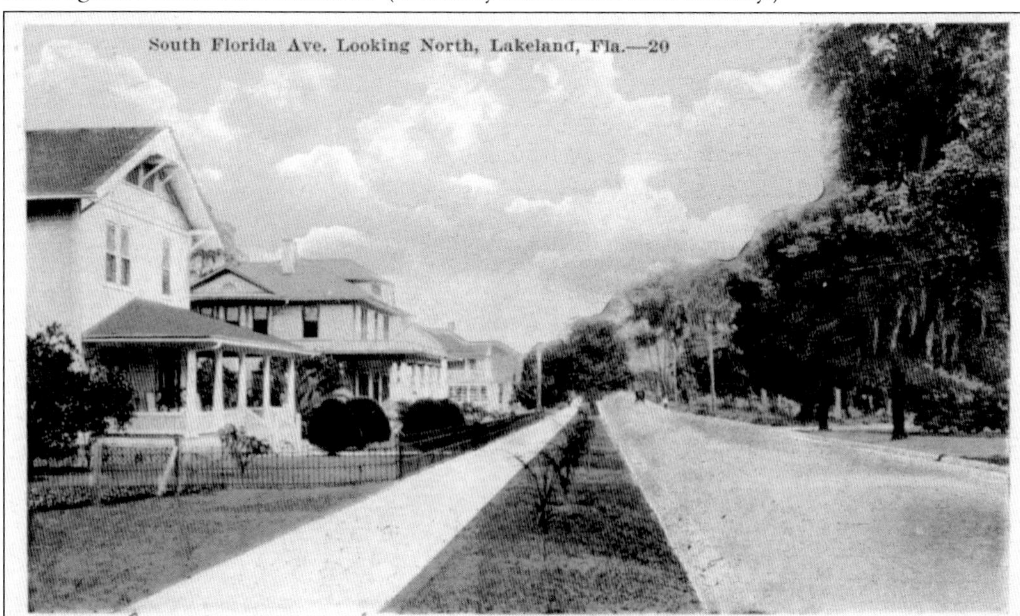

SOUTH FLORIDA AVE. LOOKING NORTH, LAKELAND, FLA. This view looks toward downtown. This postcard was probably mailed in an envelope; the note on the front reads: "Jan. 6, 1921 from Mrs. Chas. Johnson." The message on the reverse reads: "304 E. Oak St—Thanks for Christmas greeting. It has been warm here this week so we were glad to get on the shady side. This morning it is cool so I go out in the sunshine. I see so many cripples here. Florida seems to be full this winter. Has Miss Cash gone away? Best wishes to all. Sincerely Mrs. C. L. Johnson." (Courtesy Lakeland Public Library.)

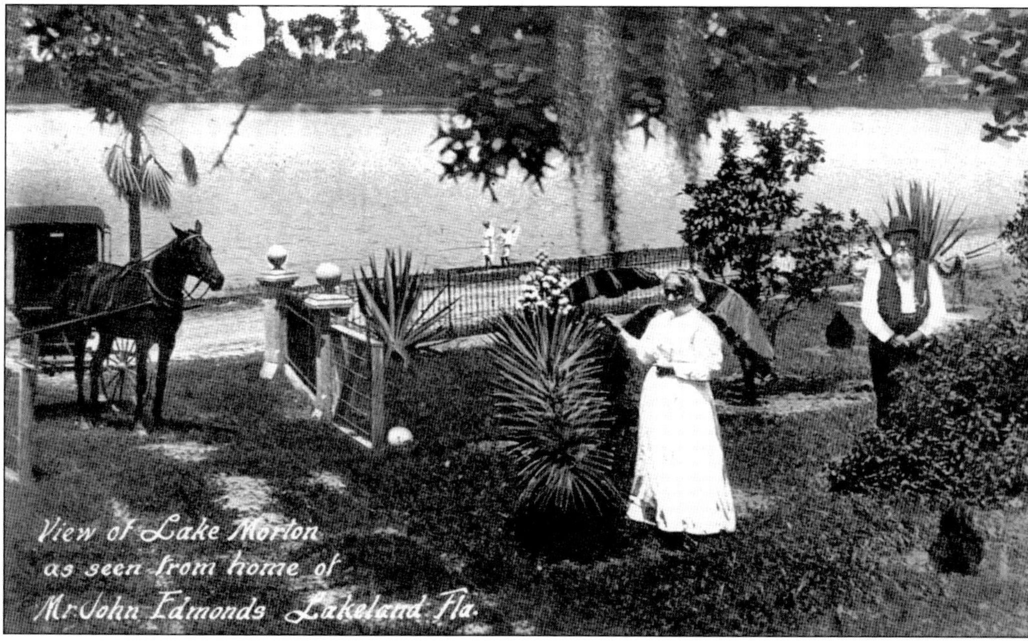

VIEW OF LAKE MORTON AS SEEN FROM HOME OF MR. JOHN EDMONDS, LAKELAND, FLA. This postcard dates from *c.* 1915. (Courtesy Lakeland Public Library.)

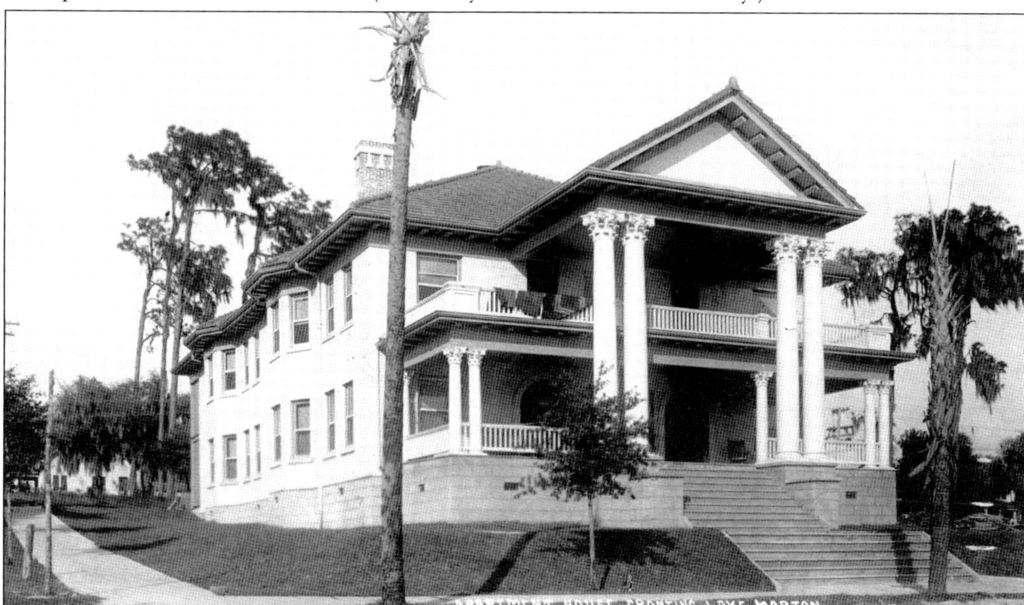

APARTMENT HOUSE FRONTING LAKE MORTON, LAKELAND, FLA. The magnificent Lakeshore Hotel (1913) was constructed at the corner of Lake Morton Drive and Iowa Avenue at a cost of $15,000 by Spence M. Stephens. Later known as the Freeman Apartment House, it was owned for a brief period by Florida Southern College and served as a dormitory. It has been renovated, and since the 1970s, it has been known as the Ruthven Building. This postcard was published by the Red Cross Pharmacy, which was located at 126 South Kentucky Avenue. (Courtesy Larry Gray.)

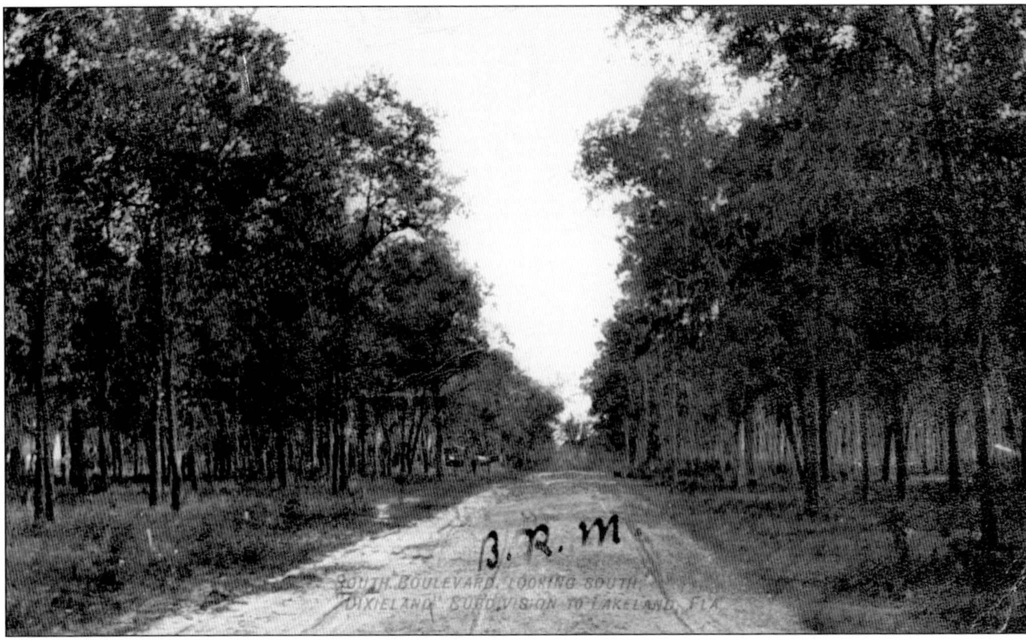

South Boulevard, Looking South "Dixieland" Subdivision to Lakeland, Fla. South Boulevard was a thickly wooded area in the early 1900s bearing little resemblance to the residential neighborhood it has since become. This was mailed from Auburndale to Akron, Ohio, in January 1908. (Courtesy Lakeland Public Library.)

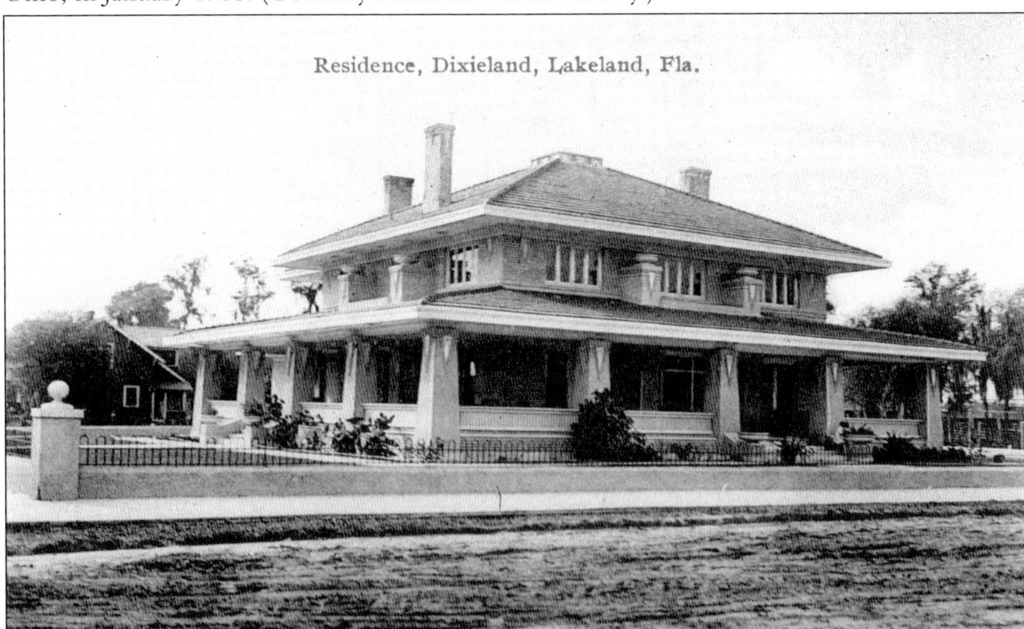

Residence, Dixieland, Lakeland, Fla. The beautiful Columbus W. Deen home, built in 1912, is on the southwest corner of Success Avenue and McDonald Street. Like many homes in the area, it served a short stint as a Florida Southern College dormitory and once as the Lambda Chi Alpha fraternity house. Deen (1861–1927) served as president of the First National Bank and had business interests in lumber, citrus, and phosphate. (Courtesy Larry Gray.)

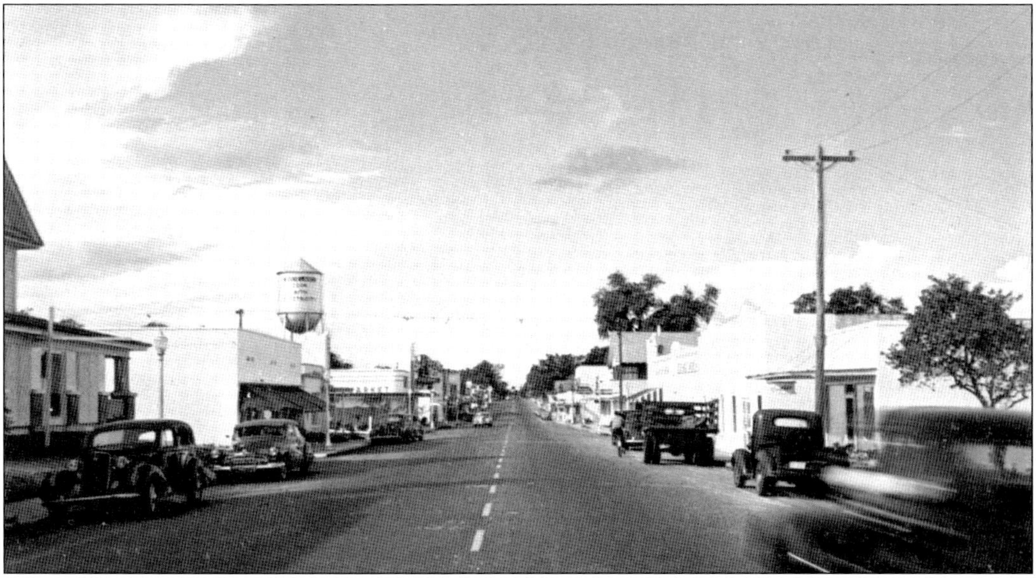

DIXIELAND SHOPPING CENTER, LAKELAND, FLORIDA. The Dixieland commercial district is located on South Florida Avenue about 10 blocks from downtown. This postcard promoted the area as "Lakeland's fastest growing shopping center." This photograph looks north toward downtown, along a stretch of Dixieland slated for extensive renovation beginning in 2005. (Courtesy Lakeland Public Library.)

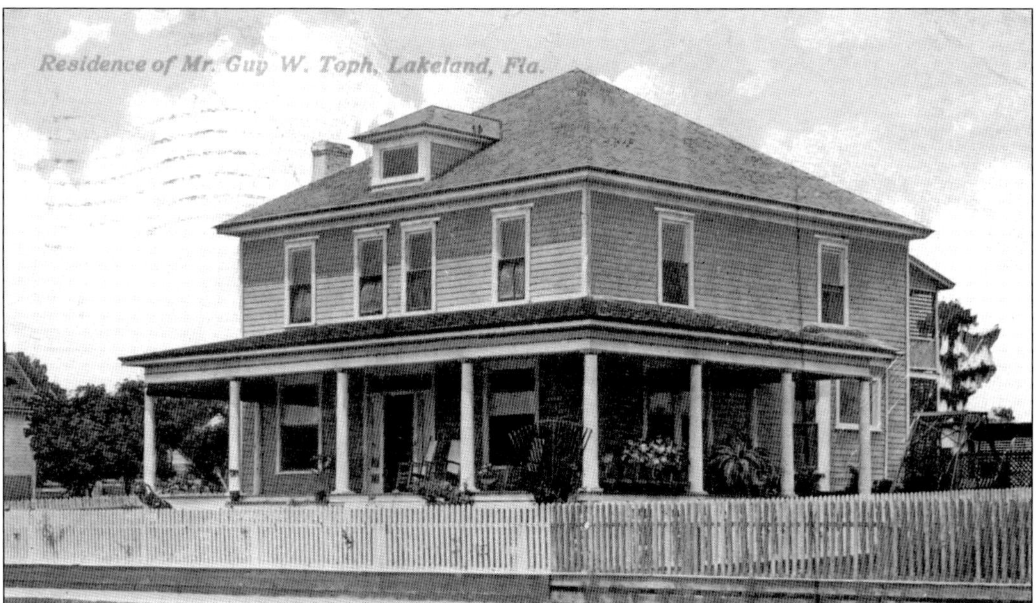

RESIDENCE OF MR. GUY W. TOPH, LAKELAND, FLA. Guy W. and Ellen E. Toph lived at 307 West Peachtree Street. Guy W. Toph was a local insurance agent. Postmarked in Tampa on January 1, 1913, this card had the New Year's greeting: "Tampa, Fla. Dec 31st, 12. Your Xmas gift rec'd and very much appreciated. Suppose the bunch of kin folks were with you for Xmas dinner. Wish I could have been one of the party. My sister's home on other side." (Courtesy Larry Gray.)

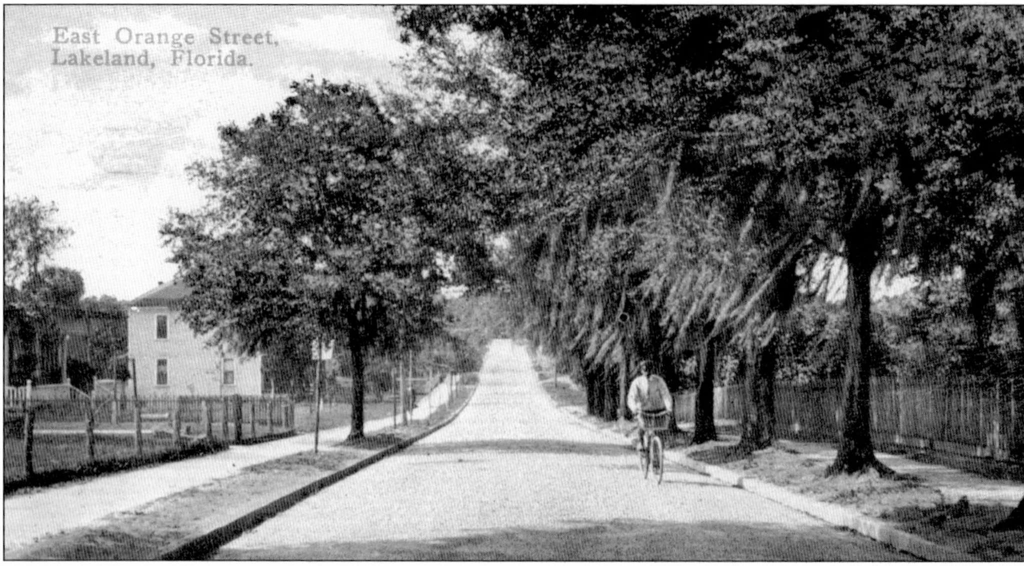

EAST ORANGE STREET, LAKELAND, FLORIDA. Postmarked July 21, 1915, this view appears to face downtown. There was not much news to report this day, but Lakeland received high marks: "Dear Marion, We are all well hope you the same had a little shower today say how do you like our town mama said it a nice place wish you was hear. With Love M. F. H." (Courtesy Lakeland Public Library.)

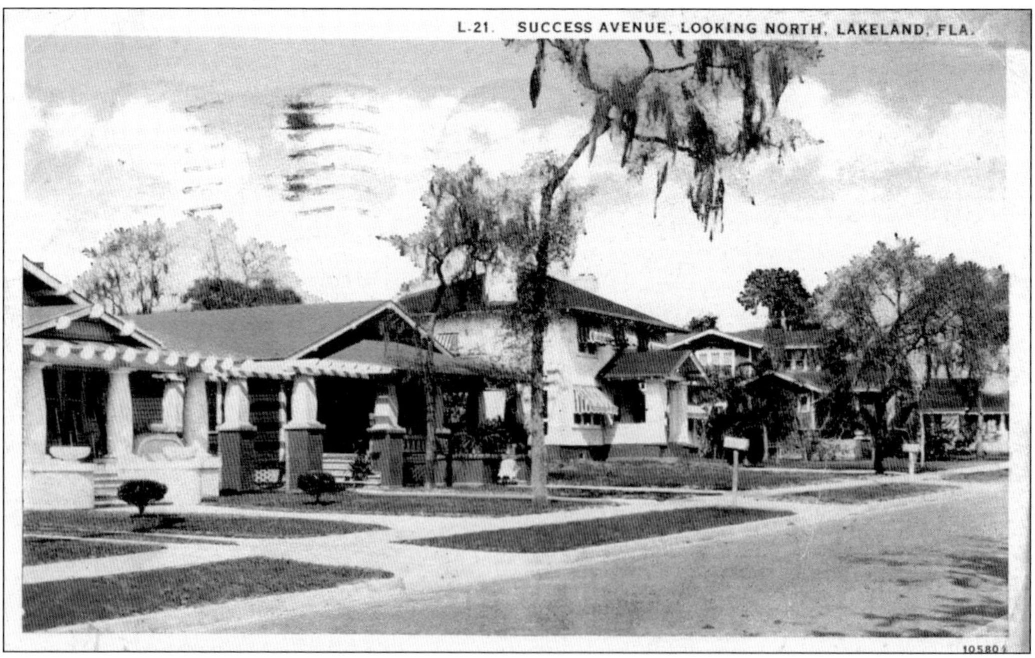

SUCCESS AVENUE, LOOKING NORTH, LAKELAND, FLA. These homes still stand on the west side of the 800-block of Success Avenue and are representative of homes built during the 1920s. A mild winter doubtless sounded appealing to the recipients of this message in Wilkes-Barre, Pennsylvania: "Feb. 24, 1928, Dear Friends, We are so busy don't have much time to write but think of you all. We are having very warm weather and the trees and flowers are all in bloom. Hope you are well." (Courtesy Lakeland Public Library.)

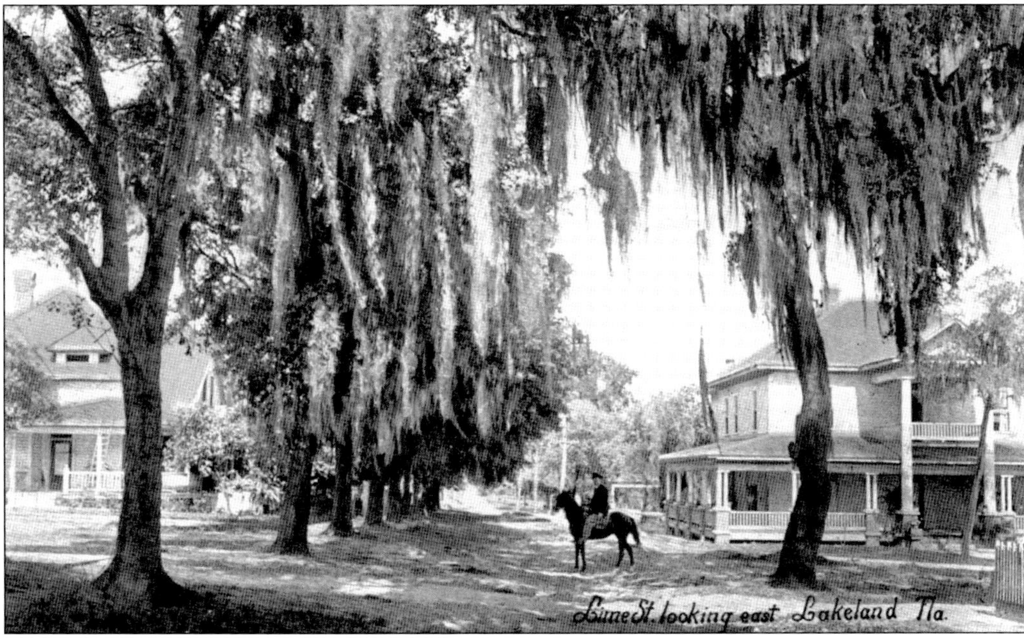

LIME ST. LOOKING EAST, LAKELAND, FLA. A man on horseback poses in a 1910s view of rural Lakeland; today this is just south of the center of downtown. (Courtesy Lakeland Public Library.)

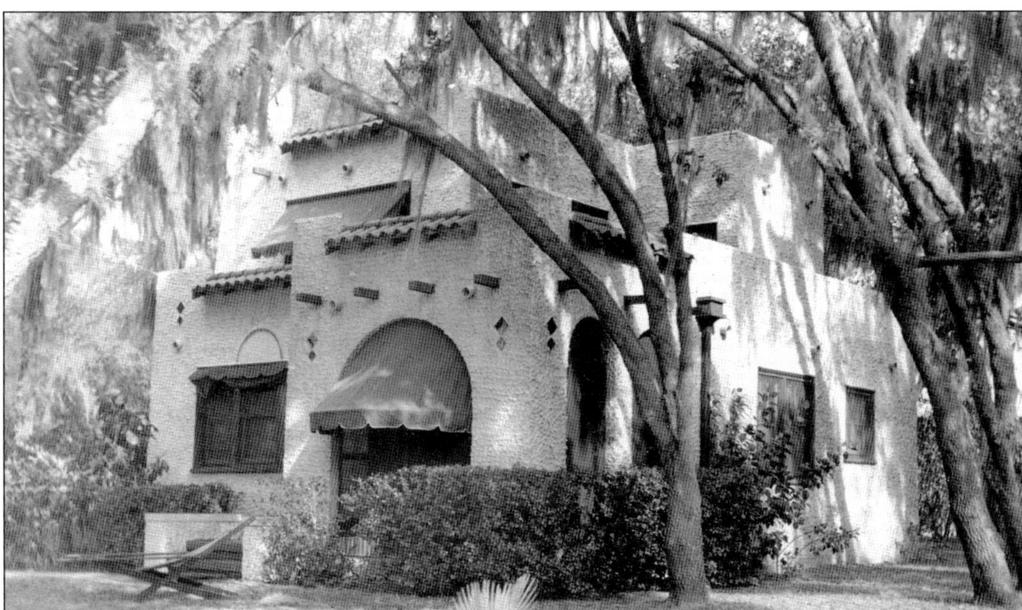

A MEDITERRANEAN-STYLE HOME. Typical of homes in Lakeland's older neighborhoods, this was a source of pride to March 1940 Lakeland residents: "Mr. C. had these made to send to his friends; he explains that the stuff hanging from the trees is moss, not snow and icicles." (Courtesy Larry Gray.)

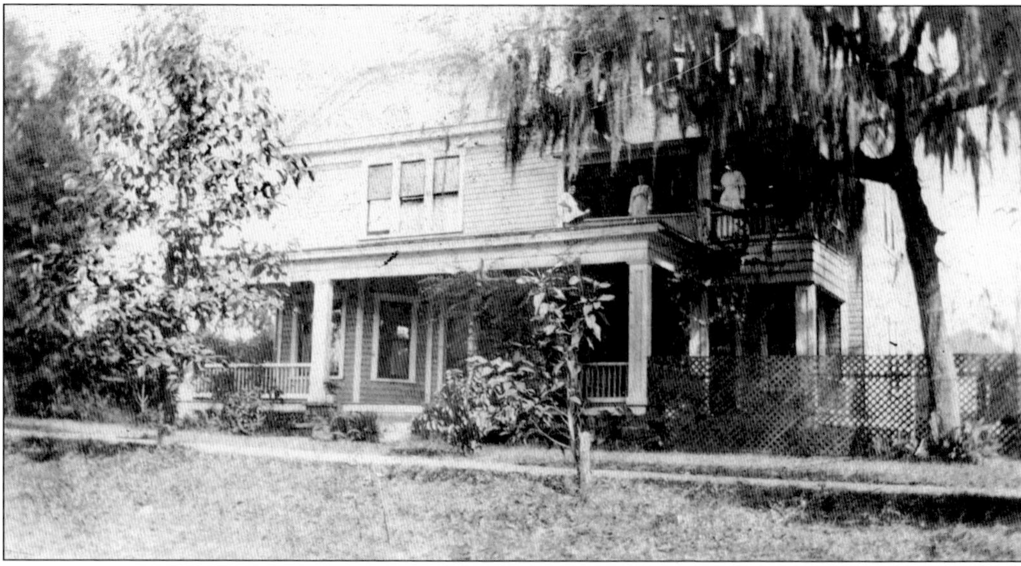

WINTER GETAWAY? A group poses on the second floor balcony of a Lakeland residence; perhaps one is the postcard writer. Postmarked February 1918 in Lakeland, it reads: "Lakeland Feb 22nd. Dear Ada, We are going to Jacksonville March 1st so direct letters there. Will be there a month. Will write you later. . . . Hoping you and family are all well. Pa & I are well and hearty. Nothing going on here today. Lovingly, Mother." (Courtesy Larry Gray.)

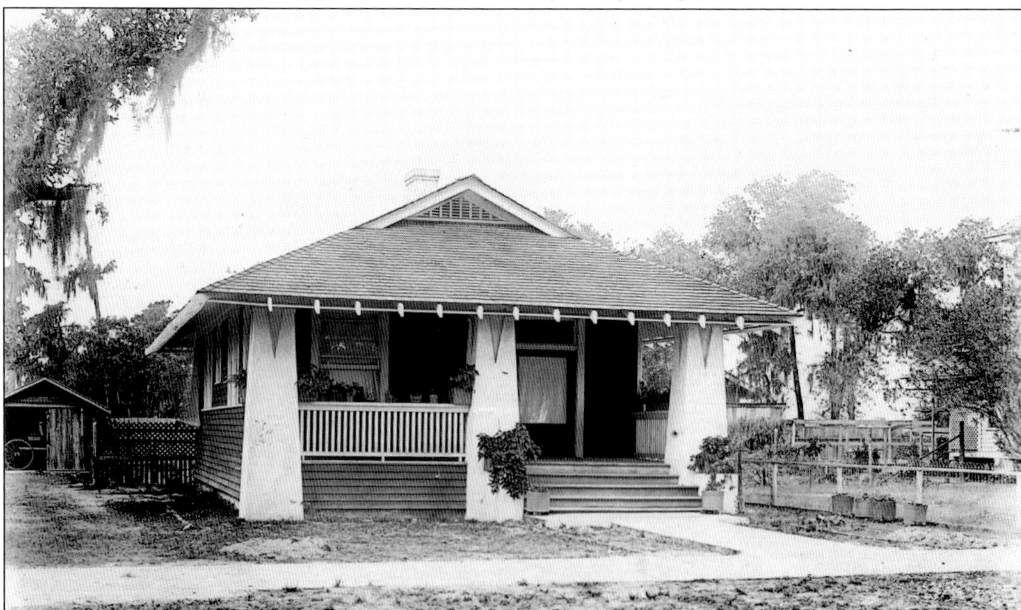

A TYPICAL BUNGALOW-STYLE HOME IN LAKELAND. A carriage is visible through the doorway of the back shed. Postmarked in Lakeland March 1913 and mailed to Boston, Georgia, it reads: "Don't you like my cozy corner? It has six rooms, just built for two, or more. See my rose garden—in those candy tubs—I planted them the 2d week in Jan. and have had several roses. I picked the first 'Bride' today. I will send you all some oranges soon. Have been waiting to send them from our grove at Avon Park. I write you a letter real soon. Kiss every body—and Ollie. 'Kilace.' " (Courtesy Larry Gray.)

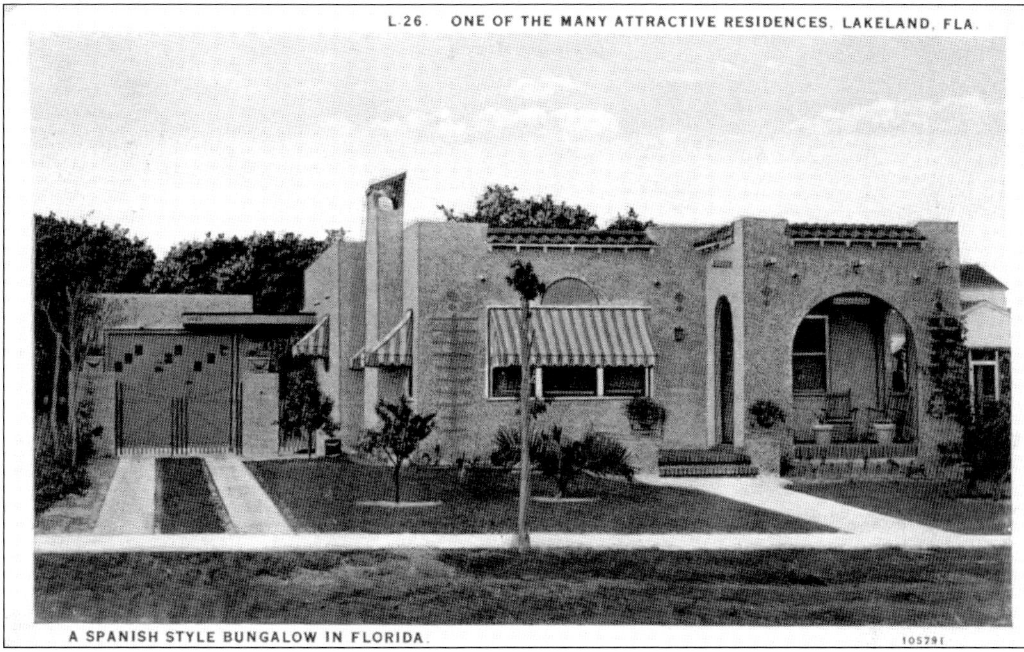

One of the Many Attractive Residences, Lakeland, Fla. A Spanish-style Bungalow in Florida. This cryptic message was mailed in February 1928: "Just thought I would have to drop you a line. No doubt Stella has told you of the misfortunes to Liz and her family. I didn't intend going down at first, but glad I changed my mind. Love Phil." (Courtesy Lakeland Public Library.)

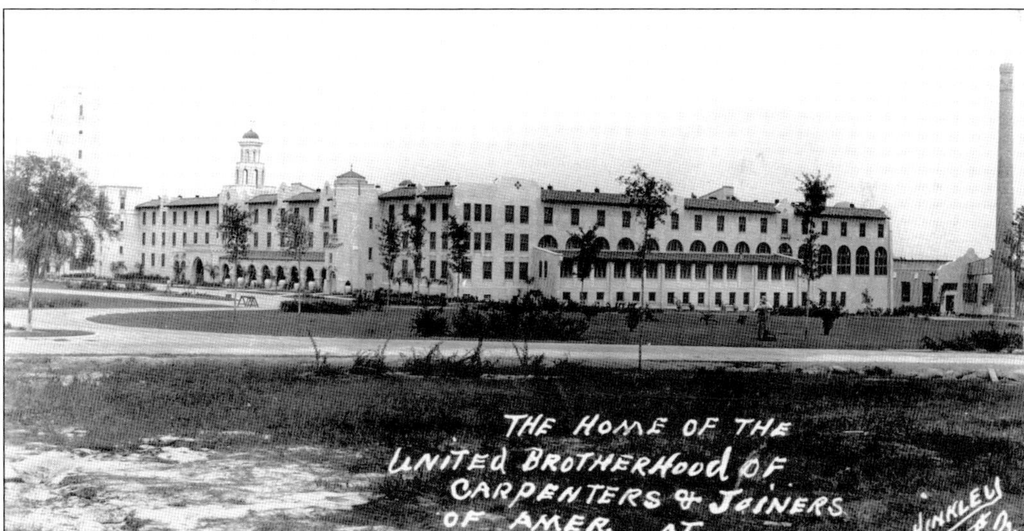

The Home of the United Brotherhood of Carpenters & Joiners of Amer. at Lakeland, Fla. These union retirement home buildings were located on a 1,700-acre site south of Lake Gibson. The property was purchased in 1923 at a cost of $70,000; construction was finished, and the home opened in 1928. Today it serves as a general retirement community. This real-photo postcard likely dates from the late 1920s. The Carpenters' Home has been featured on many commercial postcards. (Courtesy Larry Gray.)

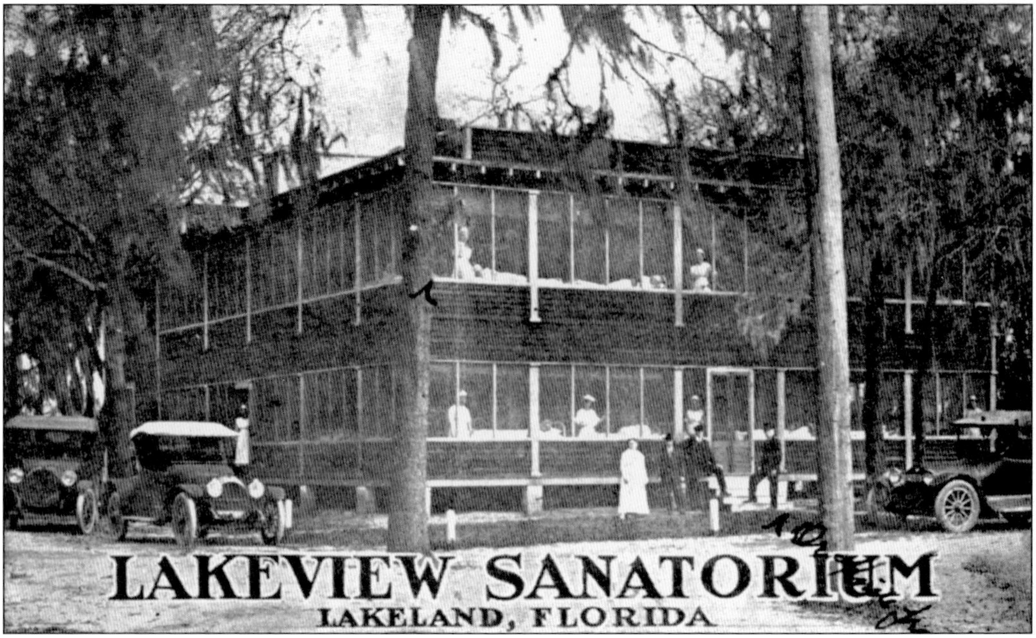

Lakeview Sanatorium, Lakeland, Florida. The sanatorium provided surgical services and treatment for tuberculosis and other chronic diseases and ailments. This brief positive review was penned by a health professional. "This is where I had a patient in corner room, very nice inside." (Courtesy Lakeland Public Library.)

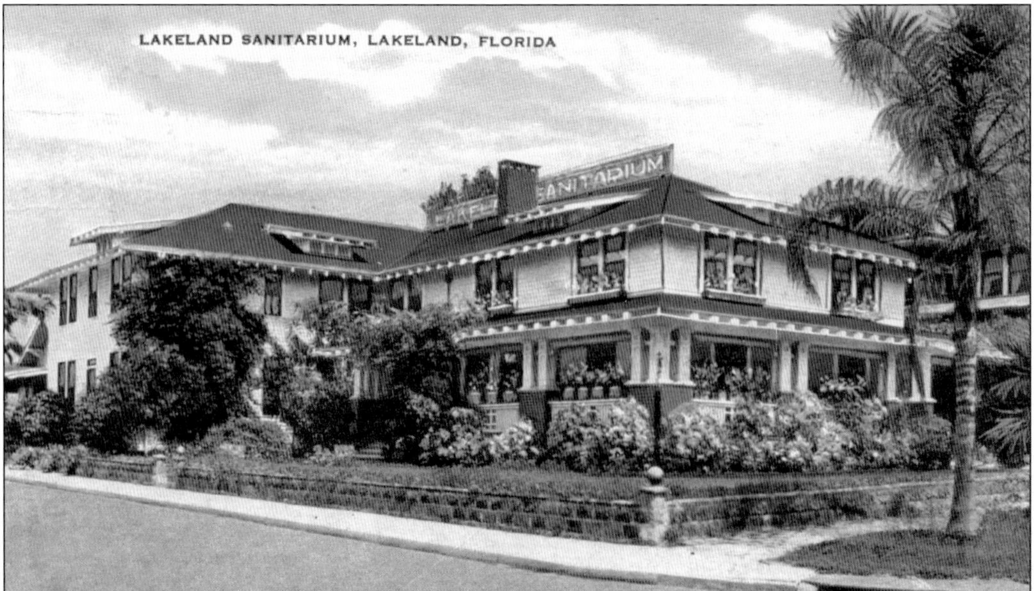

Lakeland Sanitarium, Lakeland, Florida. The sanitarium was at the corner of Main Street and Florida Avenue in 1915, and Dr. F. H. Hanna was the president. This postcard appears to date from the 1920s and shows the sanitarium at a new location. (Courtesy Lakeland Public Library.)

Seven

GOVERNMENT

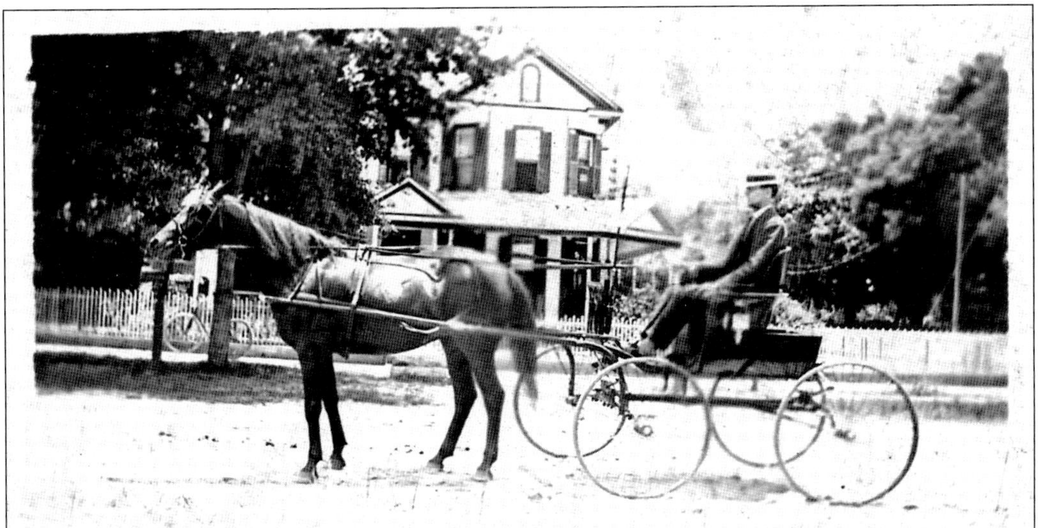

LAKELAND'S MAYOR JOHN COX. Mayor John F. Cox served Lakeland from 1905 to 1907, 1911, 1916, and 1917; he was one of the town's longest-serving mayors. Cox was a businessman and president of the Polk County Realtors Association and died in 1924. The former John F. Cox Grammar School was named in his honor. He was the son of Gen. J. A. Cox, a respected Confederate veteran and legislator. Lakeland's first mayor was John W. Trammell. During his tenure in 1885, the town was four square miles in size, and the first ordinance passed was to preserve the public peace and morals of the town. (Courtesy Lakeland Public Library.)

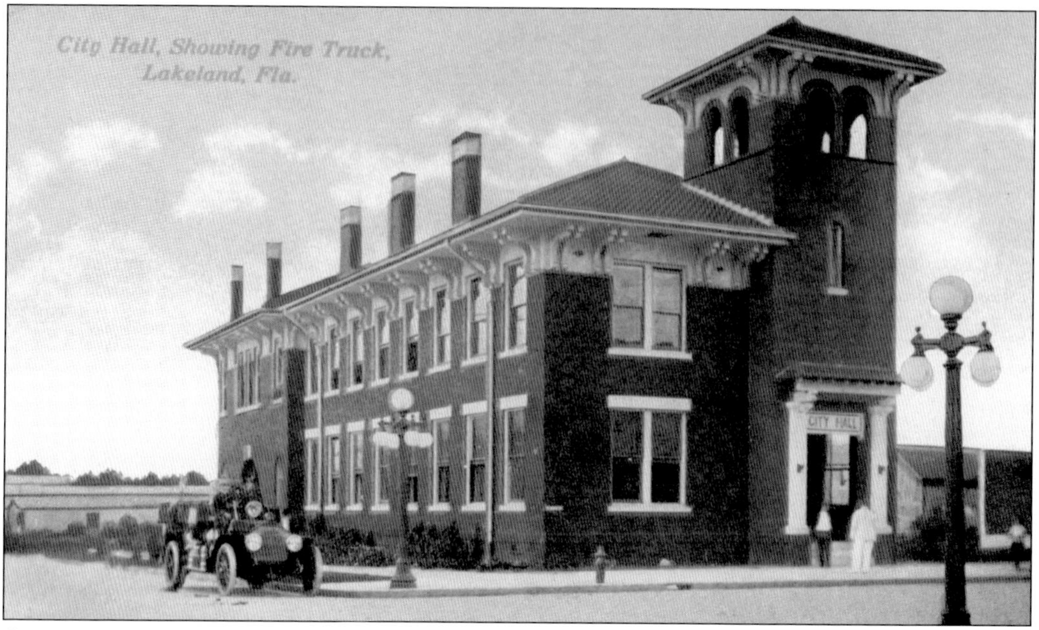

City Hall, Showing Fire Truck, Lakeland, Fla. The City Hall (*c.* 1913) stood at the northeast corner of Main Street and Florida Avenue. It was the second municipal building at this site; the first was a wooden-frame structure built in 1905 and demolished to make way for the present building. The fire department and jail were housed in City Hall. (Courtesy Larry Gray.)

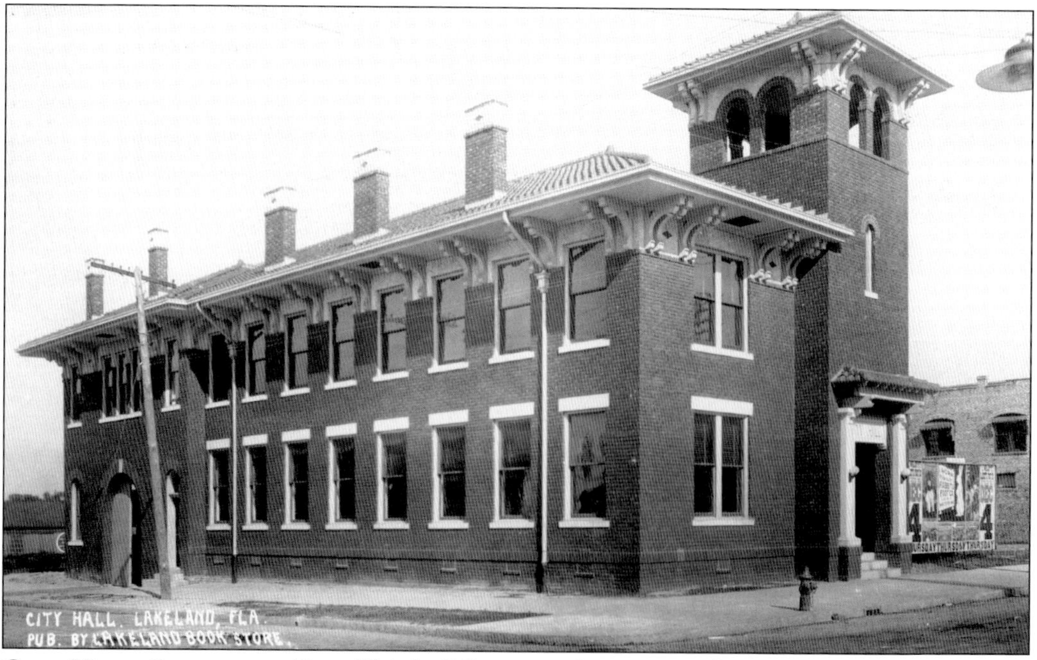

City Hall. Lakeland, Fla. This building served as City Hall until 1926, when the city's offices were moved to a new building on South Massachusetts Avenue. The distinctive southeast tower was subsequently removed, but a 1980s renovation by J. Hardin Peterson Jr. restored the building to near its original state. (Courtesy Lakeland Public Library.)

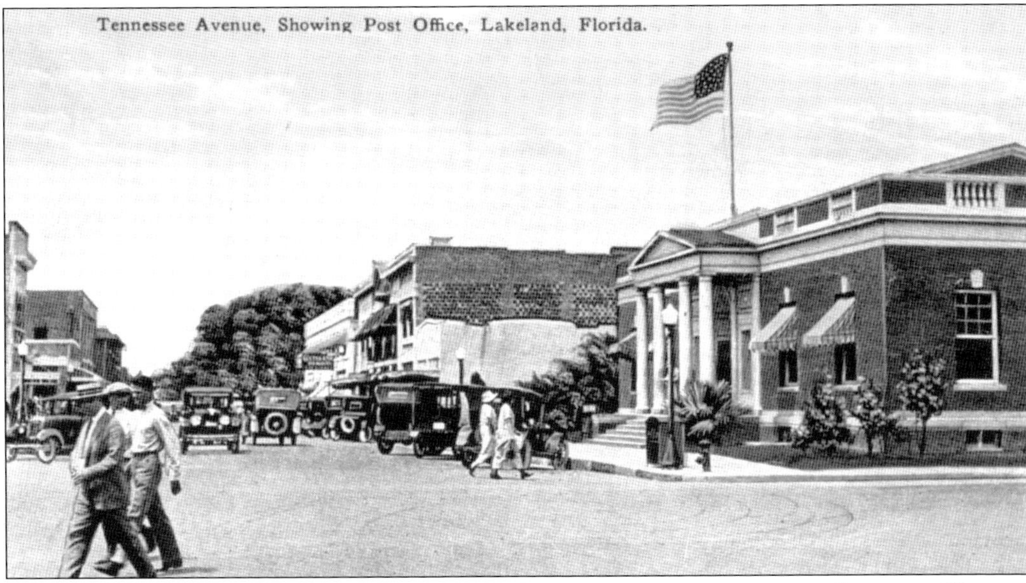

TENNESSEE AVENUE, SHOWING POST OFFICE, LAKELAND, FLORIDA. The post office was erected in 1917 at the corner of South Tennessee Avenue and Lemon Street. The post office had been in many other downtown locations but most recently was on the south side of Main Street between Kentucky and Tennessee Avenues. Early postmasters included Dr. F. L. Brooks, Capt. L. M. Ballard, W. M. Boswell, Mary Vineyard, and J. L. Skipper. The building is now known as the Federal Building. (Courtesy Lakeland Public Library.)

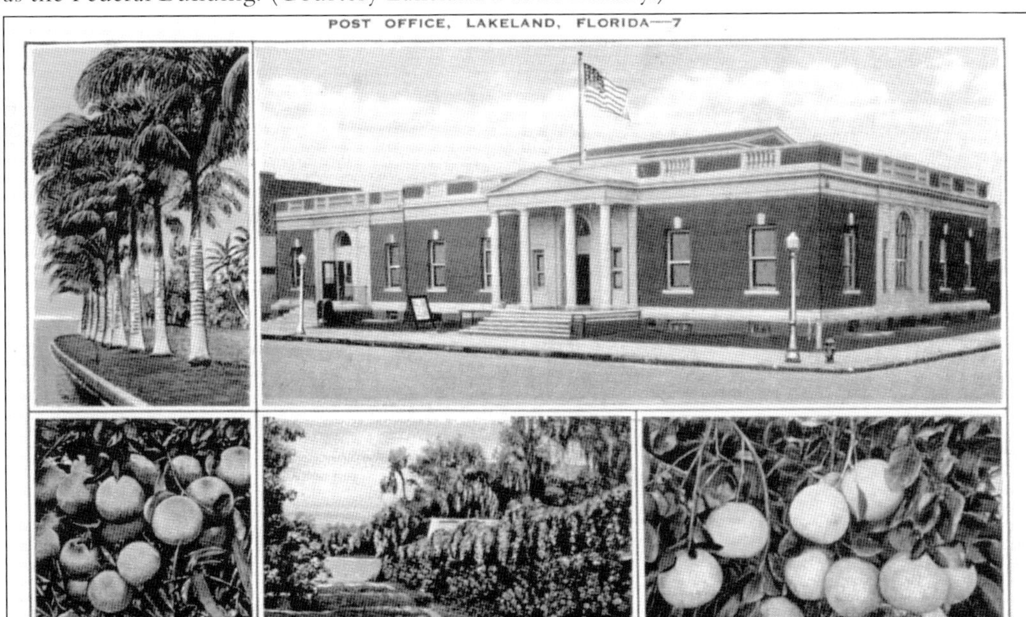

POST OFFICE, LAKELAND, FLORIDA. This multiview postcard includes the post office, stately palms, oranges, grapefruit, and flowers. The post office was built at a cost of $75,000. This 1930s card promotes the city's virtues: "Lakeland is unique—swimming, boating, fishing in 15 beautiful lakes within the city limits. Several of these lakes are only a few blocks from the business center." (Courtesy Lakeland Public Library.)

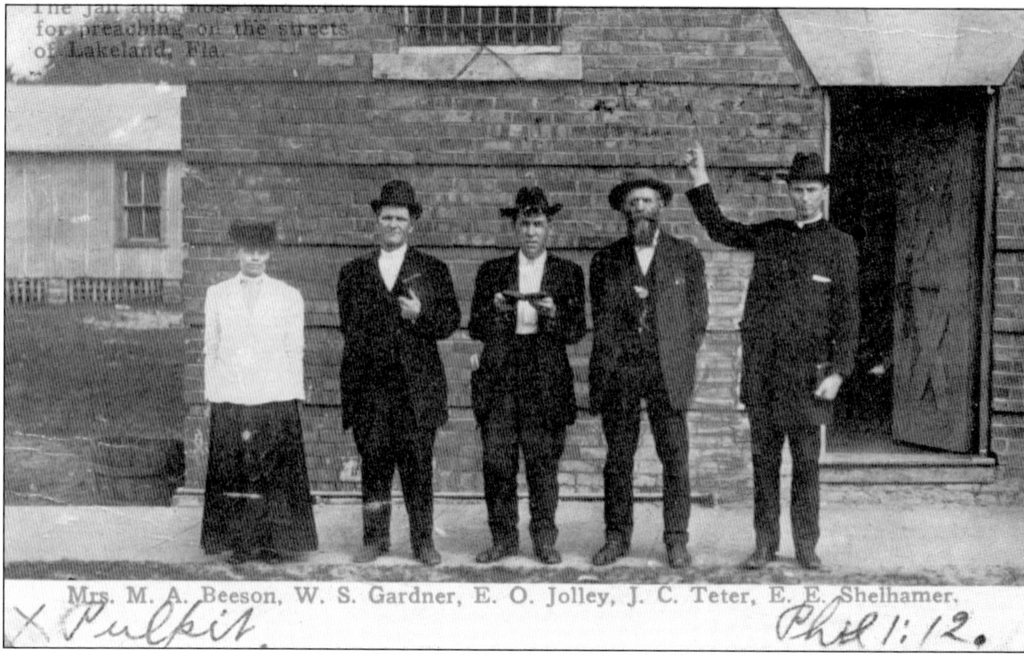

THE JAIL AND THOSE WHO WERE IN IT FOR PREACHING ON THE STREETS OF LAKELAND, FLA. This striking postcard shows Mrs. M. A. Beeson, W. S. Gardner, E. O. Jolley, J. C. Teter, and Rev. E. E. Shelhamer. Rev. Elmer Ellsworth Shelhamer (1869–1947) was a well-known itinerant Free Methodist evangelist. He mailed this card to a Georgia minister in May 1913 to arrange a worship service. Reverend Shelhamer points to the jailhouse window, and he marked an X in the window on the postcard indicating this was his pulpit. (Courtesy Larry Gray.)

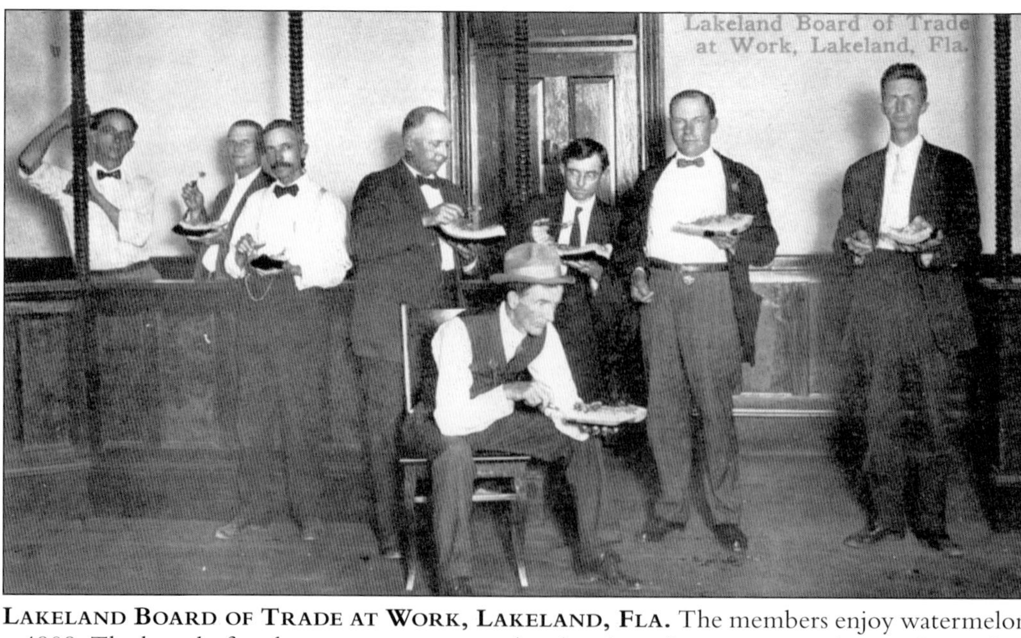

LAKELAND BOARD OF TRADE AT WORK, LAKELAND, FLA. The members enjoy watermelon *c.* 1909. The board of trade was a precursor to the chamber of commerce and, as such, worked to promote business development in the city. (Authors' Collection.)

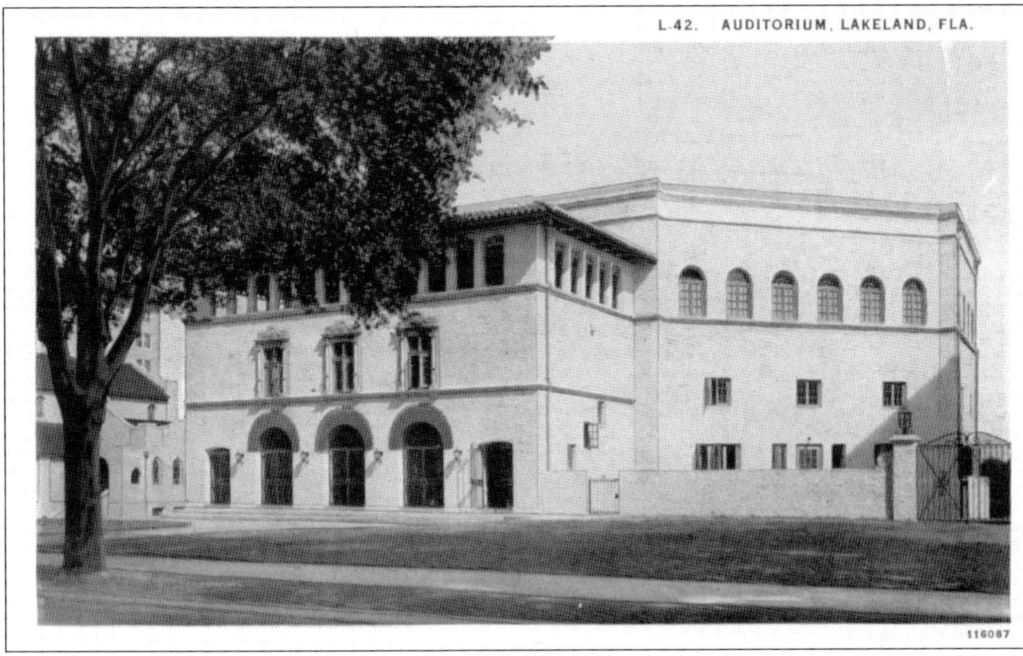

AUDITORIUM, LAKELAND, FLA. The Harry S. Mayhall Auditorium (1926) was the scene of many civic functions and also served as an auditorium for Florida Southern College. The beautiful auditorium was demolished around 1970. (Courtesy Lakeland Public Library.)

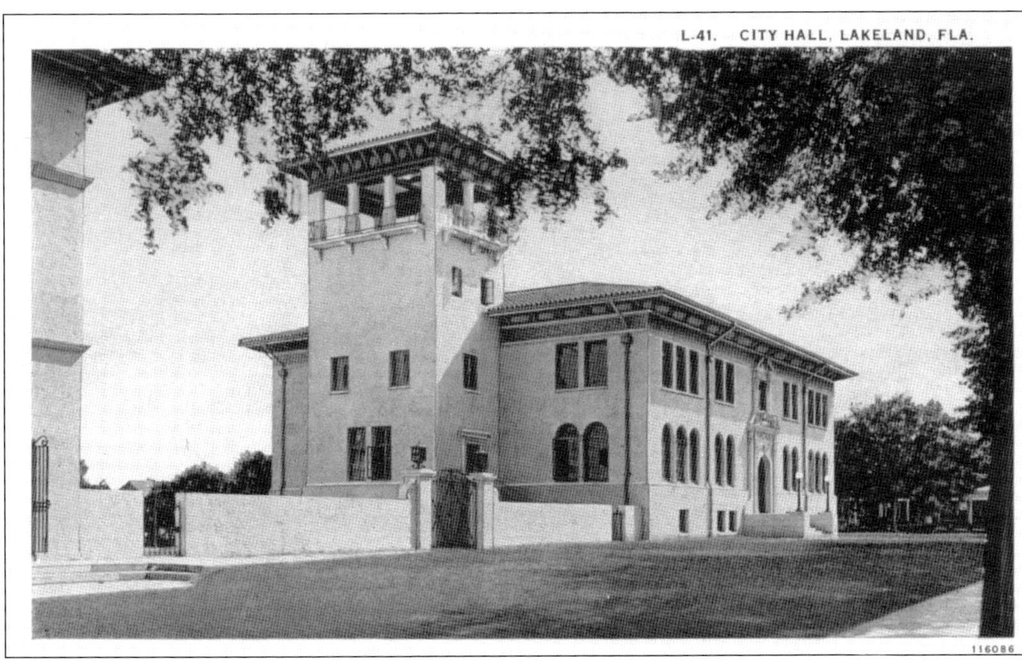

CITY HALL, LAKELAND, FLA. The new City Hall was built in 1926 and was located on the east side of South Massachusetts Avenue, south of the Mayhall Auditorium. It has been dramatically enlarged and still serves as City Hall. (Courtesy Lakeland Public Library.)

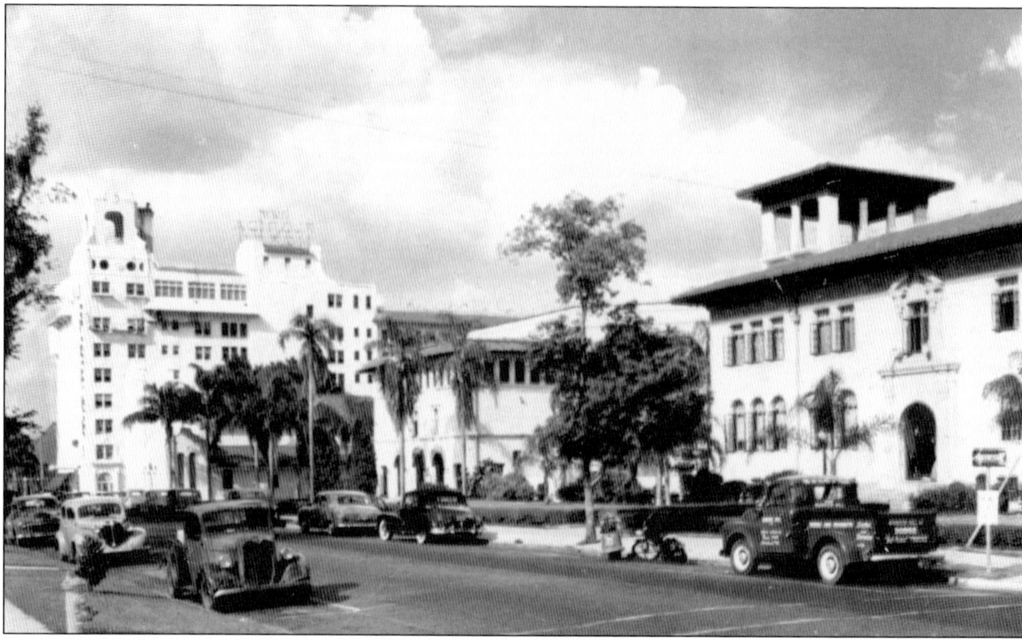

City Hall and New Florida Hotel, Lakeland, Florida. Looking north on South Massachusetts Avenue, from the left to right are the New Florida Hotel, All Saints' Episcopal Church, Harry S. Mayhall Auditorium, and City Hall. (Courtesy Lakeland Public Library.)

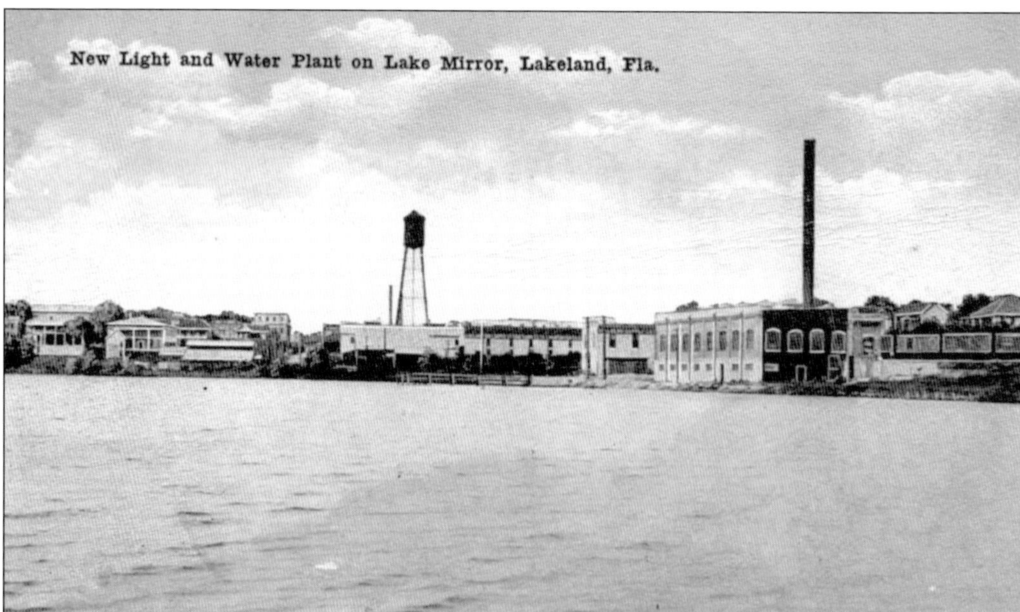

New Light and Water Plant on Lake Mirror, Lakeland, Fla. A plant with two 250-kilowatt generators was completed in 1916 on the north shore of Lake Mirror. In November 1924, Gertie wrote, "My dear Hubbie, We are having a wonderful time. The ladies here have certainly entertained us. . . . this is a grand place." (Courtesy Lakeland Public Library.)

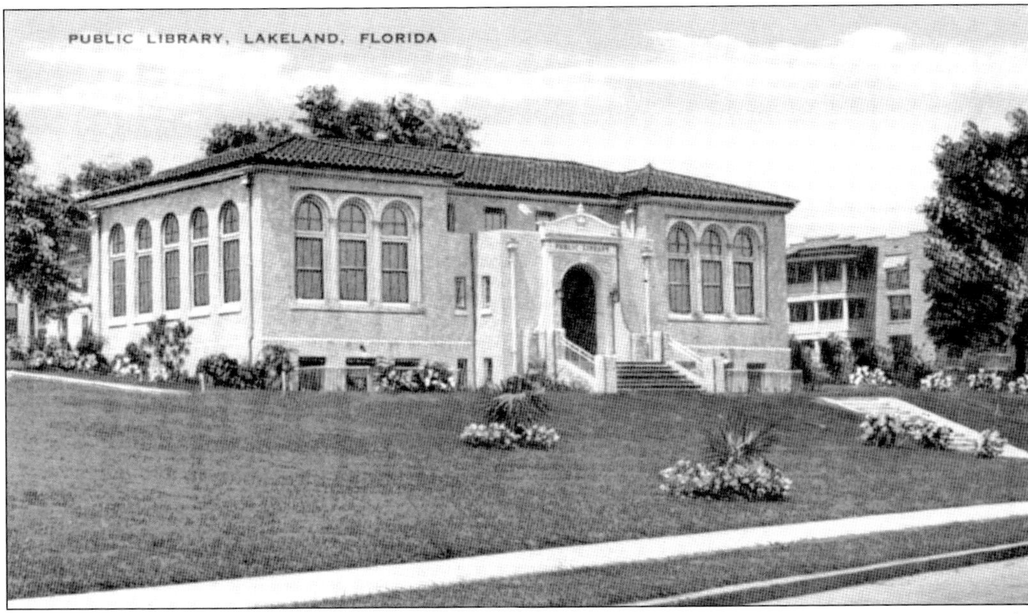

PUBLIC LIBRARY, LAKELAND, FLORIDA. The public library was constructed in 1927 on the north shore of Lake Morton. The Mediterranean-style library was designed by Tampa architect Franklin O. Adams Jr., who also designed the Mayhall Auditorium, City Hall, and the second Morrell Memorial Hospital. The library moved to the east shore site of the Lake Morton Grammar School in the 1960s. (Courtesy Lakeland Public Library.)

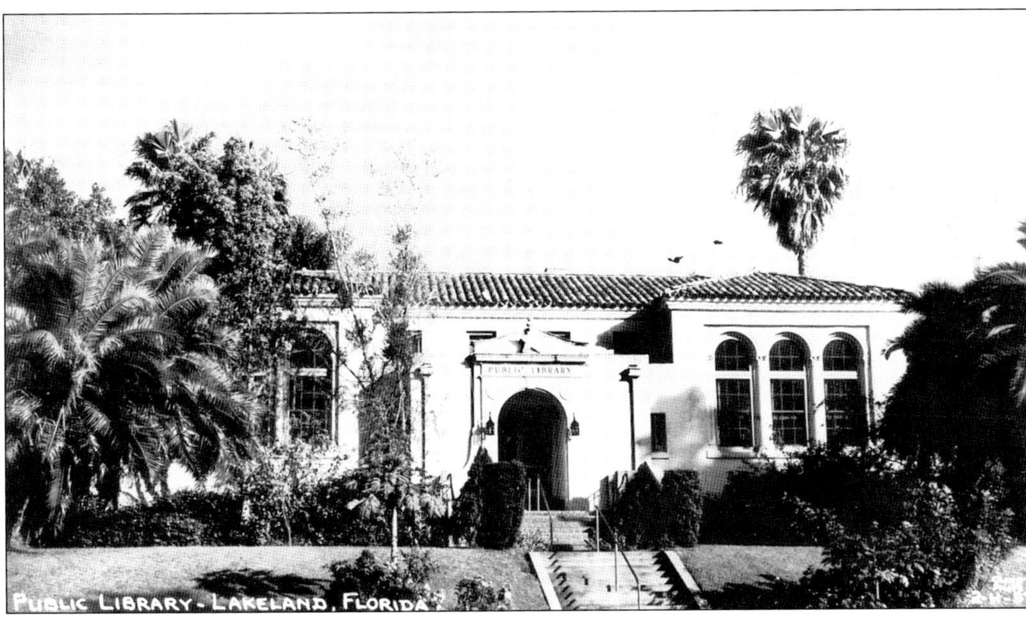

PUBLIC LIBRARY—LAKELAND, FLORIDA. The library was renamed the Park Trammell Library in 1955, and moved to new quarters in 1966. The building is now home to the chamber of commerce. Government buildings made popular postcards, as citizens were connected personally by interaction to the local government, and many of the buildings remained unchanged for decades. (Courtesy Lakeland Public Library.)

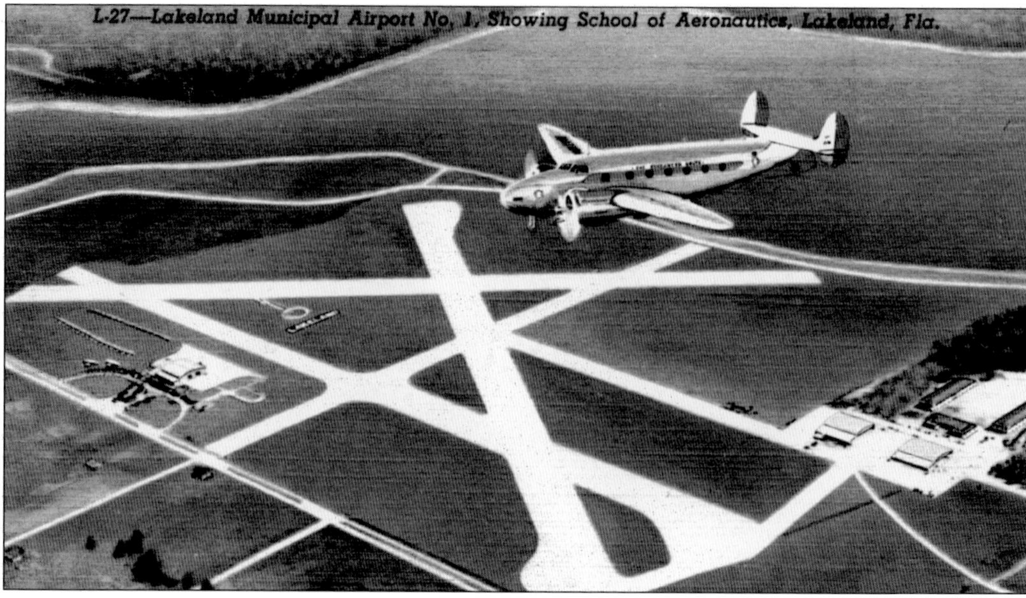

LAKELAND MUNICIPAL AIRPORT NO. 1 SHOWING THE SCHOOL OF AERONAUTICS. The airport was on the west shore of Lake Parker. During World War II, it housed the Lodwick School of Aeronautics, which provided training for British and American pilots. There have been four airports in what is now Lakeland—one near Gibsonia, the airport near Lake Parker, one near the intersection of Bartow Road and Combee Road, and the present airport (old Drane Field, now Lakeland Linder Regional Airport). (Courtesy Lakeland Public Library.)

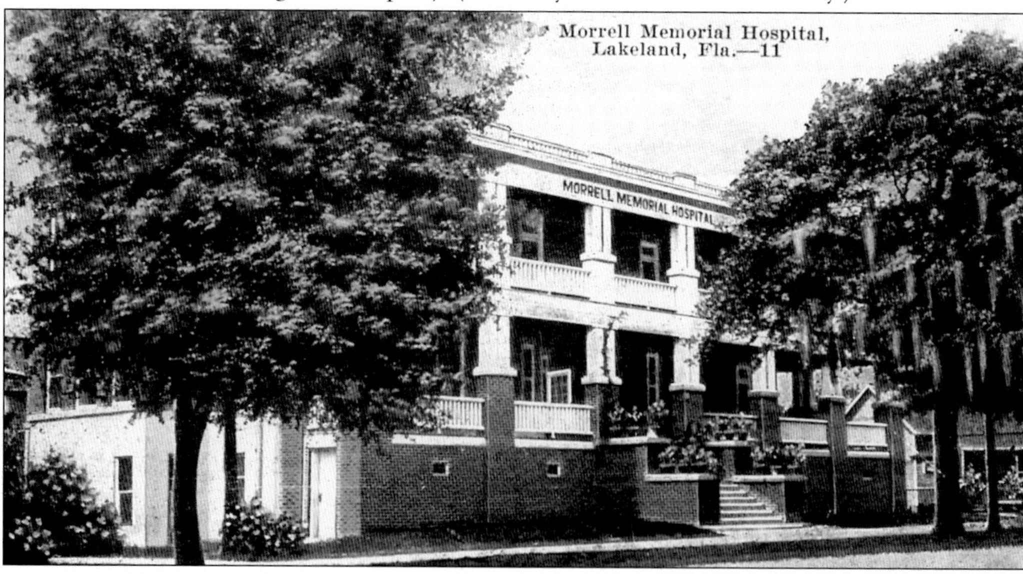

MORRELL MEMORIAL HOSPITAL, LAKELAND, FLA. The hospital was opened in 1916 thanks to the generosity of Jane Morrell, who left property to the city for a hospital. It was on the west side of South Missouri Avenue between Lemon and Orange Streets. Life in the early days of Lakeland moved at a much slower pace, and private lives were not very private. Daily reports in the *Lakeland Evening Telegram* and *Lakeland Morning Star* announced not only births and deaths but who went to the hospital and what operations were performed. (Courtesy Lakeland Public Library.)

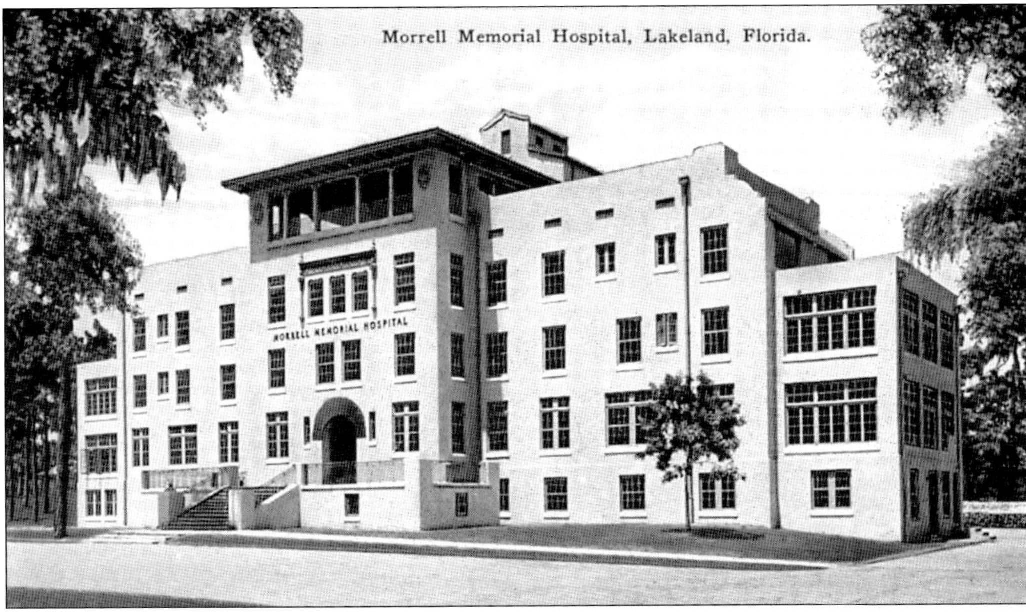

MORRELL MEMORIAL HOSPITAL, LAKELAND, FLORIDA. This 100-bed facility was the second Morrell Memorial Hospital (1926), constructed on the west side of Lakeland Hills Boulevard overlooking Lake Parker. The $300,000 building was part of the more than $1.5 million of municipal construction under way in the mid-1920s, including the Mayhall Auditorium, City Hall, and library. (Courtesy Lakeland Public Library.)

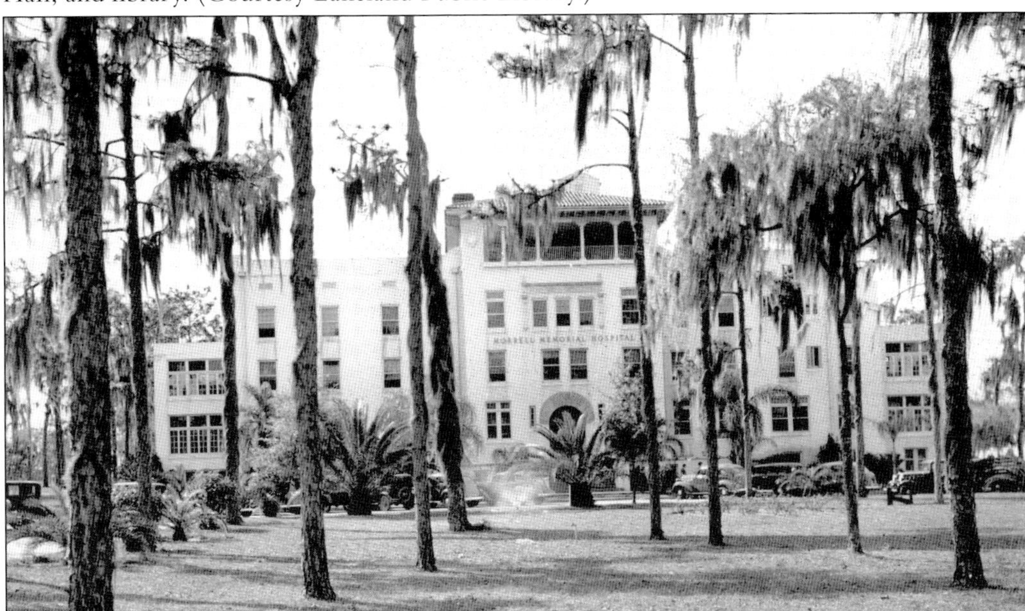

MORRELL MEMORIAL HOSPITAL, LAKELAND, FLA. This postcard was mailed in February 1947. The building was demolished in 1972 to accommodate further expansion of the newer Lakeland General Hospital, which had been built immediately to the south of Morrell Memorial. This site is largely beneath the north wing of what is now the Lakeland Regional Medical Center. (Courtesy Lakeland Public Library.)

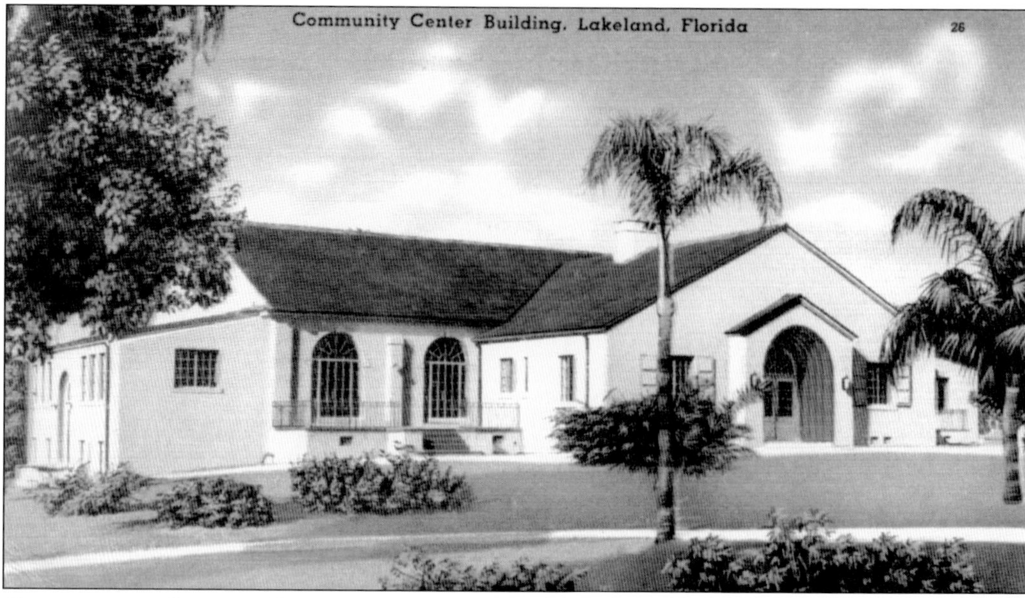

Community Center Building, Lakeland, Florida. The Lakeland Tourist Club was formed in 1922 and from 1938 met in this city-owned clubhouse, the hub of Lakeland's recreation facilities. City shuffleboard and roque courts were on the east side of the complex. The back of the building overlooks Lake Mirror; the front faces East Orange Street. Now known as the Magnolia Building, it is flanked by Hollis Gardens and the Barnett Family Park. (Courtesy Lakeland Public Library.)

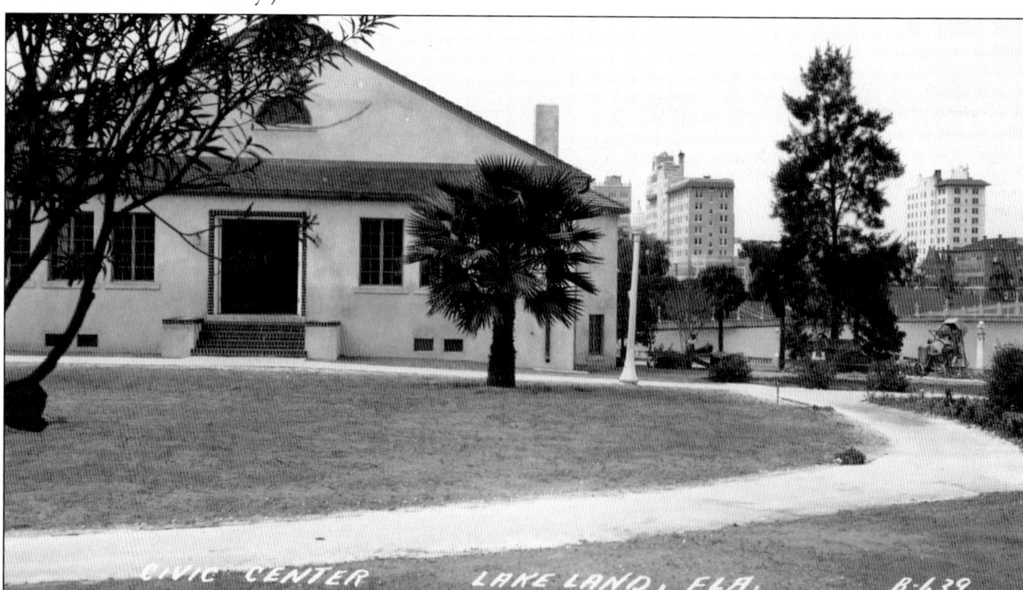

Civic Center, Lakeland, Fla. Part of the Lake Mirror Civic Center complex is shown in this 1940s real-photo postcard. This building was constructed on the southeast corner of Lake Mirror and still provides a home for Lakeland's Pied Piper Players. The complex also included the magnificent 6,900-foot Lake Mirror Promenade, dedicated in 1928. The promenade was renamed for Frances Langford (1913–2005) in 1946, honoring Lakeland's renowned singer and actress. (Courtesy Lakeland Public Library.)

Eight

Agriculture and Industry

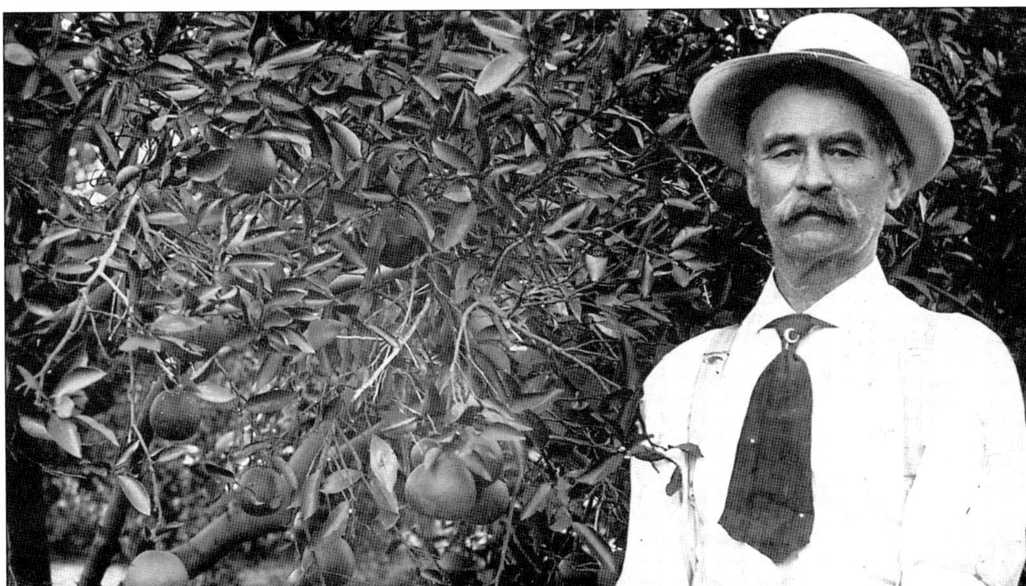

Makings of a Small Orange Grove. A man stands next to a fruit-laden citrus tree in this real-photo postcard. Mailed from Lakeland on February 1911, it reads: "How is this for high? My hammock is strung under this tree. Yours, TPS." (Author's Collection.)

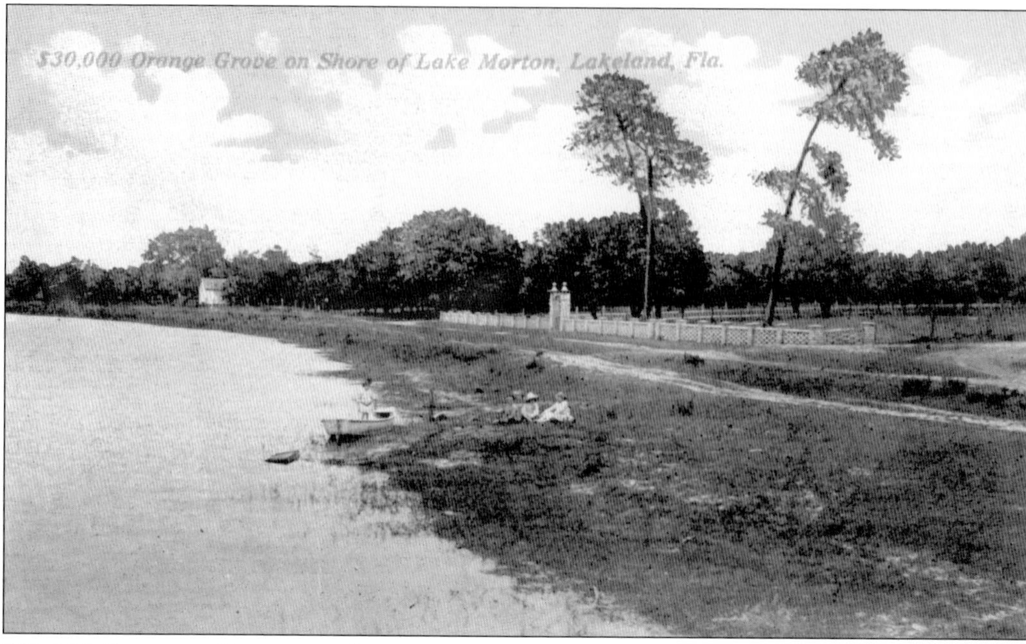

$30,000 ORANGE GROVE ON SHORE OF LAKE MORTON. Lake Morton Drive is now home to the Lakeland Public Library, the First United Methodist Church, businesses, apartments, and other residential buildings. Many of Lakeland's famous swans, some of which are descended from swans donated to the city by Queen Elizabeth II in 1957, live and are cared for around this scenic lake. (Courtesy Lakeland Public Library.)

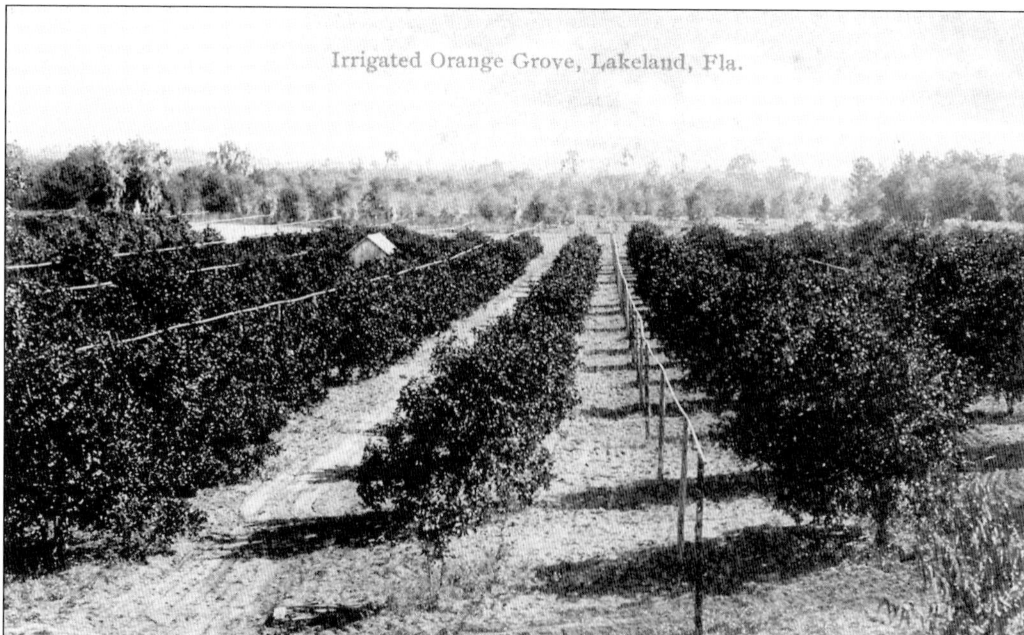

IRRIGATED ORANGE GROVE, LAKELAND, FLA. Postcards advertising Lakeland's citrus products served dual purposes; they promoted the industry worldwide and helped draw tourists to central Florida's pleasant climate. (Courtesy Lakeland Public Library.)

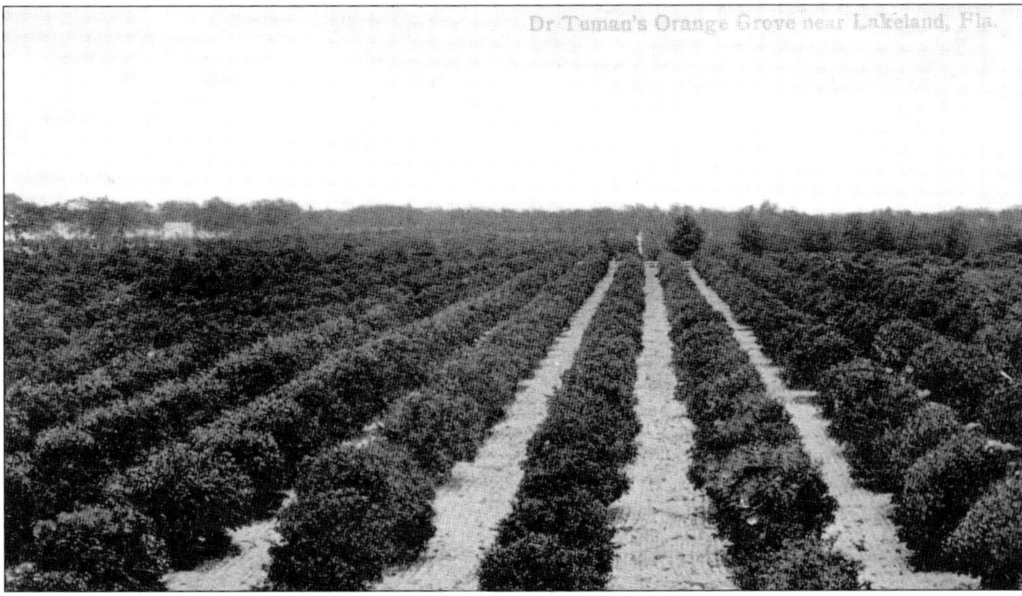

DR. TUMAN'S ORANGE GROVE NEAR LAKELAND, FLA. Early Lakeland residents depended in large measure on the land, a favorable climate, and a burgeoning industrial infrastructure. Pine forests provided lumber and turpentine, citrus and other crops grew well throughout central Florida, cattle were raised on vast expanses of open land, and phosphate mining was profitable. The rising tide lifted all ships, but those not directly involved in agricultural pursuits benefited as the community developed a solid footing and positive reputation. This unsent pre-1916 postcard shows a healthy young grove. (Courtesy Larry Gray.)

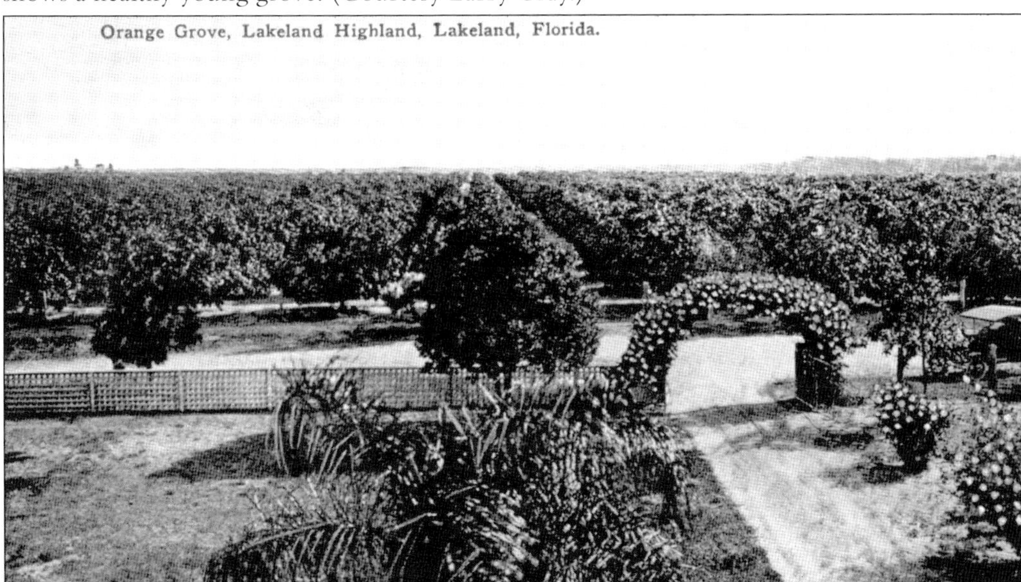

ORANGE GROVE, LAKELAND HIGHLAND, LAKELAND, FLORIDA. In 1931, a couple wrote to friends in Brunswick, Maine: "202 East Oak St. Lakeland, Fla. We are back in the sunny South and find it plenty warm just now very dry too so the crops are suffering. We are in an apartment house have 2 rooms, handy to downtown and plenty going on all the time. Hope you are both well, Dona & John." (Courtesy Lakeland Public Library.)

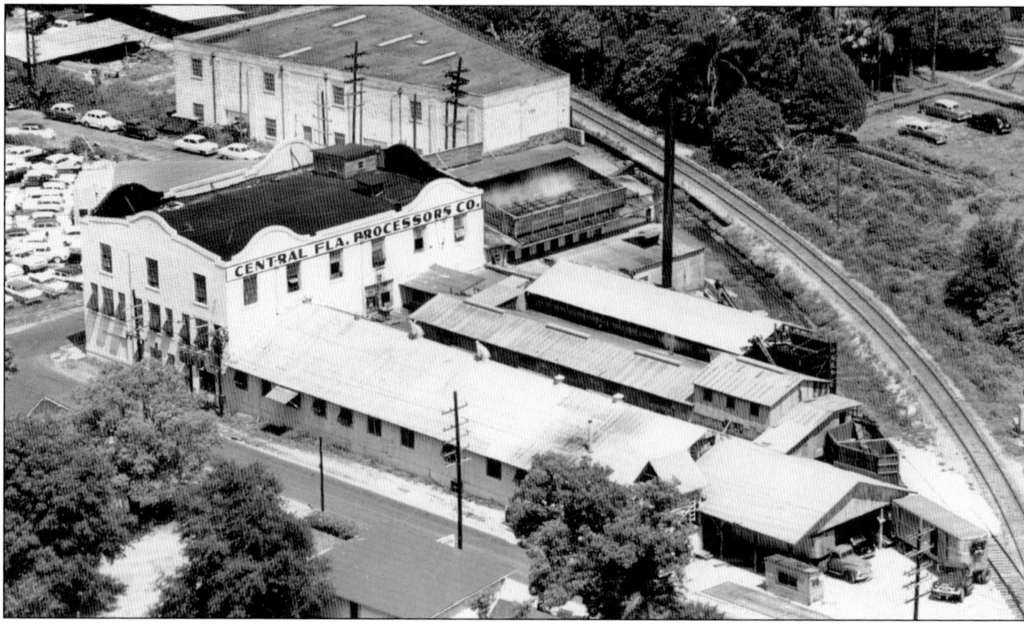

Central Florida Processors Co. This citrus packinghouse was at the northeast corner of North Lake Avenue and East Rose Street northeast of Lake Mirror. Few small packinghouses survive in central Florida. (Courtesy Lakeland Public Library.)

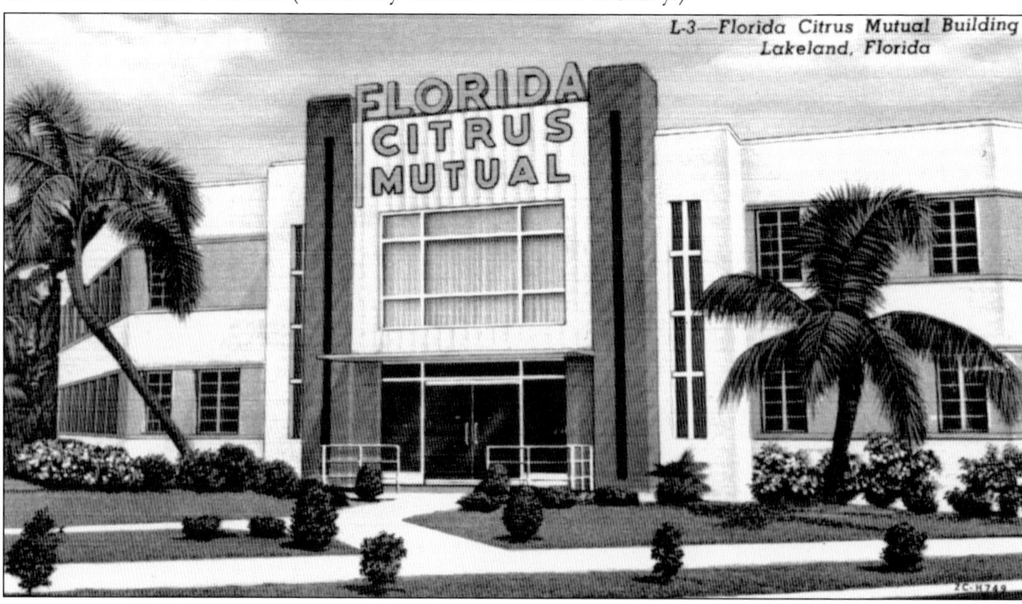

Florida Citrus Mutual Building, Lakeland, Florida. This building is located at the corner of East Orange Street and Massachusetts Avenue, the former site of Morris G. Munn's home. By the 1950s, the Florida Citrus Mutual was one of the world's largest agricultural cooperatives. It had approximately 7,000 growers as members, representing 85 percent of the citrus grown in Florida. There were 519 handlers, which included fresh fruit shippers, canners, concentrators, and cash boxers who were affiliated with the mutual. It was not a marketing agency but helped its members through establishing floor prices and furnishing current industry information. (Courtesy Lakeland Public Library.)

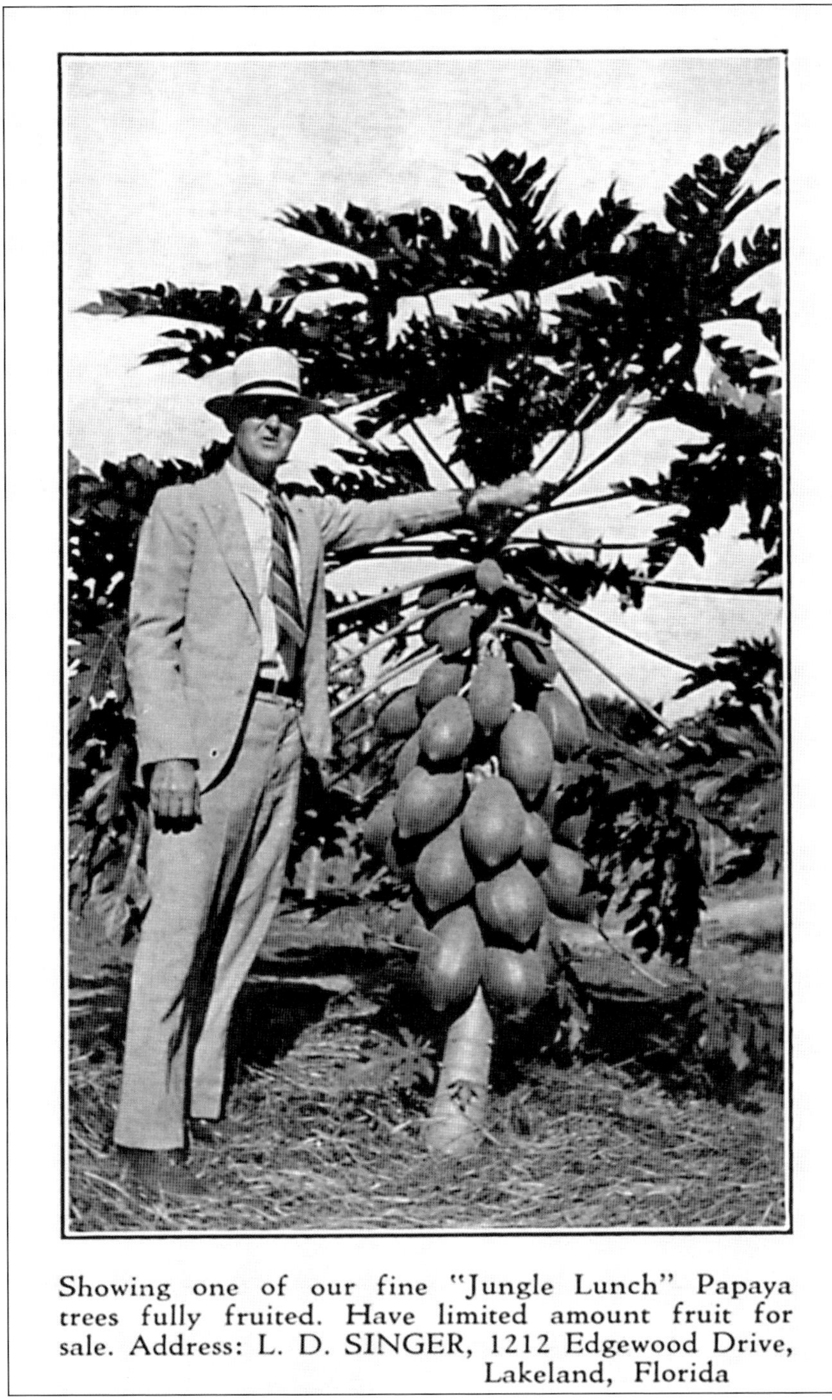

HEAVY-LADEN PAPAYA TREE. Small commercial papaya orchards could be found in south and central Florida into the 1950s, until natural pests limited their viability. This unusual postcard advertises a local grower's crop: "Showing one of our fine 'Jungle Lunch' Papaya trees fully fruited. Have limited amount fruit for sale. Address: L. D. Singer, 1212 Edgewood Drive, Lakeland, Florida." (Courtesy Larry Gray.)

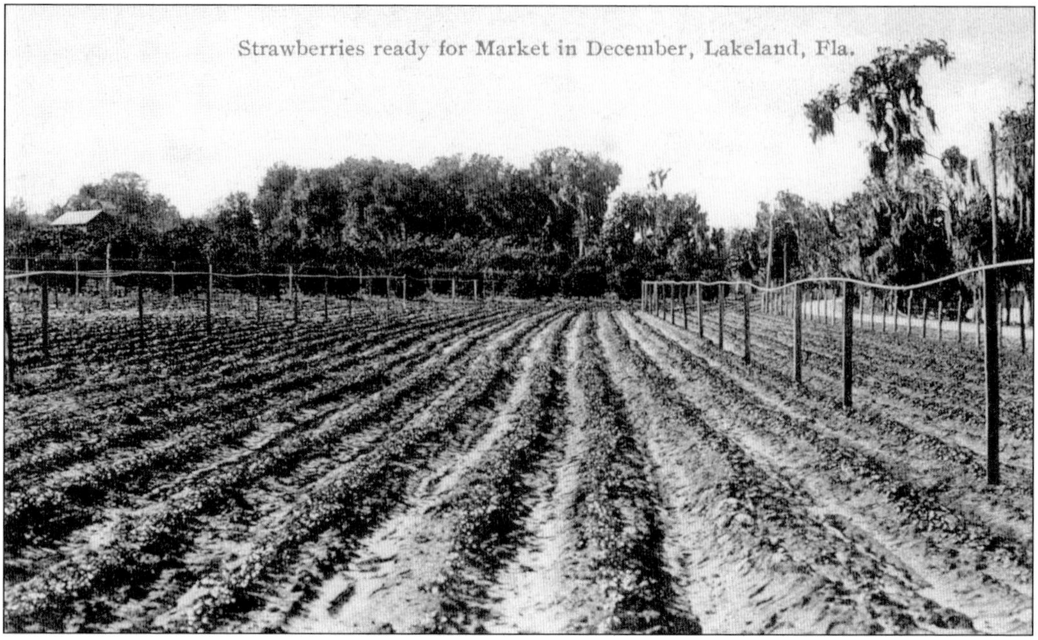

Strawberries Ready for Market in December, Lakeland, Fla. By the mid-1890s, local strawberry farms were benefiting immensely from Lakeland's busy rail service. Strawberries were planted in September and October, and the season ran from Thanksgiving to June. Strawberry farms were also in neighboring Kathleen and Providence, among other areas. Farms and groves are still found within 10 miles of the center of town. (Courtesy Lakeland Public Library.)

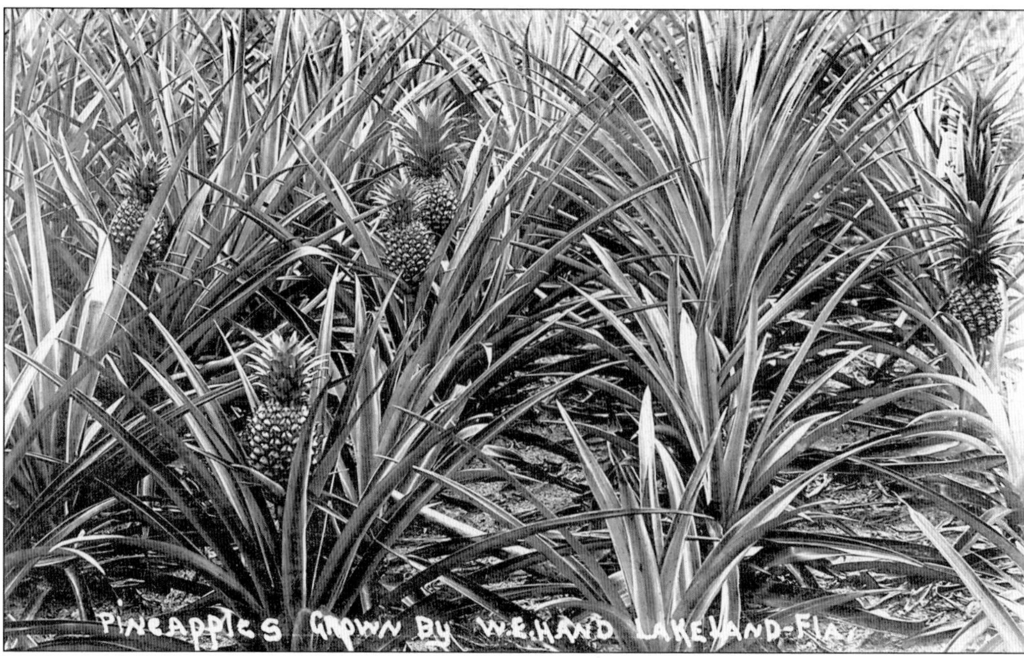

Pineapples Grown by W. E. Hand, Lakeland, Fla. W. E. Hand also grew papayas locally. (Courtesy Larry Gray.)

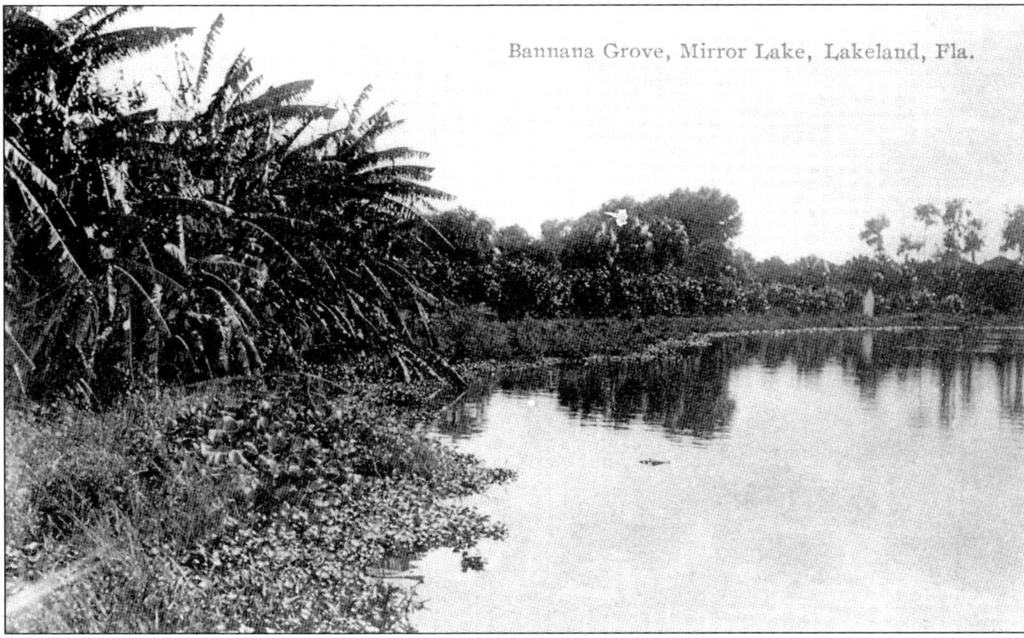

BANNANA GROVE, MIRROR LAKE, LAKELAND, FLA. Non-commercial lady-finger bananas grow very well in well-drained consistently moist soils, and it was no surprise that they would thrive in Lakeland. This lakeside grove was shown on a number of early-20th century postcards of the city. (Courtesy Lakeland Public Library.)

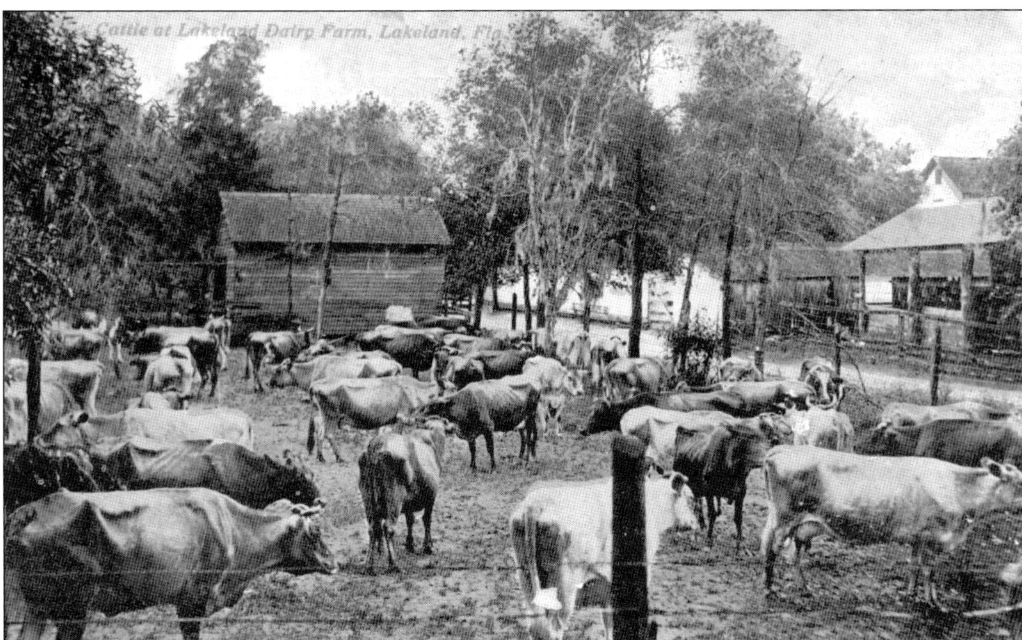

CATTLE AT A LAKELAND DAIRY FARM, LAKELAND, FLA. Cattle, citrus, and strawberries were the primary industries in early Lakeland, and there are still cattle to be found on the outskirts of the city. (Courtesy Lakeland Public Library.)

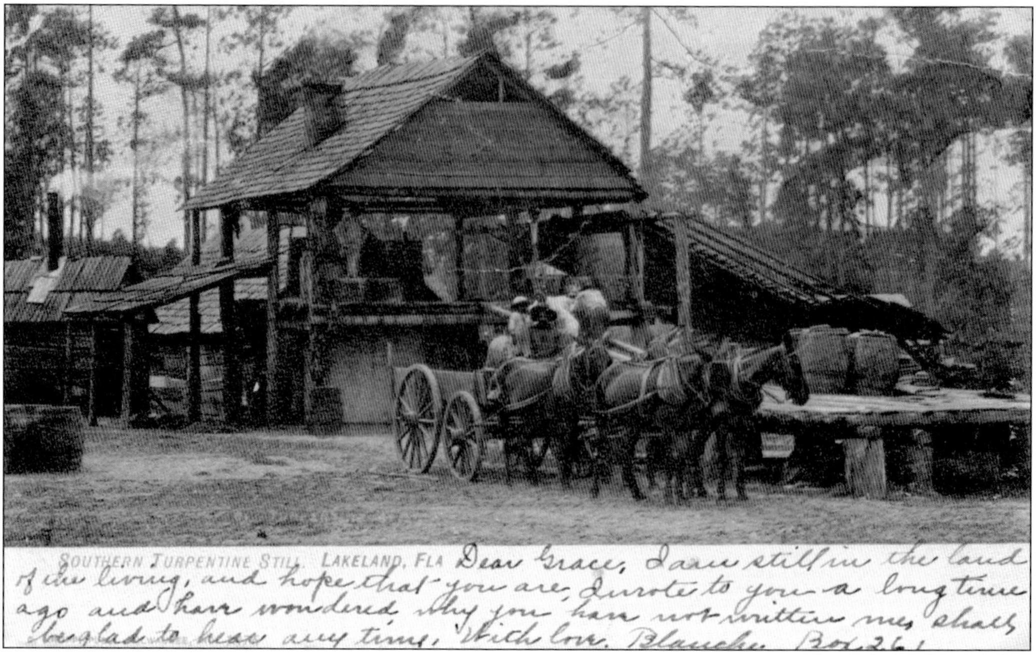

SOUTHERN TURPENTINE STILL, LAKELAND, FLA. The author reports in January 1907, "Dear Grace, I am still in the land of the living, and hope that you are, I wrote to you a long time ago and have wondered why you have not written me shall be glad to hear any time. With love. Blanche Box 261." (Courtesy Lakeland Public Library.)

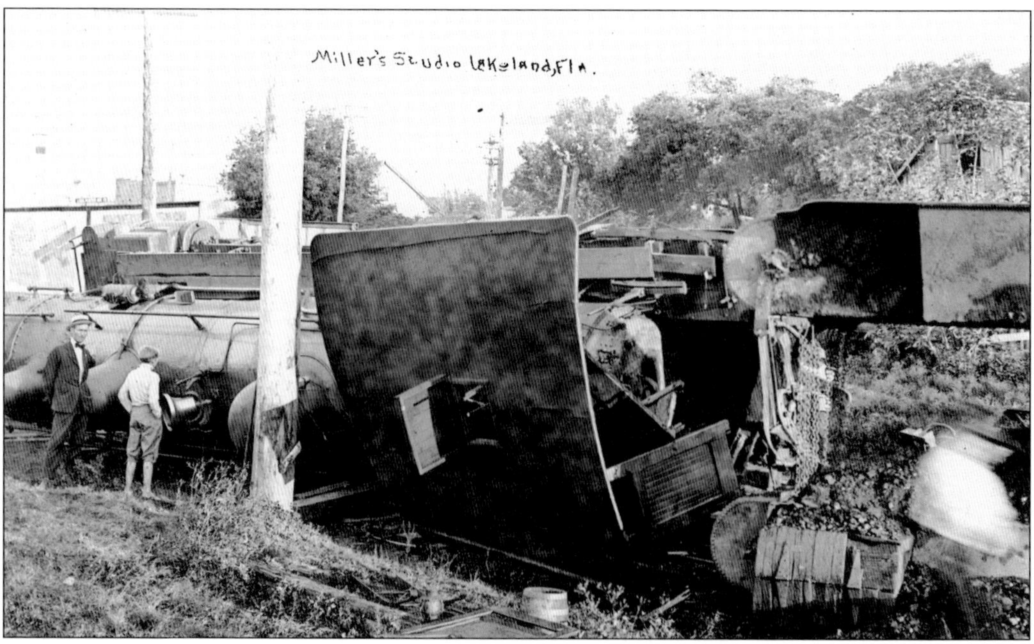

MILLER'S STUDIO, LAKELAND, FLA. This rare real-photo postcard published by an early Lakeland photographic studio shows a derailed train locomotive and tender adjacent to the city's light and water plant. This may have occurred as late as 1916. (Authors' Collection.)

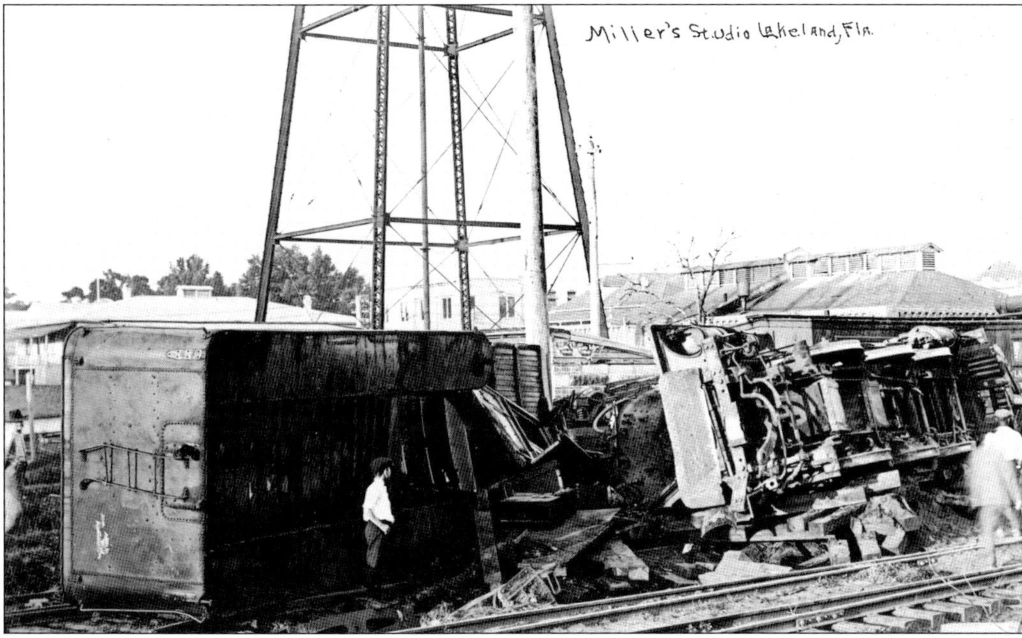

Miller's Studio, Lakeland, Fla. This is the second real-photo postcard in a series of three that records a train derailment in downtown Lakeland. Wrecks were not uncommon and, as seen here, sometimes drew crowds of youngsters in knickers. (Authors' Collection.)

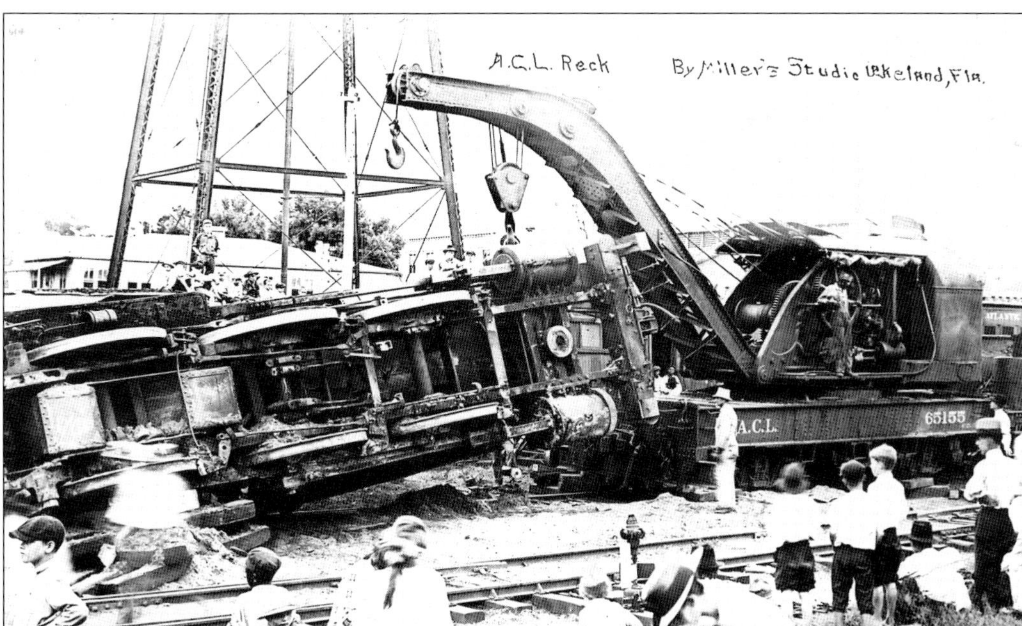

A. C. L. Reck by Miller's Studio, Lakeland, Fla. Heavy equipment was brought in to right the locomotive. Luckily the Atlantic Coast Line Railroad maintained yards and shops in Lakeland north of Lake Beulah and west of Lake Wire. (Authors' Collection.)

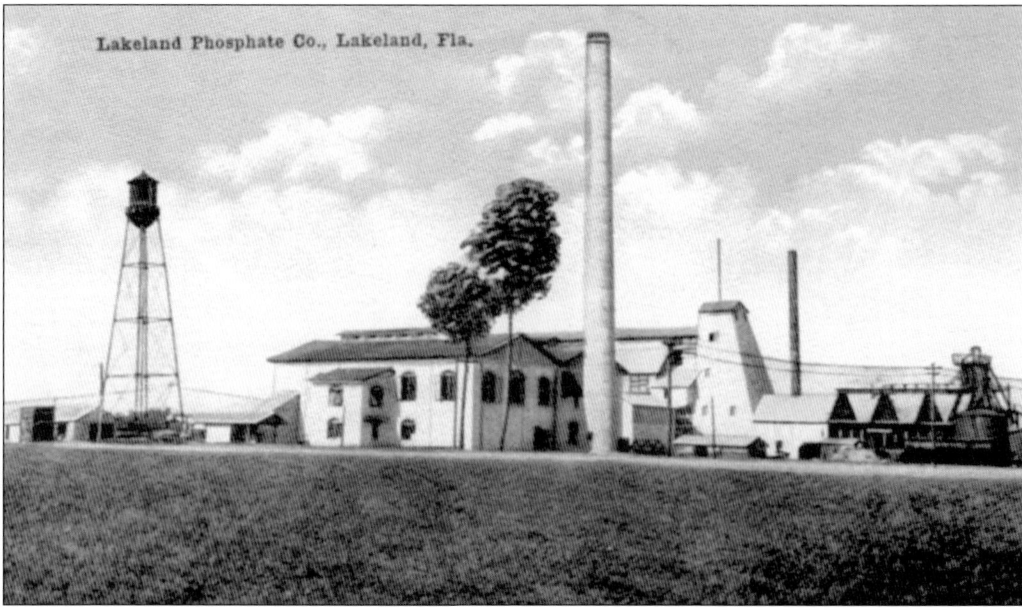

LAKELAND PHOSPHATE CO., LAKELAND, FLA. By 1914, when the company began operations, it was one of approximately 20 located in central Florida. (Courtesy Lakeland Public Library.)

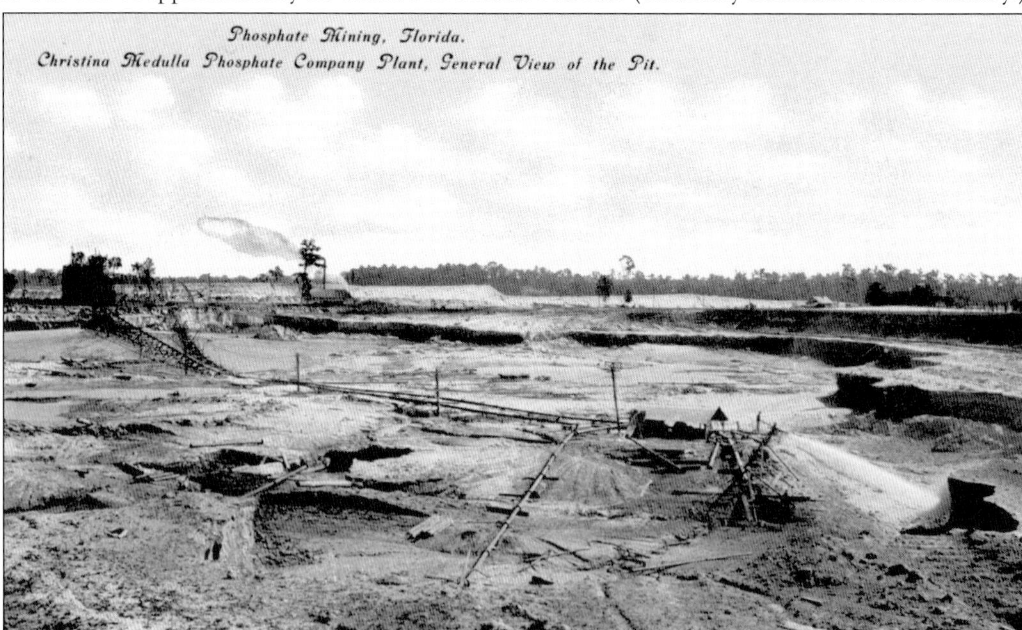

PHOSPHATE MINING, FLORIDA. This unusual postcards show the Christina Medulla Phosphate Company Plant mine pit. Christina, a mining community in South Lakeland, was founded in 1907 by Lakeland's C. G. Memminger, who changed the name of his Medulla mine to that of his only child. The mine was later absorbed by the Standard Phosphate Company. The postcard was mailed from Mulberry in April 1912 to Grace Branch in West Tampa in care of the Box Factory and reads: "4/26/12 Dear Grace—How are you today? Hope you are better. I am well and living high—would like to see you. Have you ever seen a phosphate mine before? Here is a photo of one. Bye-bye." (Courtesy Larry Gray.)

Nine

RECREATION

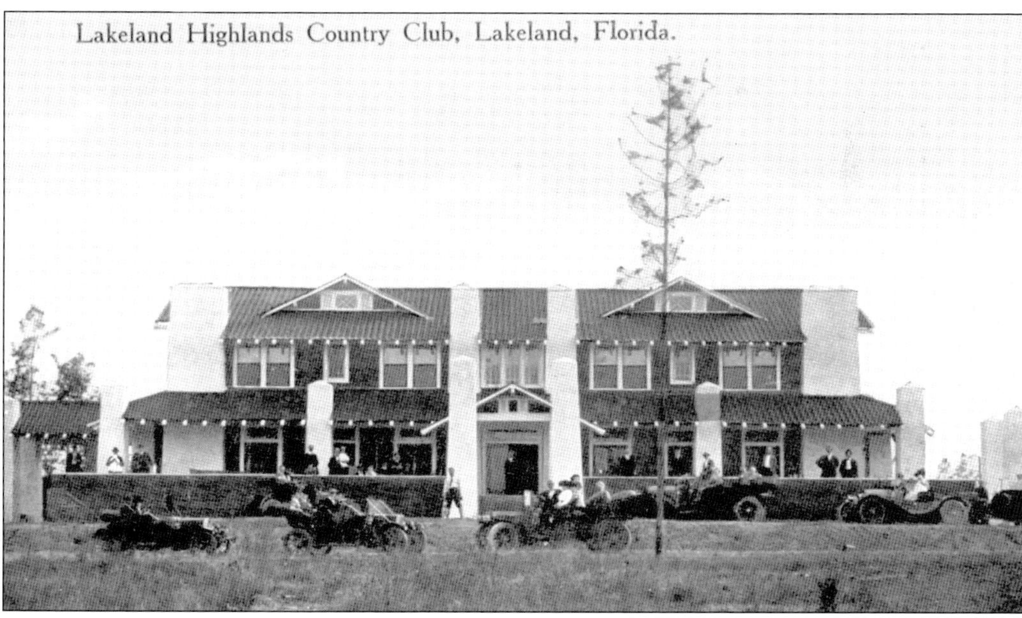

LAKELAND HIGHLANDS COUNTRY CLUB, LAKELAND, FLORIDA. This building was constructed in 1912 and torn down in 1940. It was the centerpiece of the Lakeland Highlands area south of town. The postcard is hand dated February 7, 1914. (Courtesy Lakeland Public Library.)

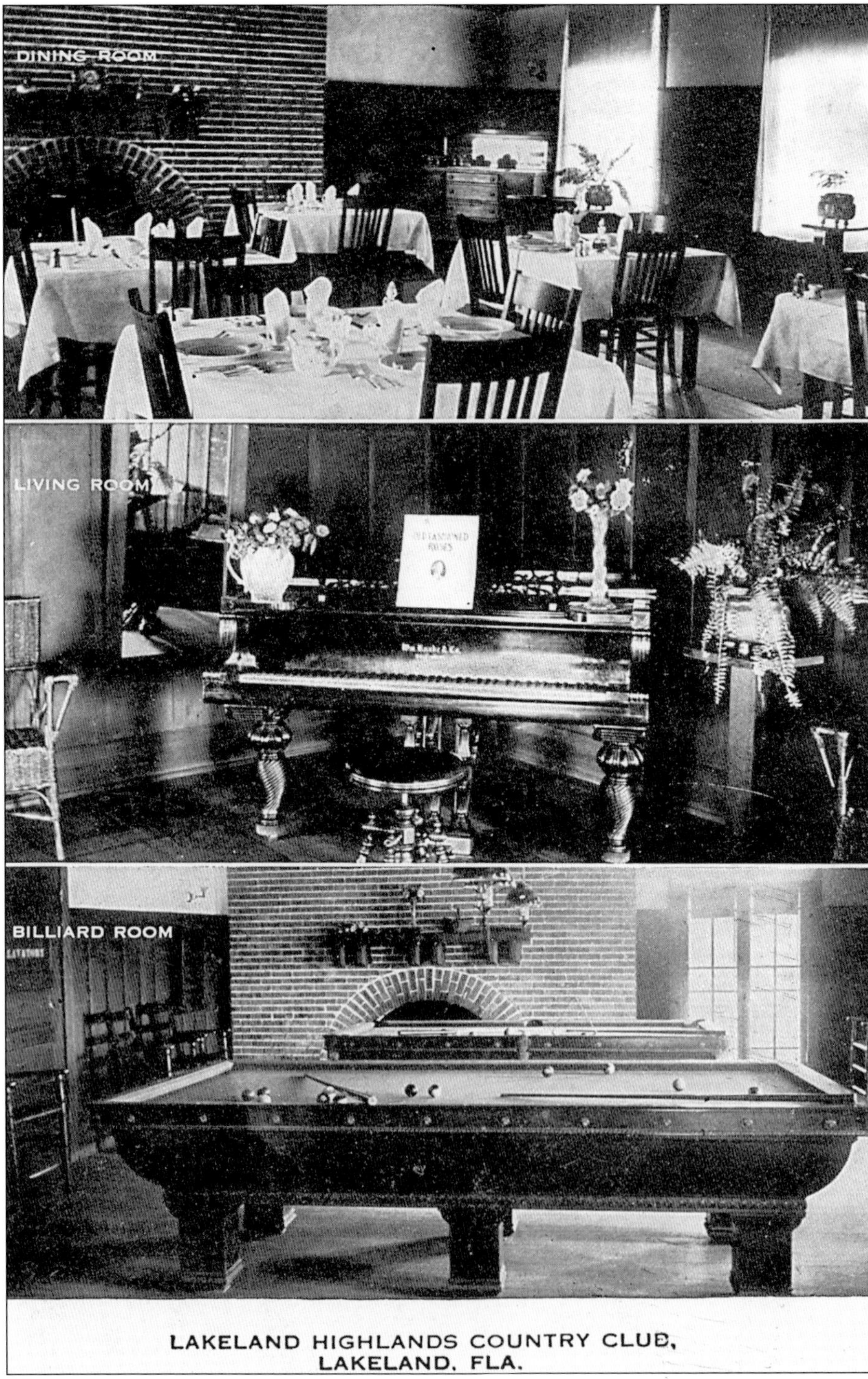

LAKELAND HIGHLANDS COUNTY CLUB, LAKELAND, FLA. The dining room, a piano in the living room, and the billiard room of the elegant clubhouse are shown. This late-1910s postcard advertised the Lakeland Highlands development, promoted by W. E. Hallman and Company. (Courtesy Lakeland Public Library.)

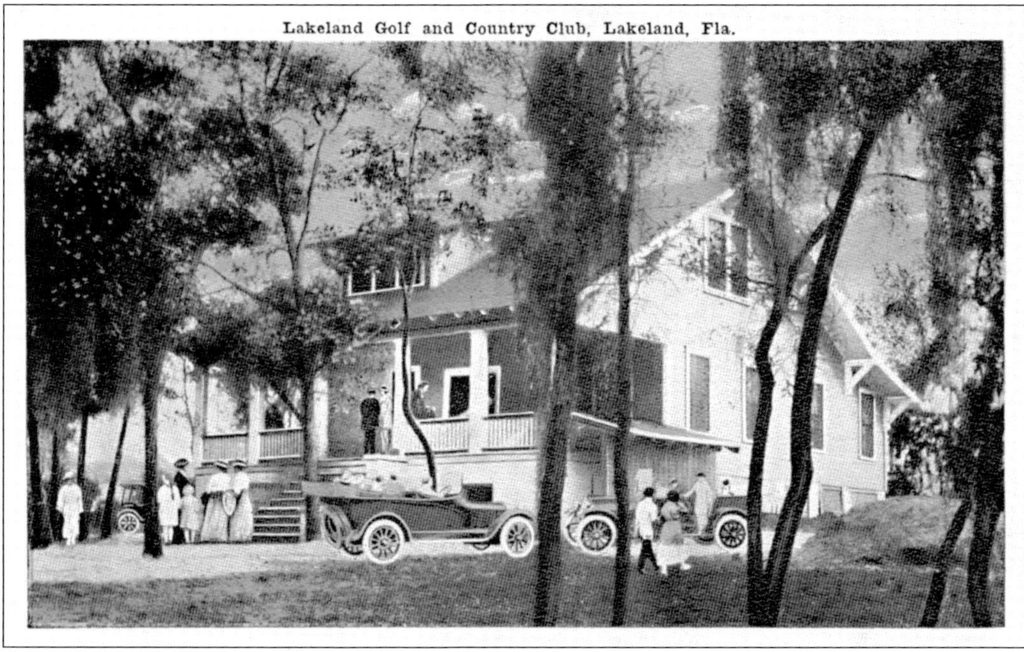

LAKELAND GOLF AND COUNTRY CLUB, LAKELAND, FLA. This card shows one of the city's earliest golf clubs *c.* 1920. Lakeland's temperate climate promotes year-round outdoor recreation. Just try to drive more than a few miles today without encountering a golf course. (Courtesy Lakeland Public Library.)

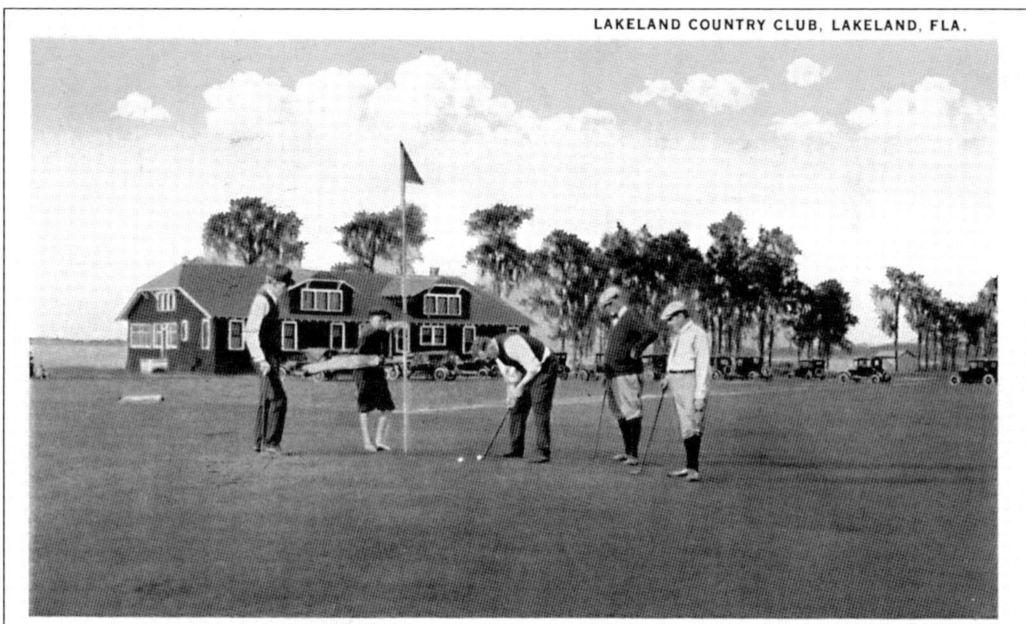

LAKELAND COUNTRY CLUB, LAKELAND, FLA. The club was organized in 1921 and opened in October 1923 on the southeast shore of Lake Parker. Water sports were particularly popular in young Lakeland: swimming, boating, fishing; camping, and hunting were other popular pastimes. (Courtesy Lakeland Public Library.)

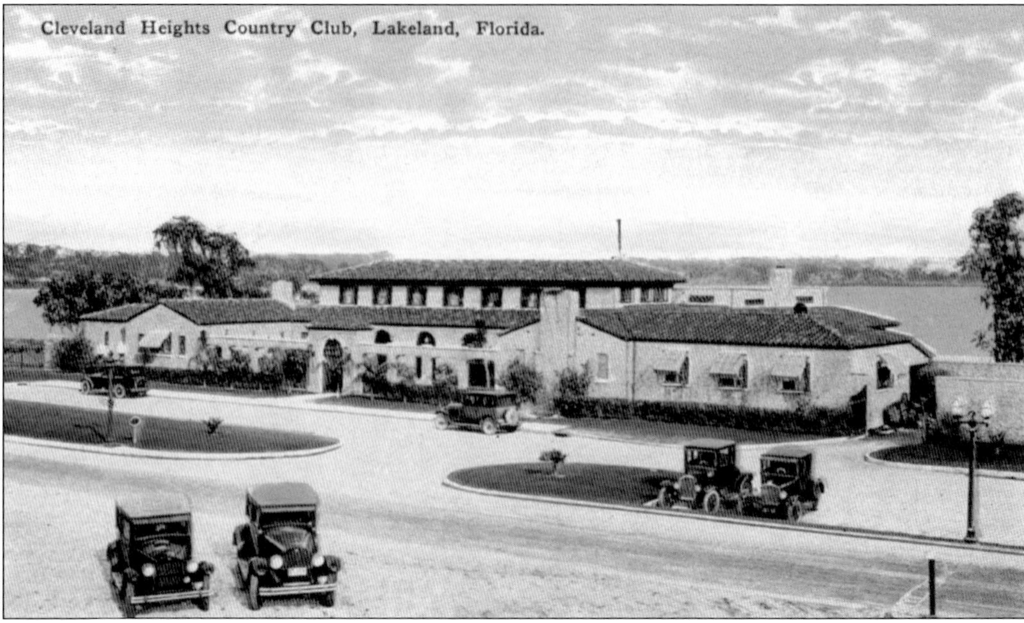

CLEVELAND HEIGHTS COUNTRY CLUB, LAKELAND, FLORIDA. The clubhouse was on Lake Hollingsworth Drive at the northern terminus of Cleveland Heights Boulevard. The country club was part of the sprawling Cleveland Heights development south of Lake Hollingsworth, which was constructed in the mid-1920s. The city assumed ownership of the building by 1930, and in 1935, it was leased to the Lakeland Yacht and Country Club. By the late 1950s, the club purchased the building. (Courtesy Lakeland Public Library.)

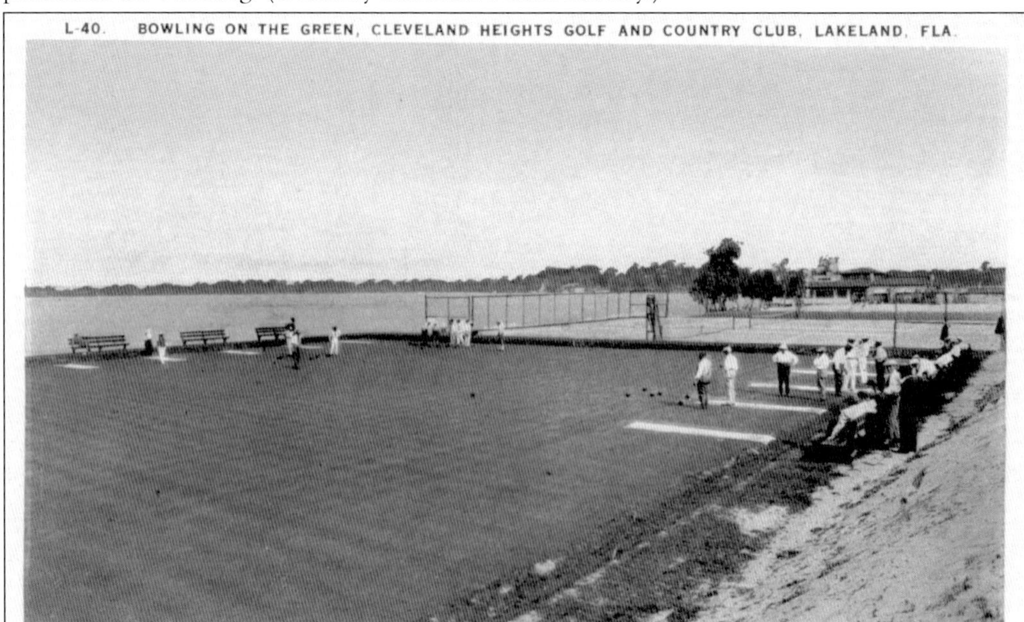

BOWLING ON THE GREEN, CLEVELAND HEIGHTS GOLF AND COUNTRY CLUB, LAKELAND, FLA. This 1920s postcard shows lawn bowling greens and tennis courts adjacent to the clubhouse on Lake Hollingsworth. (Courtesy Lakeland Public Library.)

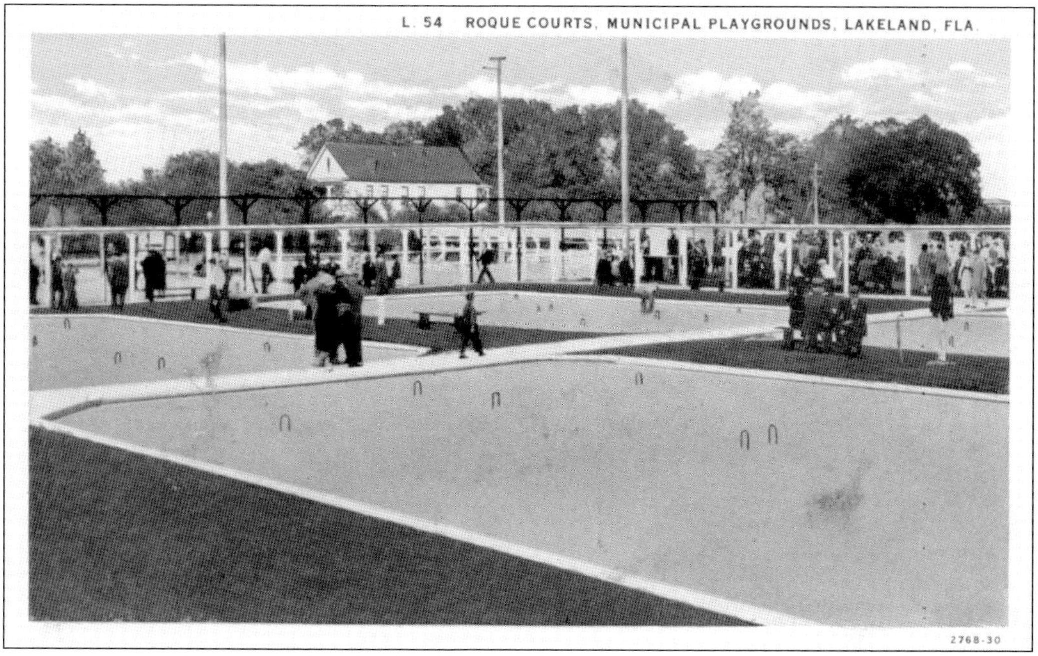

ROQUE COURTS, MUNICIPAL PLAYGROUNDS, LAKELAND FLA. Roque initiated in the United States as a variant of croquet and was especially popular in Florida during the 1920s. The playing surface is hard and is bounded by five-inch-high walls, which may be used in play, reminiscent of billiards. (Courtesy Lakeland Public Library.)

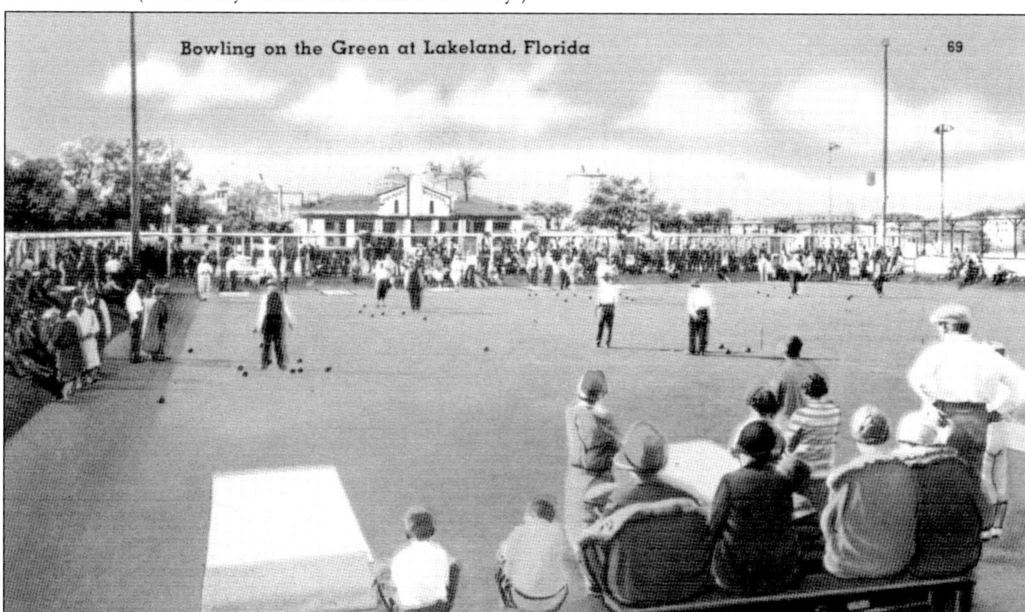

BOWLING ON THE GREEN AT LAKELAND, FLORIDA. The Lakeland Lawn Bowling Club was organized in 1923 and bowled on greens at the Lake Mirror Civic Center. The first of two fine greens was constructed in 1934, and a second was completed in 1954. Concurrent with extensive renovations to the Lake Mirror Civic Center site, a replacement artificial lawn was constructed in 2003 at Lake Parker Park. (Courtesy Lakeland Public Library.)

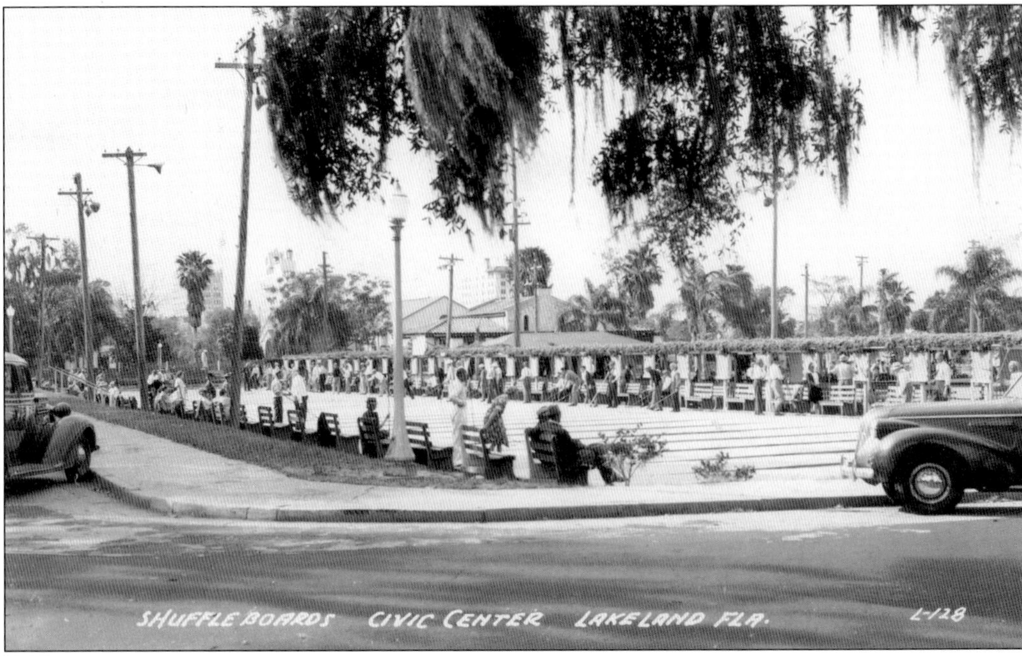

SHUFFLEBOARDS, CIVIC CENTER, LAKELAND FLA. Organized club sports drew a large following as the population increased. Shuffleboard, lawn bowling, croquet, and roque were all played in municipal parks, and the civic center provided several game fields for local enthusiasts. Shuffleboard was especially popular in the 1930s and 1940s. (Courtesy Lakeland Public Library.)

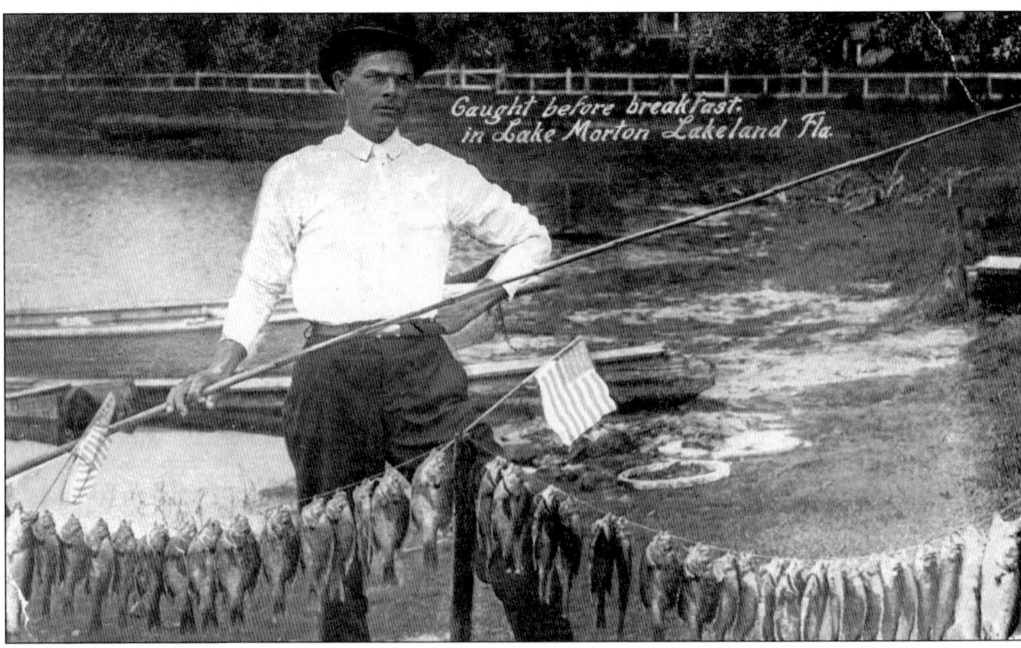

CAUGHT BEFORE BREAKFAST IN LAKE MORTON. Fishing is still a popular pastime on Lakeland's many lakes. This postcard was published by early Lakeland historian R. E. Lufsey, *c.* 1912. (Courtesy Lakeland Public Library.)

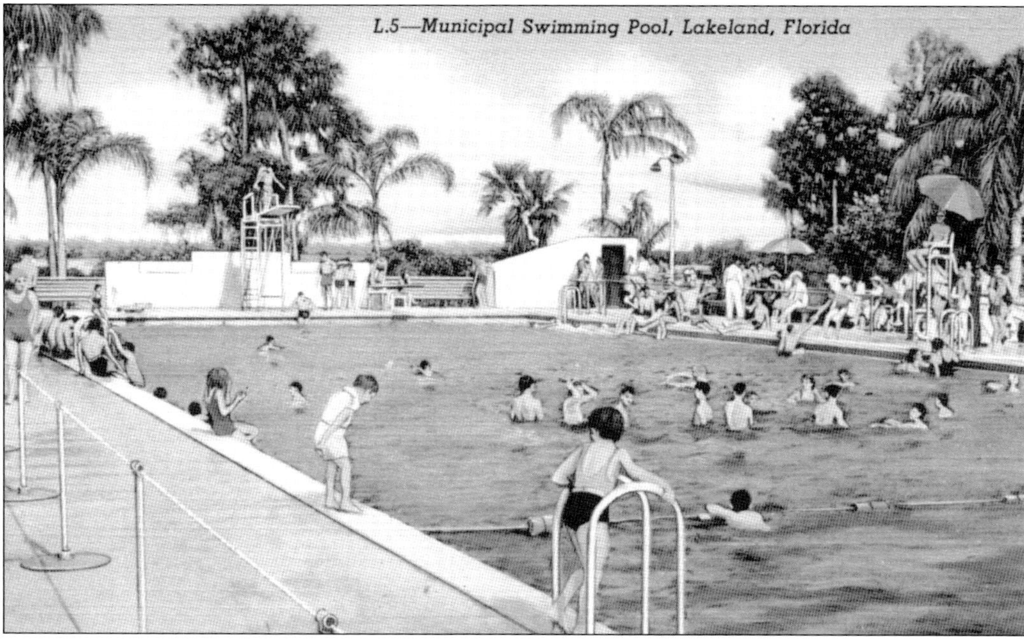

MUNICIPAL SWIMMING POOL, LAKELAND, FLORIDA. The pool was located on North Florida Avenue. This late-1930s to early-1940s postcard advertised the city's benefits: "Lakeland's recreational advantages are second to none in the state. Ideal weather conditions permit the indulgence in all forms of amusement and sport practically every day in the year." (Courtesy Lakeland Public Library.)

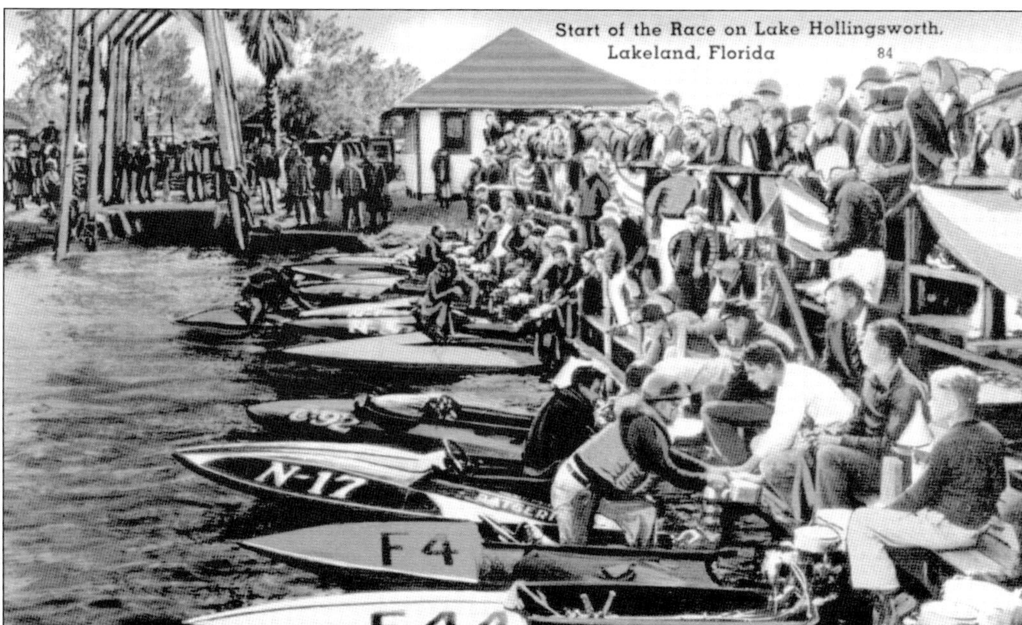

START OF THE RACE ON LAKE HOLLINGSWORTH, LAKELAND, FLORIDA. The Orange Cup Regatta—featuring record-setting powerboat racing—has been held nearly every year on Lake Hollingsworth for some 70 years. (Courtesy Lakeland Public Library.)

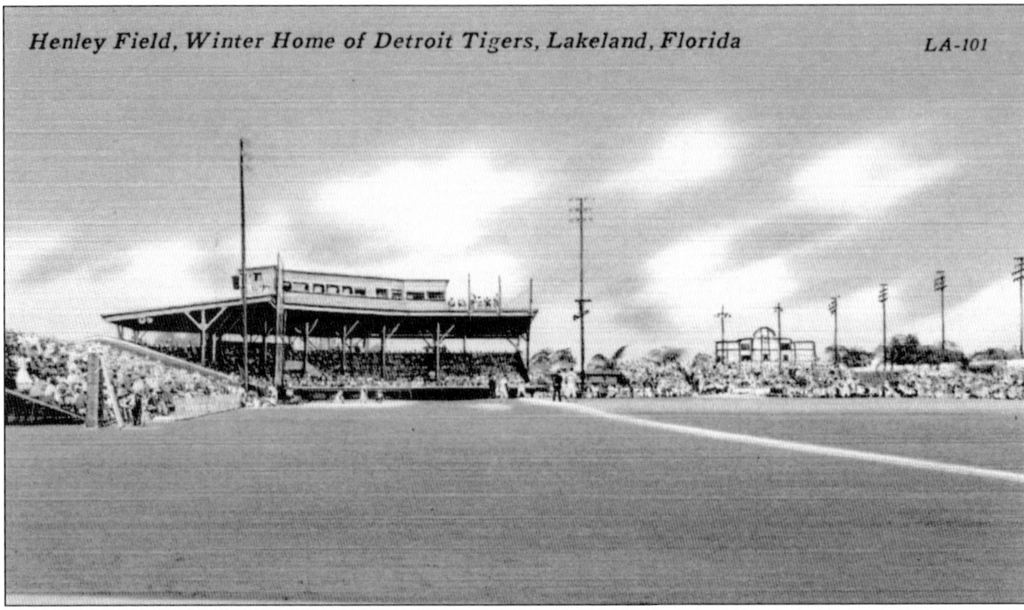

HENLEY FIELD, WINTER HOME OF DETROIT TIGERS, LAKELAND, FLORIDA. Professional baseball teams have held spring training in Lakeland for nearly 80 years—first the Cleveland Indians (1924–1927) and the Detroit Tigers since 1934. High school sports have always drawn enthusiastic crowds. The 1923 Lakeland High School football team had an impressive 10-0 record and inspired the proud "Dreadnaught" nickname. (Courtesy Lakeland Public Library.)

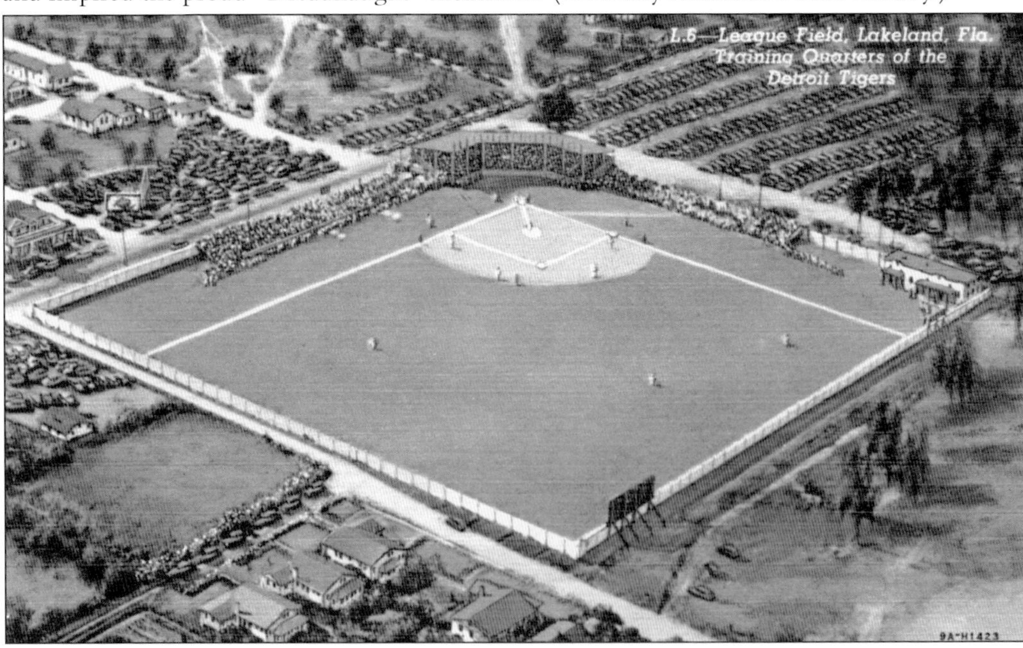

LEAGUE FIELD, LAKELAND, FLA. TRAINING QUARTERS OF THE DETROIT TIGERS. Henley Field opened in the 1920s and was later named for local pharmacist Clare Henley. The Tigers trained in this stadium until 1966, when they moved north to Joker Marchant Stadium. Henley Field is home of the Florida Southern College Moccasins, nine-time NCAA Division II National Champions. (Courtesy Lakeland Public Library.)

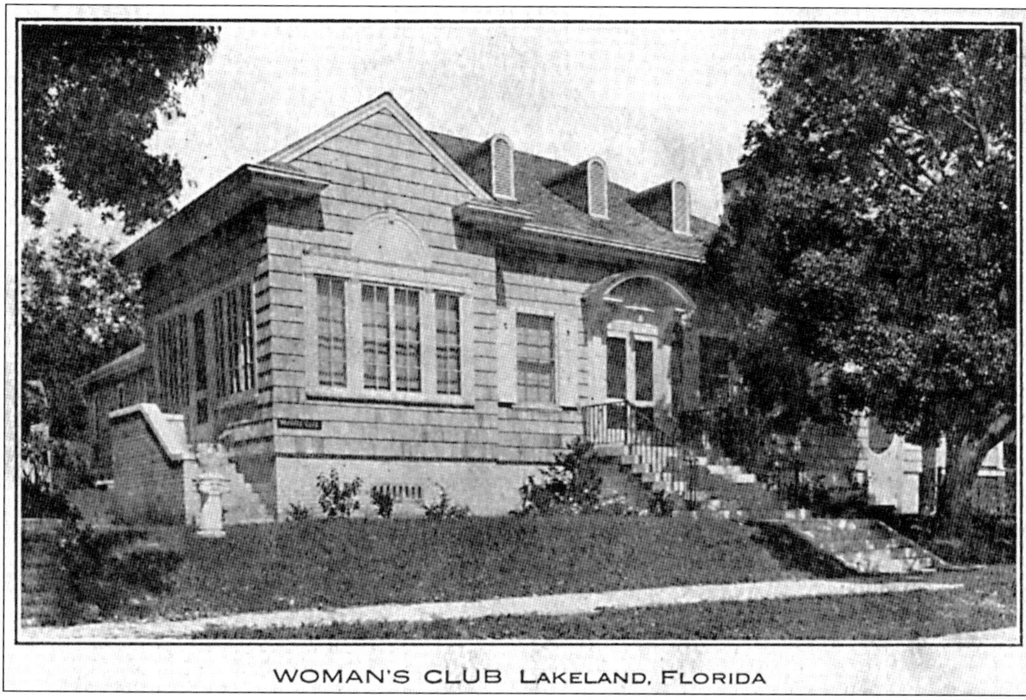

WOMAN'S CLUB, LAKELAND, FLORIDA. The club was organized in 1912, property was purchased in 1923, and this clubhouse was constructed in 1928 for $13,000. The clubhouse building remains on the northeast shore of Lake Morton. (Courtesy Lakeland Public Library.)

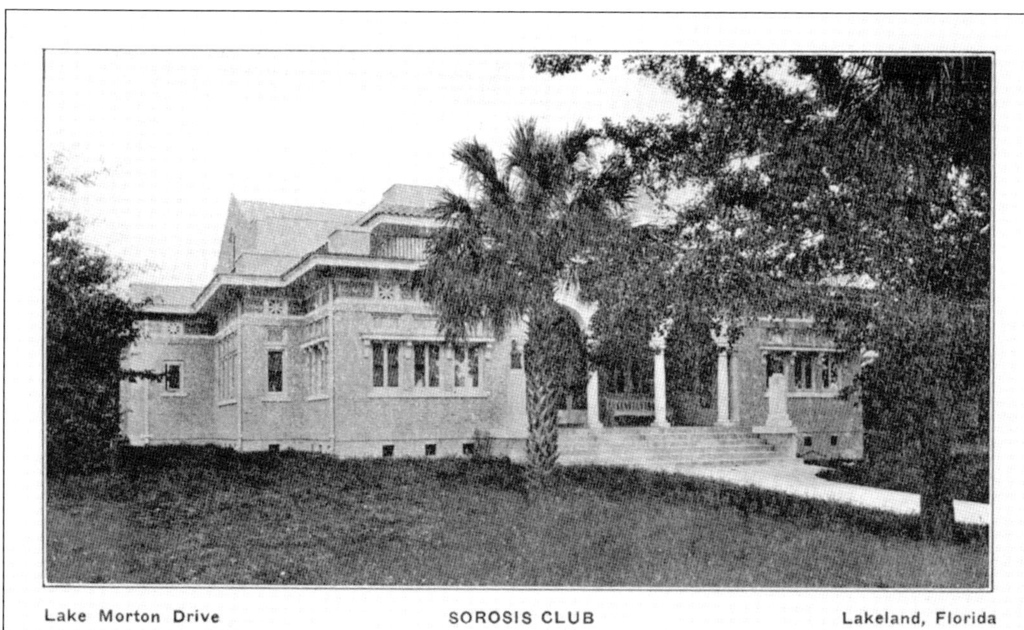

SOROSIS CLUB, LAKE MORTON DRIVE, LAKELAND, FLORIDA. The club was organized in 1922 with the $75,000 clubhouse erected in 1928. The clubhouse still stands on the east shore of Lake Morton Drive. (Courtesy Lakeland Public Library.)

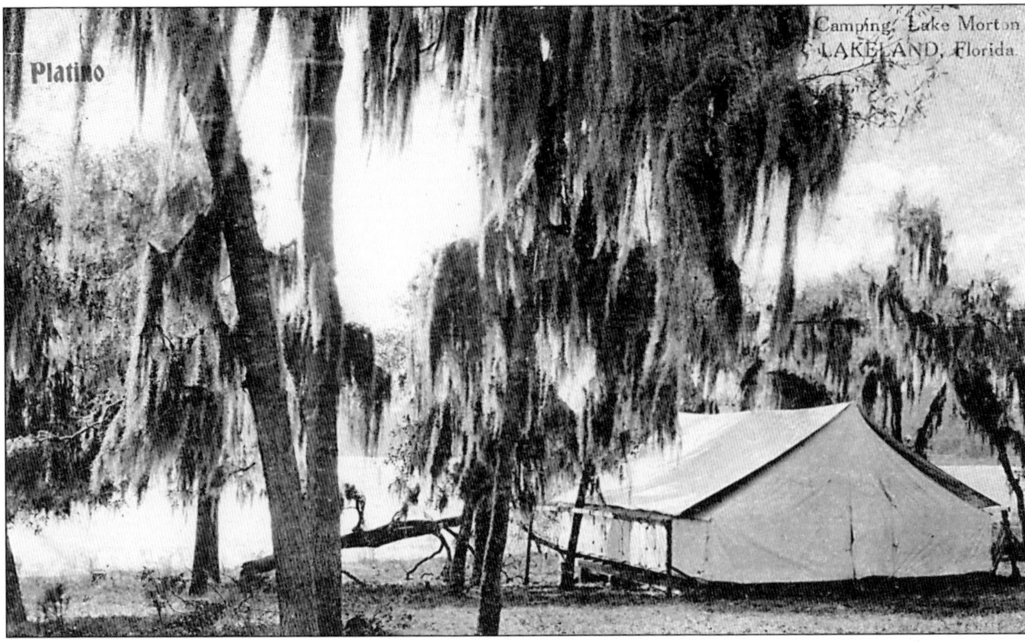

Camping, Lake Morton, Lakeland, Florida. A large canvas wall tent overlooks the lake. This tourist camp was scarcely beyond downtown and existed as late as the 1920s. (Courtesy Larry Gray.)

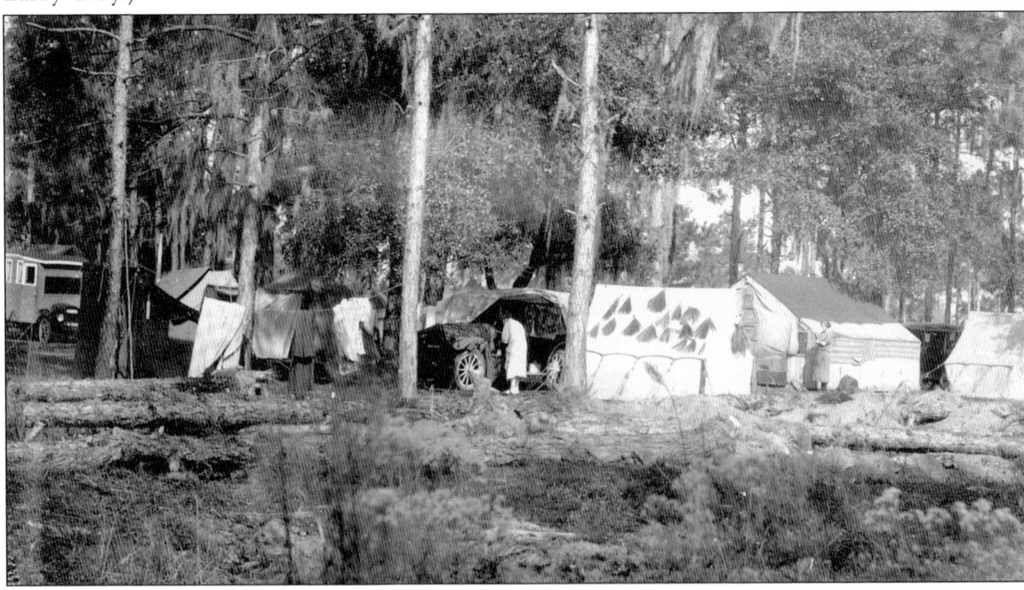

Camping at Lake Bonny. This real-photo postcard was mailed from Lakeland in February 1924. An unusual view of camping tourists is complete with what appears to be a homemade recreational vehicle at far left. The unsuspecting subject of this photograph wrote: " 'Camp Bonny' Lakeland, Fla. This picture back view was snapped when I did not know a 'Kodak fiend' was around. We expect to move on down the west coast tomorrow to Tampa and other points of interest. Hope this finds you all well. We are O.K. and having a fine time. Weather is lovely now. This only shows a small part of the camp. Sorry Will was not in picture. Lovingly, Dora." (Courtesy Larry Gray.)

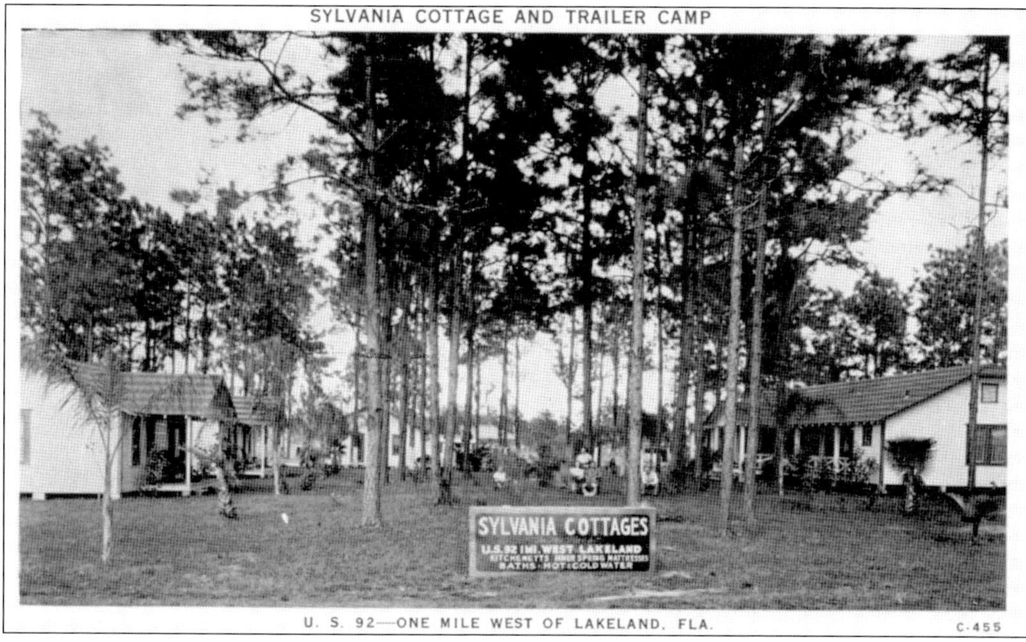

SYLVANIA COTTAGE AND TRAILER CAMP—U.S. 92—ONE MILE WEST OF LAKELAND, FLA. The Sylvania Cottage Court advertised 11 modern heated cottages with kitchenettes and private baths, hot and cold water, and innerspring mattresses. The reverse of the card endorses their proximity to area attractions: "Only a few minutes' drive to Lakeland's Million Dollar Recreation Center. One hour drive to Bok (Singing) Tower. Thirty minutes' drive to the beautiful Cypress Gardens. Fine golf courses and good fishing nearby." (Courtesy Lakeland Public Library.)

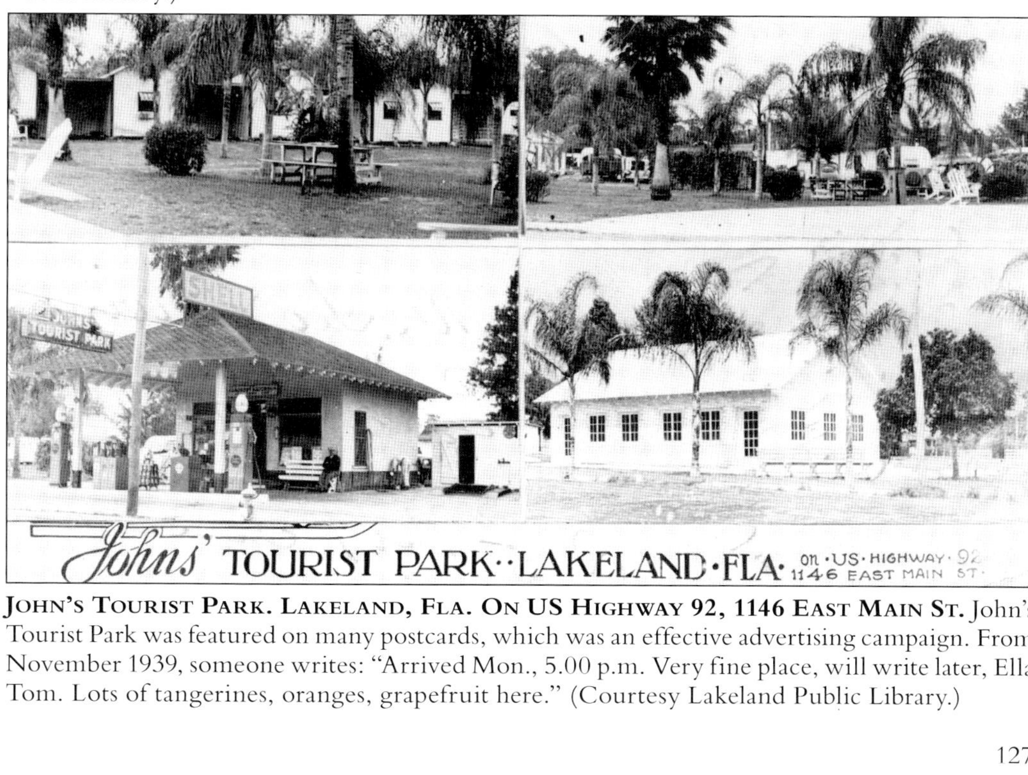

JOHN'S TOURIST PARK. LAKELAND, FLA. ON US HIGHWAY 92, 1146 EAST MAIN ST. John's Tourist Park was featured on many postcards, which was an effective advertising campaign. From November 1939, someone writes: "Arrived Mon., 5.00 p.m. Very fine place, will write later, Ella Tom. Lots of tangerines, oranges, grapefruit here." (Courtesy Lakeland Public Library.)

Sources Consulted

Davis, Joyce M. *Lakeland's Unique Architectural Heritage*. Lakeland, FL: Polk Museum of Art, 1987.

Dunn, Hampton. *Lakeland, a Pictorial History: A Revised Edition of Yesterday's Lakeland*. Norfolk/Virginia Beach, VA: Donning Co., 1990.

———. *Yesterday's Lakeland*. Lakeland, FL: City of Lakeland, 1976.

Haggard, Theodore M. *Florida Southern College, Lakeland Florida: The First 100 Years, An Illustrated History, 1985*. Lakeland, FL: Florida Southern College Press, 1985.

Homan, Lynn M., and Thomas Reilly. Images of America: *Lakeland*. Charleston, SC: Arcadia Publishing, 2001.

Lakeland and Polk County city directories, various years.

Lakeland Evening Telegram, various dates.

Lakeland Morning Star, various dates.

Pinkston, Margaret D. *Mosswood Remembered*. Baltimore: Gateway Press, 1995.

Sage-Gagne, Waneta. *Pilots in the Sun: Primary Pilot Training Schools in Lakeland and Avon Park, Florida, 1940–1945*. Lakeland, FL: Friends of the (Lakeland Public) Library, 1990.

This Was Yesterday: A History of Lakeland, Florida. Lakeland, FL: Junior Welfare League of Greater Lakeland, Inc., 1973.